Cause Marketing FOR DUMMIES®

by Joe Waters & Joanna MacDonald

WILEY

Wiley Publishing, Inc.

Cause Marketing For Dummies®

Published by
Wiley Publishing, Inc.
111 River Street
Hoboken, NJ 07030-5774
www.wiley.com

Copyright © 2011 by Wiley Publishing, Inc., Indianapolis, Indiana

Published by Wiley Publishing, Inc., Indianapolis, Indiana

Published simultaneously in Canada

For general information on our other products and services, please contact our Customer Care Department within the U.S. at 877-762-2974, outside the U.S. at 317-572-3993, or fax 317-572-4002.

For technical support, please visit www.wiley.com/techsupport.

Wiley also publishes its books in a variety of electronic formats and by print-on-demand. Not all content that is available in standard print versions of this book may appear or be packaged in all book formats. If you have purchased a version of this book that did not include media that is referenced by or accompanies a standard print version, you may request this media by visiting http://booksupport.wiley.com. For more information about Wiley products, visit us www.wiley.com.

Library of Congress Control Number: 2011932267

ISBN: 978-1-118-01130-0 (pbk); ISBN: 978-1-118-11904-4 (ebk); ISBN: 978-1-118-11905-1 (ebk); ISBN: 978-1-118-11906-8 (ebk)

Manufactured in the United States of America

10 9 8 7 6 5 4 3 2 1

WILEY

About the Authors

Joe Waters: Joe Waters is a leading expert on cause marketing and social media for nonprofits. He's the blogger behind the web's No. 1 cause marketing blog, Selfishgiving.com. Since 2004, he has shared his experiences and insights on how small companies and causes can raise money and awareness with cause marketing on a shoestring budget. Joe's the director of cause marketing for a Boston hospital where he manages a team of sales, event, and marketing professionals that develop cause marketing programs with local and national companies. A sought-after commentator on the subject, Joe is a regular speaker at Cause Marketing Forum's annual conference. He's contributor to The Chronicle of Philanthropy and Care2.com's *Trailblazers for Good* and has been featured in the Association for Healthcare Philanthropy Journal, Mashable.com, INC.com, and the Stanford Social Innovation Review.

Joanna MacDonald: Joanna works alongside Joe and is a senior member of the cause marketing team at a Boston hospital where she focuses on cause marketing sales and operations. She specializes in third-party partnerships and cause marketing events and is the yang to Joe's ying! Joanna's long career in nonprofit and for-profit work include stints at the United Way, Cablevision, and Greater Boston Chamber of Commerce. With Joe, she is the cofounder of SixFigureCauseMarketing.com, a training program for causes that want to launch effective and lucrative cause marketing campaigns.

Dedication

This book is dedicated to all the causes from whom we've learned so much about cause marketing, and to all the companies that helped make our programs so successful. We are honored to have learned and worked with them.

Authors' Acknowledgments

We're very thankful to Wiley Publishing for giving two new authors the chance to write a *For Dummies* book on such a great topic like cause marketing, which seems to be on every company's and nonprofit's to-do list.

Amy Fandrei, our acquisition editor at Wiley, expertly guided us through the process of becoming Wiley authors. Throughout the writing of the book, she offered advice, insight, direction, and even comfort. She was always upbeat and only knew one direction: straight ahead. Thank you, Amy.

Kelly Ewing, our editor at Wiley, made writing this book a lot easier. And the prose you'll find in it is much better because of her. Every writer needs a good editor. Ours was Kelly.

Kelly wasn't our only editor. We also needed a technical editor who knew and understood the topic as well as we did and could flag something that needed more explaining, tell us when we were incorrect, or just plain wrong! This heavy task fell to Portland-based cause marketer Megan Strand, a consultant with InCouraged Communication, who did an excellent job providing feedback and helping us produce a much better book.

We couldn't have written this book without access to some basic resources.

My friend and colleague David Hessekiel at Cause Marketing Forum was a wonderful resource. We found much of the information we needed right on his fantastic website (www.causemarketingforum.com).

Another tremendous resource was Cone LLC, a leading cause marketing agency based in our hometown of Boston. Its thought leadership on cause marketing is well known and respected. It's also reflected in the research and studies on cause marketing it frequently shares with the world. Having Cone to turn to was like having our own cause marketing research team a phone call or tweet away! We especially want to thank Sarah Kerkian from Cone's Insights Group for all her help.

Finally, we want to thank our families for their support while we wrote this book. While they didn't contribute directly to the research, writing, or editing of the book, they nourished the project with their love, sacrifice, and encouragement. Their patience allowed us to harness passion to prose and produce the book you now hold in your hands.

Publisher's Acknowledgments

We're proud of this book; please send us your comments at http://dummies.custhelp.com. For other comments, please contact our Customer Care Department within the U.S. at 877-762-2974, outside the U.S. at 317-572-3993, or fax 317-572-4002.

Some of the people who helped bring this book to market include the following:

Acquisitions and Editorial

Project Editor: Kelly Ewing

Acquisitions Editor: Amy Fandrei

Technical Editor: Megan Strand

Editorial Manager: Jodi Jensen

Editorial Assistant: Amanda Graham

Sr. Editorial Assistant: Cherie Case

Cartoons: Rich Tennant
(www.the5thwave.com)

Composition Services

Project Coordinator: Patrick Redmond

Layout and Graphics: Joyce Haughey, Lavonne Roberts, Corrie Socolovitch

Proofreaders: John Greenough, Lauren Mandelbaum, Evelyn Wellborn

Indexer: Cheryl Duksta

Publishing and Editorial for Technology Dummies

    Richard Swadley, Vice President and Executive Group Publisher

    Andy Cummings, Vice President and Publisher

    Mary Bednarek, Executive Acquisitions Director

    Mary C. Corder, Editorial Director

Publishing for Consumer Dummies

    Kathy Nebenhaus, Vice President and Executive Publisher

Composition Services

    Debbie Stailey, Director of Composition Services

Contents at a Glance

Table of Contents

Introduction

· ·

We both entered the workforce about the same time in the early 1990s. Joanna worked in the community relations department of a cable company, and Joe did fundraising for the Muscular Dystrophy Association. Despite being in different organizations with different responsibilities, we both found ourselves at the intersection of marketing, philanthropy, and business.

We had a lot of different names for what we did. Corporate giving. Sponsorship. Community relations. Neither of us thought to call our work cause marketing, a practice that had only been around a decade. Only in the late '90s did we begin to view ourselves as cause marketers and truly understand this new, dynamic field.

About This Book

Today, cause marketing is on the tongue of just about every cause and company you talk to — and rightfully so. An industry that saw just $120 million in spending in 1990 is now projected to be at $1.7 billion in spending in 2011, according to the latest IEG Sponsorship Report.

But the growth in cause marketing has been uneven, as it generally hasn't included the small companies and causes that are the backbone of American business. This book looks to correct this issue by focusing on three major themes:

- ✔ Traditional cause marketing, such as point-of-sale and purchase- and action-triggered donation programs, which companies and causes of any size can execute.

- ✔ The introduction of social media and how it can be effectively combined with cause marketing to level the playing field with larger competitors, raise money, and build awareness.

- ✔ The future of cause marketing and how it's unfolding with mobile technology and location-based services, such as Foursquare, Facebook Places, and Gowalla. These developments promise further advantages for smaller companies and causes, if they will only embrace them.

More than anything else, this book is about what works now or what will work in cause marketing in the years ahead. We speak from experience; we've personally tested most of the things we talk about. We're also confident that what did work for us is not a fluke. The tactics, tips, suggestions, and insights we offer can be repeated by anyone and produce the same successful results.

If your goal was to pick up a book that was practical, actionable, tested, and detailed, you've come to the right place.

Conventions Used in This Book

For us, cause marketing is not the marketing of causes, as it is for some people. Cause marketing is a partnership between a nonprofit and a for-profit for mutual profit. This book is about win-win partnerships between companies and causes.

We wrote this book with causes and companies in mind, but specific sections address issues that are unique to businesses and nonprofits. Both have challenges and opportunities. And while they share much in common, there are times when we treat them separately.

The fact that companies and causes are so different is one of the reasons their partnerships are so strong. They complement and complete each other. That's why treating them as one and the same would be a mistake to our readers and a disservice to these powerful partnerships.

Throughout this book, we include URLs (web addresses) where you can go to find out more information relating to cause marketing. You can easily identify these links because they appear in a different font — for example, www. dummies.com.

Foolish Assumptions

As we were writing this book, we pictured small companies and causes staring awestruck at the cause marketing campaigns executed by their larger counterparts. Although these companies were impressed, they were frustrated that such success was well out of their reach.

But we're passionate that these causes and small companies have the same ability to execute successful programs as the larger organizations do, if they only had someone to teach them how. That's what we're here to do.

As we wrote this book, we made the following main assumptions about you, the reader:

✔ If you're a cause, you're looking for a new way to raise money and build awareness. If you're a company, you want to help good causes and give yourself a powerful competitive edge.

✔ You're open to a new way of thinking about how causes and companies work together. Cause marketing is not philanthropy, corporate giving, or sponsorship. Are you ready to wear a new hat?

✔ Your interest extends beyond causes and companies and how technology, social media, and location-based services will drive cause marketing in the months and years ahead. Hey, you're a hipster and follow the coolest trends!

How This Book Is Organized

This book is made up of six parts that introduce you to the traditional world of cause marketing (for example, point-of-sale, purchase-triggered donations, message promotion) and the online cause marketing world that is emerging with social media and location-based services.

Part I: Getting Started with Cause Marketing

Part I is all about getting you up to speed on what cause marketing is (and isn't) and choosing the right approach for your cause or company. This part also looks at what no cause marketing program can do without — a partner. We explore how partners are not so much found as they are detected. Finally, we show you how you can make your best qualities work for you. Like good partners, assets are uncovered, not discovered.

Part II: Promoting Your Cause Marketing Plan

Part II covers the actual selling of your cause marketing program. We take you from making the initial phone call and dealing with gatekeepers to the meeting and using PowerPoint effectively. (Don't worry: We don't leave you hanging at the slideshow!) We take you to the most important step — the close.

Part III: Implementing Your Cause Marketing Program

Part III begins with a look at the best type of cause marketing, point-of-sale. We show you how to create a timeline; work with operations staff; and how to navigate your printing and shipping options. Taking your cause marketing program from the back office to the storefront, we look at the key role managers and cashiers play in your success and how to maximize their involvement. Lastly, we switch gears and look at creating and executing the second major cause marketing strategy, purchase- and action-triggered donations.

Part IV: Taking Your Cause Marketing Program Online

The web, social media, and location-based services will play a key role in the growth and development of cause marketing. Part IV examines how group buying services, question-and-answer sites, and Facebook Likes, among other online tools, are creating new opportunities for win-win partnerships and are making cause marketing more transparent and ubiquitous than ever.

Part V: Expanding Your Cause Marketing Plan

Part V takes your cause marketing program to the next level. We explain how to build on your first program, even when you hit a few bumps on the road with your new partner. We also look at advanced cause marketing strategies: tapping the power of events, celebrities, text-to-give, and third-party partners.

Part VI: The Part of Tens

Like all *For Dummies* books, this one has a Part of Tens. These chapters list the ten commandments of cause marketing, ten mistakes to avoid, ten low-budget cause marketing ideas, ten cause marketing programs we wish we could take credit for, and ten ways to nail your next cause marketing presentation. Phew! We love lists of ten! And we think you'll agree with us that some of the most important advice in the book is found in this easy-to-read and helpful section.

Icons Used in This Book

The little pictures (called icons) you see in the margins throughout this book emphasize a point to remember, a danger to be aware of, or information that we think you may find helpful or will make a task easier. Here's what each of those icons mean:

Tips are bits of information that you may find useful or that make something you need to do easier.

We use this icon to point out situations that can get you into trouble.

When you see this icon, take special note of the information so that you remember it later.

If you're a business owner interested in cause marketing, you'll want to watch for these icons. We wrote this text especially for you.

Where to Go from Here

You don't have to read this book front to back, but you may want to. As much as possible, we follow a chronological progression with *Cause Marketing For Dummies* that takes you through the steps of creating and executing a cause marketing program.

Of course, the great thing about this book, and *For Dummies* books in general, is that each chapter stands alone, so you can use this book as a reference. The detailed table of contents is a big help in finding the specific information you're seeking.

Not sure where to begin? If you're new to cause marketing, start with Chapter 1 so that you can fully understand what cause marketing is and how our perspective on it may be different from how others have talked about it. If you aren't interested in one particular aspect of cause marketing, then you can proceed sequentially as we begin with basic offline strategies and move to more advanced campaigns involving social media and location-based services.

If you're somewhat familiar with transactional cause marketing and are fortunate to already have a partner to work with, you can skip the first few chapters and jump into the cause marketing tactics that might make sense for a partnership program.

If you're interested more in the future of cause marketing and the direction it will take in the years to come, or if you are just looking for some quick tips, resources, or inspiration, start with Part V.

Part I
Getting Started with Cause Marketing

The 5th Wave — By Rich Tennant

"That's very innovative, but I'm just not interested in buying a box of Girl Scout Cigars."

In this part . . .

Part I lays the foundation for cause marketing success by explaining what cause marketing is, the different types of tactics, and how to find what every program needs: a partner. We also show you how you can maximize the success of your program with training, motivation, and incentives.

Chapter 1

Getting to Know What Cause Marketing Is All About

Cause marketing isn't the marketing of causes, nor is it a catchall for every type of promotion or fundraising program between a company and cause. Cause marketing is its own unique practice that has parameters, tools, and techniques. You don't play tennis with a bat, and you don't perform surgery with a pen (ummm, unless you have to). You also don't want to begin using cause marketing if you're unready or ill-equipped for the job.

In this chapter, we dig into what exactly cause marketing is. We also explore the most common types and talk about which ones are the best for you.

What Is Cause Marketing?

Cause marketing is a partnership between a nonprofit and a for-profit for mutual profit. For example, you may be familiar with the partnership between Komen for the Cure and athletic shoe maker New Balance. Komen licenses its signature pink ribbon to New Balance, which is included on a line of products, including walking and running shoes.

Komen profits from the sale of these products and gains valuable exposure. New Balance enhances its favorability with a key demographic, women shoppers, and owns the rights to a must-have product for Komen's many walking and running events across the country.

Pinpointing exactly when the first cause marketing campaign was created is like asking who discovered America. The Vikings? The Chinese? The English? The Native Americans who lived here?

Regardless of who was the first to marry cause and company together for charity and commerce, the "Columbus moment" when people became aware of this new world was 1983 when American Express partnered with the Statue of Liberty restoration project. In this arrangement, the restoration project received a penny for each use of the American Express card, and a dollar for each new card issued. In just four months, $2 million was raised for the project. American Express was a big winner, as well. Credit card activity increased 28 percent, and cause-related marketing, or cause marketing, as it's more often called, was born.

Exploring the Most Common Forms of Cause Marketing

Cause marketing isn't one-size-fits-all. In fact, it comes in many different forms. At the checkout lane at your favorite store, a cashier might ask you to donate a dollar to the American Red Cross. You could stroll to another store and buy a mug, a percentage of which goes to UNICEF and ensures clean water for people in third-world countries. Yet another trip to the store may have you purchasing a product that's part of a licensing deal between the company and cause.

Cause marketing isn't just about raising money. Employees volunteer for non-profit projects; companies put their advertising might behind producing and promoting videos, advertisements, billboards, magazine ads, and a host of other promotional tools.

Lastly, cause marketing has expanded into the ether, the online world of the Internet and social media, as men and women of all ages blog, Facebook, check in, and tweet, among other things, for the causes they care about.

This section explores them all and takes a candid look at which forms of cause marketing are best for you.

Point-of-sale cause marketing

Point-of-sale cause marketing is when a consumer is solicited at checkout for a donation. Point-of-sale can take on two forms:

- ✔ **Active cause marketing** is when a cashier asks the consumer to donate to a cause. This type is one of the most effective forms of cause marketing because it's direct (one-to-one and timely because the consumer literally has his wallet out) and personal (people give to people).

For example, in Figure 1-1, this *pinup* — our name for icons like this one that are sold and usually displayed in businesses — is sold annually by servers at Chili's Grill & Bar restaurants nationwide, benefiting St. Jude Children's Research Hospital in Memphis, Tennessee. The pinup, also advertised as a coloring sheet during the brand's *Create-A-Pepper to Fight Childhood Cancer* campaign, sells for as little as $1 (although there is the option to donate more, which we like!), and sales have been hotter than a chili pepper! Since 2002, Chili's has raised more than $35 million for St. Jude.

✔ **Passive cause marketing:** This, too, happens at the checkout, but signage or electronic displays do the asking. For example, an increasingly popular way to ask consumers to support a cause is to have the electronic terminal solicit a donation after the customer swipes their credit card for payment. Shoppers can choose to add a $1 or more to support a cause. Other times, you may see a sign with a code for the cashier to use when the customer requests to make a donation (see Figure 1-2).

Figure 1-1: Some of the most successful cause marketing campaigns are point-of-sale programs that involve selling a pinup, such as this one sold at Chili's Grill & Bar (back).

MAKE A DONATION TO ST. JUDE AND COLOR A BRIGHTER TOMORROW FOR THOUSANDS OF KIDS.

$1_____ $5_____ $10_____ $_____

100% of the purchase price of this coloring sheet will go to St. Jude Children's Research Hospital®

createapepper.com   St. Jude Children's Research Hospital   ALSAC • Danny Thomas, Founder   stjude.org

THANK YOU!

100% of the purchase price of this coloring sheet will go to St. Jude Children's Research Hospital®

Figure 1-2:
Passive
cause
marketing
can involve
a simple
sign at the
register like
this one
at Whole
Foods.

Most active cause programs involve more than just the cashier asking shoppers to donate money. They usually (but not always) include some type of pinup that the shopper adds his name to and then it's displayed somewhere in the store (see Figure 1-3).

Purchase or action-triggered donations

A purchase or action-triggered donation occurs when a consumer performs a particular *action* — donating a coat, liking a Facebook page, and so on — or *purchases* a product or service. In both instances, a donation is made to a cause (see Figure 1-4). For example, when you buy the RED app for iPhone and iPod touch, Shazam contributes 20 percent from the $5.99 price tag to the Global Fund to invest in HIV/AIDS programs.

Figure 1-3:
If you've ever donated to a cause at a store, you may have been asked to sign your name to a pinup, which is then hung in the store.

Figure 1-4:
An example of a purchase-triggered donation.

Licensing

Licensing is when a company pays a fee to use a nonprofit's brand on its product. Licensing typically includes a certification process by the nonprofit before the company is allowed to use the logo. A longstanding licensing pact is the Arthritis Foundation's Ease-of-Use Commendation for the Advil Caplets Easy Open Arthritis Cap (see Figure 1-5).

Cause marketing licensing is practiced by only large causes with the iconic brands, such as Komen for the Cure and the American Heart Association. These well-established causes can drive consumer buying and have the legal teams to ensure that pacts are executed properly. Cause marketing licensing is not a realistic option for small companies and causes.

Figure 1-5:
Arthritis Foundation's Ease-of-Use Commendation for the Advil Caplets Easy Open Arthritis Cap.

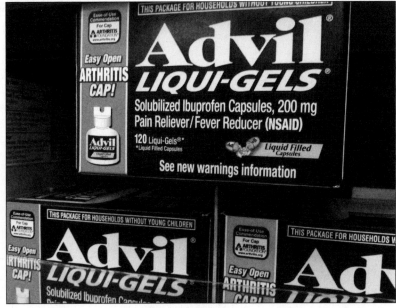

Message promotion

Message promotion is when a business puts its resources to work to promote a cause-focused message. For example, pet food company Iams recruited celebrity spokesperson Hilary Swank, a two-time academy award winner and the owner of two adopted dogs, for ads in support of the Helen Woodward Animal Shelter. Swank's voice was used in a pair of moving public service announcements showing shelter dogs and cats bonding with their new owners. "The real reward in adopting a pet," Swank says, "is when the pet adopts you."

To watch this video, scan the QR code to the left with your smartphone or visit `http://youtu.be/gqpOKsJUkYc`.

Sometimes message promotion is combined with a charitable gift. In the case of "Red, White & You" from New England Confectionary Company (NECCO), their print ad was combined with a $75,000 donation to the United Service Organizations (USO) and enough sweetheart candies for 3,000 care packages (see Figure 1-6).

Figure 1-6: NECCO's Sweethearts *Red White & You.*

Employee engagement

Employee engagement is when a company leverages its workforce for social good. Employee involvement with a cause marketing campaign can range from employees supporting a point-of-sale program at the register to volunteer programs that take employees out of the workplace and put them to work on a community project. A great example of this was The Home Depot's partnership with KaBOOM!, which involved nearly 100,000 Home Depot employees building *1,000 Playgrounds in 1,000 Days* (see Figure 1-7).

Figure 1-7:
In addition to volunteers, Home Depot donated $25 million to building 1,000 playgrounds in 1,000 days.

Digital programs

The web, social media, and especially *location-based services* — services like Foursquare, Facebook Places, and SCVNGR that use mobile technology to track and engage users — will dramatically impact cause marketing and change the way we execute current cause marketing tactics. To leave out digital programs or to lump them in with another area like message promotion is to leave out the future of cause marketing and how cause and companies will partner in the years to come.

One example of the intersection of cause and digital is TwitChange, a celebrity tweet auction created by Shaun King, an Atlanta pastor during the summer of 2010 (see Figure 1-8). The concept of TwitChange was simple: Celebrities auctioned off their Twitter influence to the highest bidder. The typical celebrity Twitter package on eBay looked something like this:

> *"Ryan Seacrest will follow you on Twitter for a minimum of 90 days, will retweet one of your tweets, and will send out a tweet including your @twitterhandle."*

TwitChange was a big hit. Its first campaign raised over $500,000 for aHomeInHaiti.org.

Figure 1-8: TwitChange was so successful in September 2010 that it now plans to run four to six campaigns a year.

Maybe you don't have the luxury of a celebrity partner. Digital programs can be used by anyone, especially if you have a Facebook page. For example, for each Like of its Facebook page earlier this year, Gerber donated $1 up to $500,000 to Rachael Ray's cause Yum-o!

You can find out more about digital tools and how to master them in Part IV.

Making the Case for Doing Cause Marketing in the First Place

We're excited about cause marketing, but we understand that you may be just curious, or maybe even a bit nervous on whether it's right for you. Here are five good reasons to love cause marketing and to jump in with both heart and feet:

✓ **Cause marketing is a growth industry.** In 2010, corporate cause sponsorship was up 6.7 percent to $1.62 billion, making it the fastest growing sponsorship category that IEG, a company that provides measurement information to the global sponsorship industry, tracks. By comparison, in 1990, cause sponsorship was a $120 million industry. Causes and companies of all sizes can be part of cause marketing's bright future.

✔ **Consumers want more cause marketing.** Despite cause marketing's tremendous growth, consumers would like to see even more. According to the 2010 Cone Cause Evolution Study, 83 percent of Americans wish more of the products, services, and retailers they used would support causes. Not only is cause marketing growing, but consumers want and expect companies and causes to work together on cause marketing pacts.

✔ **Consumers want companies to act locally.** This point is critical for local causes and businesses that may feel that cause marketing is only for bigger charities and companies. Nearly half of the respondents to the Cone study said companies should focus on issues that impact local communities. And 91 percent said that companies should support an issue in the communities where they do business (Cone, 2010).

✔ **Technology is leveling the playing field.** If large causes and companies had an advantage in the past, that's changing thanks to new technologies, such as social media, the mobile web, location-based services, and *quick response codes* (QR codes) — offline hyperlinks that smartphone users can scan to access online content — which promise to arm local companies and causes with the tools they need to compete. Check out Chapter 10 where we discuss enhancing your program by using QR codes.

✔ **Consumers are fans of transactional cause marketing.** Shoppers surveyed actually prefer point-of-sale (81 percent) and purchase-triggered donation (75 percent) cause marketing. This news is great for local causes and businesses as they both have an easy point of entry and generate excellent revenue and awareness.

Why cause marketing is the Borg

The battleground is anywhere in the world. Governments are out of money, and museums, historical sites, and cultural institutions are turning to the private sector and to consumers to keep their doors open and visitors moving through the turnstiles. For example:

✔ Shiny electric cars sit outside one Rome museum after a business paid $110,000 for a sponsorship.

✔ The Louvre in Paris is exploring licensing its name to a line of elegant watches.

✔ In Spain, an art museum is keeping its lights on by promoting its utility partners.

Everyone talks about the growing reliance on corporate partnerships, but it's only the beginning of the commerce and consumerism nonprofits will have to adopt to survive. And cause marketing will be part of the vanguard.

With government funding decreasing annually and limits on how much donors will pay for tickets to a gala or an exhibition, nonprofits have to be more creative than ever in generating revenue, exploring untapped assets, and watching expenses.

Beautifully situated on the left side of the Seine, the Musee d'Orsay , a museum in Paris, has leveraged its location for profit by displaying giant posters for Air France and even H&M Clothing.

The days of going hat-in-hand are over, as nonprofits have to hold onto their hats — and keep their heads — amid charges and retreats, victories and setbacks. Cause marketing may straddle both cause and commerce, but consumerism and elitism will always be wary of the other.

In the *Star Trek: The Next Generation* series, the Borg was a relentless race of antagonists that expanded and conquered the universe despite human efforts to contain them. The Borg's mantra was "Resistance is futile." It's a mantra that could be a battle cry of good for cause marketers and others who want to see funding flow to the causes they care about and are open to new, innovative strategies.

Will some of the world's most famous paintings be sponsored by Starbucks, Target, and Walmart? No one can predict the future. But we are sure of this: Resistance is futile.

"Resistance is futile."

Benefiting from Cause Marketing

The essence of cause marketing is win-win — good for the cause, good for the company. But the benefits of cause marketing will vary. Your local food bank will profit differently than the restaurant chain it partnered with. The key is knowing the unique rewards of each so that you can land a partner (see Chapter 3), execute a program, and measure your success when it's finished (see Chapter 11).

For the cause

The benefits of cause marketing to nonprofits are clear — new revenue, greater awareness, and more opportunity:

- **Cause marketing is a new source of revenue from companies.** While the community relations arm of a company awards grants, and senior management are prospects for individual gifts, cause marketing taps the marketing muscle of the company. It opens a new door in the corporate suite.

- **Cause marketing generates awareness.** This awareness is invaluable for causes that neither have the expertise nor resources to promote themselves. Cause marketing gives these causes a voice, a presence, in an increasingly crowded and competitive world.

✔ **Cause marketing opens new doors.** We speak from experience on this point. Our involvement with cause marketing has led to a more progressive and innovative approach to fundraising. As cause marketing evolves, we've kept pace with advances that have benefited our work and our cause. Nothing more clearly illustrates this point than the link between cause marketing and technology. At the beginning of the new millenium, we had to learn how to use the web for new campaigns and promotion. Next came social media and tapping Facebook, Twitter, and blogging to enhance our efforts and to raise money. Today, we're opening doors with location-based services and mobile technology — key drivers on the road ahead. Technology is a journey we must keep up with if we are to grow and compete.

✔ **Cause marketing can reach new donors.** Many causes want to target a new, younger generation of donors. It's hard to find a group that's more enthusiastic about cause marketing — except perhaps moms — than *Millennials,* the men and women of today that are in their 20s and 30s and came after Generation X. In the 2010 Cone Cause Evolution Study, questions to Millennials on influences of social/environmental causes on making brand decisions had affirmative answers as high as 90 percent (see Figure 1-9).

Figure 1-9:
2010 Cone
Cause
Evolution
Study.

How moms and Millennials compare:			
Shopping attitudes and behaviors:	Total	Millennials	Moms
Believe cause marketing is acceptable	88%	94%	95%
Bought a cause product/service in past 12 months	41%	53%	61%
Likely to switch brands	80%	85%	93%
Willing to try a NEW brand or one they've never heard of	61%	73%	73%
Willing to buy a more expensive brand	19%	26%	27%
Cause branding is important when they decide:	Total	Millennials	Moms
Which companies they want to see doing business in their communities	79%	88%	90%
Which products and services to recommend to other people	76%	86%	88%
What to buy or where to shop	75%	84%	88%
Where to work	69%	87%	79%
Which stocks or mutual funds to invest in	59%	79%	74%

For the business

Businesses benefit from cause marketing with increased favorability and loyalty with two key audiences — household decision makers (usually moms) and employees:

✔ **Cause marketing builds favorability and drives sales.** The Cone Study reports that 85 percent of those surveyed believe that companies that support causes should be rewarded with a positive image. The study also found that 1 in 5 consumers will pay more for a cause-related product. A cause will prompt 61 percent to try a product they've never heard of. And a whopping 80 percent of consumers would switch to a brand that supports a cause when price and quality are equal.

✔ **Cause marketing targets the key consumer.** Moms are the primary household shoppers and are overwhelmingly supportive of cause marketing. According to the 2010 Cone Cause Evolution Study, moms are by far the nation's most active cause consumers. A near-unanimous 95 percent find cause marketing acceptable, and 61 percent have purchased a cause-related product in the past 12 months.

✔ **Cause marketing attracts and keeps employees.** Sixty-nine percent of Americans consider a company's social and environmental commitments when deciding where to work. Once employed, employees active in company causes are happier; 93 percent say they're proud of their company's values, while 92 percent say they feel a strong sense of loyalty to their company.

Understanding What Cause Marketing Is Not

Many people have the perception that cause marketing is anything that involves marketing with causes or corporate giving. But cause marketing is something we clearly define as a win-win partnership between cause and company involving specific tactics. We strongly believe that if cause marketing doesn't stand for something, it won't mean anything.

Part of understanding what cause marketing truly is means clearly understanding what it is not:

✔ **Cause marketing is not philanthropy.** While philanthropy is one of the goals of cause marketing, giving is not its primary end. As the name indicates, it's about cause *marketing* (marketing is the things we say and do to get and keep customers). If a company just wants to engage in philanthropy, it could just donate money to the cause, anonymously if it wanted. And if a cause was just interested in raising money, it could stick with proven fundraising practices like individual giving and grants from foundations. Cause marketing has benefits for both cause and company that extend well beyond the dollars raised or received. (See the section "Benefiting from Cause Marketing," earlier in this chapter, for more information.)

✔ **Cause marketing is not sponsorship.** It's easy to confuse sponsorship with cause marketing. *Sponsorship* like cause marketing is win-win. What distinguishes the two are tactics. Consider the longstanding sponsorship of the Boston Marathon by financial services giant John Hancock (see

Figure 1-10). Is it a win-win partnership between a cause and company? Yes (the marathon is managed by the Boston Athletic Association, a nonprofit). Is it cause marketing? No. Cause marketing goes deeper and involves a close partnership between cause and company to execute a point-of-sale, purchase or action-triggered donation, licensing agreement, or other type of program for mutual gain. The good news is you can relax. Knowing the difference between cause marketing and sponsorship is not as important as knowing how the two can work together.

✔ **Cause marketing is not the road to riches.** Based on our own experiences and what we've seen in the nonprofit world, we believe most causes can raise an additional 5 to 15 percent of their revenues from cause marketing. So if you're a $2 million organization, with time and effort, you may one day raise an additional $100,000 to $300,000 from cause marketing. This estimate is modest. Some nonprofits raise more, some less, but what they will all share are modest results in raising money with cause marketing. No one is hitting the lottery. Even for large causes like Susan G. Komen for the Cure that annually raises $35 million and more from pink sneakers, mixers, and pens, cause marketing is very visible but modest compared to the $265 million they raise from other sources. Yoplait, for example, has donated $25 million to Komen for the Cure over the past 12 years through a variety of programs (see Figure 1-11).

✔ **Cause marketing is not impossible for small companies and causes.** Any organization can do cause marketing by using the strategies we outline in this book and by following the lead of bigger causes and companies. But you need to scale them for your organization and be realistic about what you can accomplish. A clear understanding of what cause marketing is and how it works and its function for both causes and companies is critical to your success.

Figure 1-10: John Hancock's support for the Boston Marathon is a good example of sponsorship, not cause marketing.

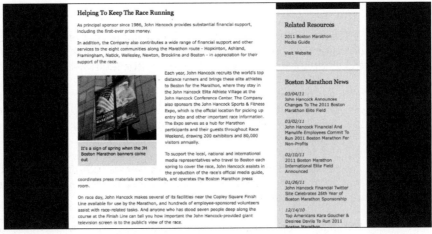

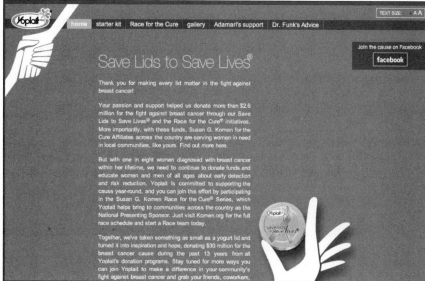

Figure 1-11:
While not
as lucrative
as some
other forms
of fundrais-
ing, monies
raised from
cause mar-
keting can
be 5 to 15
percent of a
nonprofit's
revenue.

Preparing for the End of Corporate Philanthropy

Nestle SA Chairman Peter Brabeck-Letmathe is just one of the top business leaders to recently make the case against corporate philanthropy. His concern is that corporate philanthropy may lead to a misuse of funds. What businesses like Nestle are more in favor of are social investments that align with business goals.

While not everyone is thrilled with charitable support being driven by business decisions, social investing is the future of corporate giving for both small and large businesses. Thankfully, the timing is right for several reasons.

With the drumbeat of earnings and return on investment stronger than ever, companies can no longer fund generous philanthropy programs. Investment in causes, not giving, must be the mainstay if companies are to continue to play a meaningful role in addressing societal issues.

Thoughtful consumers get it. Research shows today's consumers understand that companies have to turn a profit but also believe that they can be engines for social change at the same time.

To engage more small and medium size businesses with causes, partnerships need to be win-win as only the biggest companies can afford big budgets for philanthropy.

But the shift away from corporate philanthropy won't be easy for many causes. Going from receiving generous handouts to working for a living will take a bit of getting used to, and not all nonprofits will survive.

Here are three ways nonprofits can begin the shift away from corporate philanthropy:

- ✔ **Embrace the brave new world.** Nonprofits shouldn't feel guilty that they have to engage businesses as, well, businesses and not donors. Remember, companies still want to make a difference, but they want to help you and society while they help themselves. Think win-win-win.

- ✔ **Make it easy for companies to work with you.** Don't lay on the guilt just because you have to work for the money you originally just got in the mail for doing nothing. And don't wait for companies to tell you to step up your efforts and offer them more. Connect the dots so that they don't have to. Create opportunities and programs that are tailored to their needs and goals.

- ✔ **Use what you learn from this book.** Whether you use point-of-sale, purchase or action-triggered donations, or online programs, cause marketing can help reduce your dependence on corporate charity and give businesses a new way to work with you.

Don't worry; corporate philanthropy won't just disappear. It will be reduced, perhaps a lot. But corporate philanthropy will always be there. Keep your tin cup handy. Just don't expect to use it as much, which we think will be a good thing.

A world with *less* corporate philanthropy is here. The challenge for causes is to adapt or die. What seems like the end of corporate philanthropy will actually be a new beginning of opportunity for nonprofits that are up for the challenge.

Is it an ending or a beginning for your cause? Only you can decide.

Chapter 2

Launching a Successful Cause Marketing Program

In This Chapter

▶ Choosing the right cause marketing tactic

▶ Getting the right pieces in place for success

▶ Working on your cause marketing message

▶ Creating a powerful and balanced brand for your cause

*B*efore you head out on a road trip, you should check to make sure that you have everything you need for a successful journey. Getting ready for your cause marketing campaign is not unlike the preparations you'll make for a trip. And sometimes even one missing item can spoil the fun.

This chapter looks at the basic things you need to achieve cause marketing success. We talk about cause marketing approaches and why a support structure and powerful cause marketing message are important. Finally, we look at how real, transformative cause marketing is a road that's open to all, but is travelled by few.

Determining Your Cause Marketing Approach

The cause marketing tactic you choose will vary depending on your goals and the company or cause with which you're working. But regardless of which tactic you choose, they all share common traits that are closely connected to our definition of cause marketing (see Chapter 1).

First, all these approaches involve partnerships between a nonprofit and for-profit. If there is no partnership between cause and company, there is no cause marketing.

Second, they all are win-win. The nonprofit raises money and/or awareness and the for-profit enhances its favorability with consumers and employees, which can deliver a powerful competitive edge.

The three main cause marketing tactics are

- ✔ Point-of-sale
- ✔ Purchase or action-triggered donations
- ✔ Digital programs

To these tactics, we add three additional tactics that are worth exploring:

- ✔ Employee engagement
- ✔ Message promotion
- ✔ Licensing

Giving at the point-of-sale

Point-of-sale (POS) cause marketing is when the consumer is asked to donate a dollar or two to a cause at the point of checkout. Because these transactions often happen at a checkout register, they're sometimes called *register programs.*

POS is one of the most common forms of cause marketing, and our favorite, with good reason:

- ✔ **POS is lucrative.** Some of the most successful cause marketing campaigns through the years have been point-of-sale. Cause marketing programs, such as the *Thanks and Giving* campaign for St. Jude's Children's Research Hospital, Miracle Balloons for Children's Miracle Network, and Shamrocks for Muscular Dystrophy Association, raise millions at the register. Locally, we've raised hundreds of thousands of dollars with POS working with retailers with 9 to 100 locations in New England. We believe POS should be the cornerstone of any local cause marketing program.

✔ **POS is cost effective.** Point-of-sale programs frequently use *pinups* (see Figure 2-1) — sometimes called paper icons, mobiles, paper plaques, or scannables — that are sold at the register, signed by the shopper, and hung at the store as a sign of the shopper's and the store's support for the cause. Pinups are inexpensive to produce. Some campaigns use the credit card terminals at the register, which eliminates the printing expense and the inevitable waste of pinups all together (see Figure 2-2).

Figure 2-1: This pinup only cost 5 cents to produce.

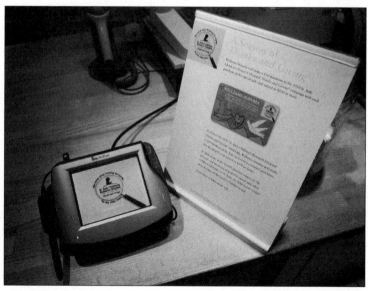

Figure 2-2: This credit card display allows shoppers at Williams-Sonoma stores to donate to St. Jude Children's Research Hospital when they use their credit or debit card, as part of the St. Jude *Thanks and Giving* campaign.

✔ **POS is easy to execute.** Every fundraiser or marketing program requires work, but in our experience, POS requires less than most. Once you sign a partner on to a program, you design a pinup, have it printed, deliver them to stores, train employees on how to sell them, wait a few weeks, and pick up your check. While you could add a few more steps to what we just outlined, you probably couldn't compress the duties of your last fundraiser into such a short list.

✔ **POS plays well with others.** This is perhaps the most compelling aspect of POS. You can add it to whatever fundraiser you're working on. Planning a walk? Recruit POS partners instead of traditional sponsors. Need a campaign to integrate well with social media channels, such as Twitter, Facebook, or Foursquare? POS is the perfect vehicle because it's flexible and promotional.

✔ **POS is a sales driver.** It's a great way to drum up business for partners as it engages the shopper at the register when she has her wallet out and is interested in saving money. Tactics such as comarketing with coupons can attract new shoppers and increase sales. And what business isn't interested in more business?

Working with purchase and action-triggered donations

In a purchase-triggered donation (PTD), a consumer's purchase triggers a donation to a cause. This donation usually takes the form of a percentage or portion of the sales or profit going to the cause.

For example, the wireless company Sprint agreed to donate $2 to The Nature Conservancy's Adopt an Acre initiative for every recyclable Samsung Reclaim handset sold. The $500,000 raised protected 10,000 acres of habitat.

But the donation isn't always money. Sometimes it's an in-kind donation. For example, work apparel maker Dickies donated $25,000 and 5,000 pants to the Salvation Army of Metro Detroit. In addition, Dickies pledged to donate one additional pair of pants for each pair sold over a specified time-frame and made a total donation of 10,000 pairs of pants. Another wrinkle to this approach is that the donation is triggered by an action instead of a purchase.

Take this program from Specialized Bikes (see Figure 2-3). For every 1,000 Likes of its official Facebook page, Specialized Bikes donates a bike to CYCLE Kids, a nonprofit fighting obesity and inactivity among youth.

Figure 2-3: Facebook Likes resulted in bike donations.

Digital programs

Here's our prediction: The web, smartphones, social media, and especially *location-based marketing services* (when consumer marketing is done through smartphones based on a shopper's location; see Chapter 10) will change cause marketing forever. *Digital cause marketing programs* utilize these online platforms to engage consumers around a cause and may unlock corporate donations or other benefits for causes.

Here's how digital tools will change cause marketing and nonprofits:

- **The web is creating a new platform for nonprofit/for-profit partnerships.** Online contests are engaging consumers where they "live" online and giving companies an alternative to in-store programs. Online round-up programs are bringing point-of-sale and purchase-triggered donations to e-tailers. With hundreds of millions of active users, Facebook has become the platform of choice for digital cause marketing campaigns for companies of all sizes.

- **Smartphones have made the web and your cause portable.** Critics complain that cause marketing is too transactional and is more marketing than mission. Some shoppers don't even know what cause they're giving to at the register. They just want to give! Ideally, consumers should be able to connect with causes where they give, even if that's a checkout line at the supermarket. The good news is that smartphones are making this a reality! Cutting-edge technology like QR codes (see Figure 2-4) allows consumers to use their smartphones with a free QR reader application to view all sorts of online content from websites and testimonials to pictures and video. When shoppers know what they're supporting, it makes the cause, and the company's support for it, more meaningfully.

Figure 2-4:
QR codes
are offline
hyperlinks
to all types
of content.

✔ **Location-based services will put POS and PTD on the map.** We believe point-of-sale and purchase-triggered donations will be enhanced, if not eventually replaced, with location-based services (LBS) that use mobile technology to — among other things — target consumers when and where they shop.

Scenario 1: You visit your local Target and use your smartphone to check-in on your favorite location-based service (ours is Foursquare — see Chapter 10). "Welcome!" the screen says. "All this month you can support the Children's Miracle Network at the register [point-of-sale]. When you do, you'll save 5 percent off your total purchase today."

Scenario 2: You visit your local Target and check-in on your favorite location-based service. You get a list of all the pink products in the store that, when purchased, trigger a donation to the Breast Cancer Research Foundation. As an additional incentive, if you use your smartphone to scan the barcodes of any specially pink products, a donation is made to Breast Cancer Research Foundation whether you buy them or not. (We're not talking science fiction here. Have you ever used the *Red Laser* application on a smartphone to scan a barcode on a product to find a better price? *Red Laser* has been downloaded over 8 million times!)

Location-based services won't change cause marketing overnight. But its eventual impact will be important, dramatic, and beneficial to the field. While learning how to do POS and PTD will be important to your success as a local cause marketer, your future will hinge on your ability to integrate these traditional practices with the web, smartphones, and social media. We discuss location-based services in detail in Chapter 10.

Looking at other approaches

Although our focus is on point-of-sale, purchase and action triggered donations, and digital cause marketing, we touch upon at least three other cause marketing approaches in this book.

- ✔ **Employee engagement:** Harnessing the power of workforces to affect social change is just what The Home Depot did when it launched *1,000 Playgrounds in 1,000 Days*. Employers are supporting employee activities with paid time off to volunteer and by matching employee gifts, like General Electric did in the aftermath of the Haiti earthquake.

- ✔ **Message promotion:** In this approach, a business puts its resources to work to promote a cause-focused message. Dawn dishwashing liquid, in partnership with the Marine Mammal Center and The International Bird Rescue Research Center, ran a spot showing how Dawn could be used to safely wash animals affected by oil spills. Dawn took the extra step of highlighting that for every bottle of Dawn purchased and activated online, the company donated $1 to the two organizations. You can watch this video online by scanning the QR code to the left with your smartphone.

- ✔ **Licensing:** This is when a company pays a fee to use a nonprofit's brand on its product. Licensing may include a certification process by the nonprofit before the company is allowed to use the logo. For example, the American Heart Association's stamp of approval on numerous cereal boxes, including Joe's favorite, Cheerios, is a licensing agreement that includes a certification process. The product is first certified as meeting the American Heart Association's low-fat and low-cholesterol standards and then General Mills, the company that owns Cheerios, pays a fee to include American Heart Association's Heart Check icon on its box.

Determining What You Need for Success

From our experience working on dozens of cause marketing programs, we've compiled a list of five things you should do before you ever reach out to that first prospective partner:

- ✔ Get your boss on board
- ✔ Identify people that can help you

> ✔ Create a place of "yes" that celebrates success and failure
>
> ✔ Identify assets to get you started
>
> ✔ Slow down! Be realistic

Doing these things first will ensure that you

> ✔ Work effectively with your boss.
>
> ✔ Don't go crazy juggling cause marketing with the rest of your work responsibilities.
>
> ✔ Work in a permission culture that encourages creativity and risk.
>
> ✔ Have the right assets and expectations to succeed.

Get buy-in from your boss

Despite being around for more than 30 years, cause marketing is still a relatively new practice, especially for many local businesses and nonprofits. A lot of misunderstanding still exists on what cause marketing is, how it's executed, and what it can and can't accomplish.

Don't expect your boss to fully understand what cause marketing is and what it can accomplish after just one meeting. Even if he says he "gets it," as is common with bosses that want to come across as all-knowing, assume that he doesn't and tread carefully.

Without the support of your boss, you may not have access to the resources and contacts you need to make the program a success. You also may need someone to catch you if you fall.

In short, your boss needs to be your ally, not your adversary or a passive observer. Here's how to keep your boss close when it may seem like you're worlds apart.

> ✔ **Persuasion is incremental.** Do you really expect your boss to change her mind overnight? People don't generally change their minds quickly or easily, so you need to be realistic about what you can accomplish with each interaction. Setting goals that can move your agenda forward will keep you and your boss engaged, in sync, and motivated.

✔ **Keep your eye on the prize — benefits, not features.** While it's tempting to share every detail with your boss — remembering that some managers expect that level of information — if your boss is results-oriented, focus on sharing the benefits of your activities to your cause or business.

Cause marketing helps nonprofits raise money and build awareness, while for companies it enhances their favorability with consumers and employees and may help drive sales.

✔ **Take baby steps.** You can ramp up a cause marketing program in many ways. Many companies and causes already engage in or benefit from corporate giving and sponsorship. Begin your cause marketing effort with small steps. For example, if you're a manager that runs a chain of bagel stores, you might start by making a small company gift of cash or food to a local shelter. Next, you might put coin canisters in your stores to help your chosen cause. And then only after these successes will you be ready to hear other cause marketing ideas.

✔ **Share the glory.** Just as you have a boss, your boss has one, too — even if it's a board of directors. It's important that you find sincere, constructive ways to highlight your boss's support and commitment to your efforts. Cause marketing takes a team effort. And every team member should be acknowledged and credited for his work, including your boss.

Commit staff or staff time

Employees performing multiple jobs is a reality of our overworked society. The director of sales also heads up marketing and human resources. Event directors also solicit major gifts and run the annual fund. Employees have to shoulder more and more these days, so you may be tempted to put cause marketing on a colleague's already overflowing to-do list.

This is a big mistake.

The prospecting and project work associated with cause marketing requires time and a lot of energy. Cause marketing is worth doing, but like anything worth doing, it requires work and a dedicated staff.

You might have a current team member suited for this role. But because of the unique skills cause marketing requires, many organizations hire someone or contract out the role. To choose the right person for the job, keep the following in mind:

- ✔ **Most cause marketers are made, not born.** You won't find many people with cause marketer in their title or on their resume. A cause marketer is not like a grant writer or major gifts officer, which are everywhere in the nonprofit world. If you plan to pick someone from your current team, consider someone that has an aptitude and interest in marketing and sales. Choose the person on your team who has been talking your ear off about cause marketing; she may be a good choice because interest is key. Cause marketing is a fast-changing field, and passion is a prerequisite for keeping up.

- ✔ **Be open to candidates from other industries.** Good cause marketers can come from sales, marketing, promotions, retail, advertising, media, and other lines of work. While some of the cause marketers on our team came from the cause world, others came from media and retail. Their unique backgrounds and skills have helped us create and deliver better cause marketing programs.

- ✔ **Hire slowly; fire quickly.** Take your time to find the right cause marketer but realize that you may have to kiss a few frogs before you have the right person to lead your program. Hiring someone and then asking them to leave isn't fun for anyone. But don't compound a poor hiring decision by letting the wrong person linger in the position. Move on and hire someone else! Some programs have rocky starts. It happens. But don't let your program strike a rock and sink.

If you don't have someone you can directly learn cause marketing from, don't worry. Examples of successful campaigns abound. Cause Marketing Forum (www.causemarketingforum.com) has plenty of case studies you can read for free on its website. As shown in Figure 2-5, CMF also hosts an annual conference, where it presents the Halo Awards for excellence in cause marketing programs.

To see the impressive list of Halo Award winners, scan the QR code to the left with your smartphone or visit http://bit.ly/jvzuPE.

When we first started in cause marketing, we had few people to learn from. Fortunately, we live in a city with two strong, local cause marketing programs: The Jimmy Fund, the fundraising arm of the Dana-Farber Cancer Institute, and Children's Hospital Boston. We started the cause marketing program at our hospital by applying some of the things that had worked for them. And what worked for them worked for us, too! So don't underestimate the power of looking around you and learning from others in your community.

Figure 2-5:
The "Halo Awards" are presented at the annual Cause Marketing Forum conference, for outstanding cause marketing.

Bring entrepreneurial spirit to the team

The best cause marketers are progressive, curious, competitive, savvy, creative, fearless, headstrong, realistic, and opportunistic. (Hey, what can we say, we're biased!) Fundraising departments are generally conservative, passive, static, accommodating, and unrealistic.

Can you see how the two might not mix well together?

That's why, for cause marketing to thrive, you need an environment in which people can experiment, try new things, get mixed results, and even fail — sometimes a lot in the beginning.

How to get a job in cause marketing

A week doesn't go by that we don't get a call or e-mail from someone looking to "get into" cause marketing. We wish we could offer them better advice. Cause marketing is a nontraditional profession, which means there aren't a lot of advertised openings for cause marketers. The good news is that we believe that there are jobs in cause marketing, but you won't find them in the Help Wanted section of the newspaper or through online career sites, such as Monster.

Here's our advice for where the jobs are in cause marketing and how you can prepare yourself to get one:

✔ **Cause marketing jobs aren't so much born as they are made.** Few nonprofits have staff dedicated to cause marketing. In Boston, where we live and work, there are only a handful of cause marketing teams. This means that you'll have to pitch a prospective employer on creating a cause marketing job for you. Remember that you're living in the real world and probably won't do just cause marketing. You may do events, marketing, major gifts, and so on. That's just how things are in the nonprofit world. One person wears many hats. But at least one of those hats will be cause marketing! But before you go calling nonprofits that have corporate partners, strong events, a good brand, a social media footprint, and are just downright innovative — the things we would look for in an employer! — read this next point.

✔ **Get some experience in cause marketing.** Few nonprofits would hire a newbie to run their cause marketing program. The key is to work in the field a bit so that you can learn the ropes and see what's involved. We hire volunteers of all ages who become full-fledged team members with real responsibilities. But you don't have to come and work with us. Volunteer with another organization for which you feel passionate. Ask them if you can work on cause marketing. We'll bet you a stack of pinups it's something they're not currently doing. If you're in college, you could intern at an agency that focuses on cause marketing. A few good ones that come to mind are MSL Group and Cone in Boston; Barkley in Kansas City; Edelman in New York; For Momentum in Atlanta; and Roscia in Paramus, New Jersey.

If you don't have someone to learn from, examples abound of successful cause marketing efforts (Be sure to read about resources for cause marketing learning in Chapter 12). When we first started in cause marketing, the field was still new, and we had no one to learn from except from what we saw and read. Fortunately, we live in Boston with two strong, local cause marketing programs: The Jimmy Fund at the Dana-Farber Cancer Institute and Children's Hospital Boston. We applied some of the things that had worked for them, and they worked for us, too!

You can work in cause marketing. But it takes smarts, savvy, experience, and drive. Do you have what it takes?

We were always lucky to work in an environment that understood that cause marketing took time to develop and constantly needed to be tweaked. Progress at times was slow, but our risk-friendly culture encouraged open discussion about what did and didn't work and encouraged real innovation.

Your cause marketing staff should be held accountable for their work and results. However, progress, especially in the beginning, is more important than success. (To find out how to measure the success of your cause marketing program, see Chapter 11.)

Analyze your existing assets

Here's an analysis of the assets that can contribute to a successful cause marketing program:

- ✔ **Corporate partners:** Do you currently have relationships with companies that can kick off your cause marketing efforts? When we started our program, we had the CEOs of two local retailers that had personally been longtime supporters of our nonprofit and were eager to explore a cause marketing partnership. Those two partners helped us grow our cause marketing program to as many as 40 partnerships. Remember, this all started with two CEOs that were personal contributors to our cause!

  One day we shared this story with a Boston charity. "That's wonderful," they said, "but we don't have any supporters like that."

  "Really, you don't?" I said. "Can I see a list of your board of trustees?" Halfway down the list, I hit solid gold when I saw the name of the founder of one of the largest discount retailers in New England. "I would start with him," I said.

  Every cause has a company or contact that can help them kick off a cause marketing program. It's not always as easy as looking at a list of trustees, but these first partners are usually a lot closer than you think. We like to say they're not discovered as much as they are detected.

✔ **Events:** If you don't have a good business prospect, you'd better have a great event. Unfortunately, events aren't leveraged enough for cause marketing. But a well-attended event with some existing sponsors is an excellent beginning for a cause marketing program. In turn, cause marketing can drive attendance to your event and sponsor return-on-investment, as you can see from our experience in Figure 2-6.

If you're reading this and thinking of an event your cause runs that you're proud of, hold on to that thought or refer to Chapter 15.

✔ **Message:** Can you say in one simple, powerful sentence what your cause does? That's your message. Our cause provides exceptional healthcare to poor, sick children and their families. That's our message. Some messages are better for cause marketing than others. Most cause marketing is health and social service-related — for example, American Cancer Society, Feeding America, St. Jude Children's Research Hospital, Share Our Strength, Product (RED), Salvation Army, American Heart Association — but even if yours isn't, that doesn't mean you can't do cause marketing. What's important is that consumers can relate with your message and mission. This might be easier if your cause treats children with cancer. It may be more challenging when your cause focuses on a narrow, less common niche, such as saving rodents from scientific experimentation.

✔ **Constituents:** One of your greatest assets are your existing supporters. Are they vast in number or stand tall in the community or have political clout? Or perhaps you're lucky to have a group of diehard supporters that can move mountains. Don't overlook your human assets.

Figure 2-6:
Halloween Town's 15,000 guests were a key audience for companies and helped us recruit cause marketing partners for this event and others.

Identifying a good cause marketing program sometimes requires a trained eye. In Chapter 11, we help you quickly determine whether your cause marketing program has what it takes to be successful.

Corporate partners, events, and messages aren't so much prerequisites for cause marketing success as they are stepping stones that can help you progress more quickly and easily. That's why we call them assets, not necessities.

Set realistic expectations for your campaign

No nonprofit or business lives by cause marketing alone. Causes raise money in a variety of ways, including grants, direct mail, major gifts, and through cause marketing. The mix is different for every cause. Our experience has been that causes can increase their revenues 5 to 15 percent using cause marketing. So if you're a $2 million organization, it's possible to raise $100,000 to $200,000 more from cause marketing. You may raise more or less money, but if you expect to raise an additional $2 million from cause marketing, you're not being realistic.

Even cause marketing powerhouses, such as Komen for the Cure, St. Jude Children's Research Hospital, Children's Miracle Network, and Muscular Dystrophy Association, raise relatively small amounts from cause marketing compared to other, more lucrative fundraisers.

Companies need to be realistic on how much cause marketing can impact their bottom line. Plenty of studies show that cause marketing is an important and legitimate part of the marketing mix for businesses. But it's only one piece of the puzzle, and it doesn't replace a comprehensive marketing strategy.

A company relying on cause marketing as its only marketing tool is being as unrealistic as a cause that expects it to double its revenues with it.

Crafting a Strong Cause Marketing Message

When we started our cause marketing program, one of our first partners was a New England party retailer. Our first program together was a POS program involving pinups with cashiers asking shoppers to donate a dollar to the hospital.

At first, the results weren't as good as we had hoped, so we camped out at a store and watched the register. When the cashier asked the shopper to support the hospital, they generally said no — except when the cashier asked the shopper to donate to help "poor sick kids," to which the shopper almost always said yes. With a little research, we discovered that shoppers weren't against giving to our hospital. They just didn't know much about us, so it was easier to say no. Being relatively unknown to shoppers hurt our cause at the register. But when we focused on our issue — poor sick kids — they donated.

That's when we decided that our cause marketing campaigns would never again be undermined by poor messaging. And thanks to this section, neither will yours.

Pinkwashing shouldn't color your thinking

Regardless of the season — but especially in October during Breast Cancer Awareness Month — you can always find cause marketing for breast cancer causes in stores. Seeing pink everywhere — and we do mean *everywhere* — may brainwash you into thinking that only causes with cancer messages can do cause marketing successfully. Everyone else needs a special dispensation from the Pope of Pink, Komen for the Cure founder Nancy Goodman Brinker.

Nothing could be further from the truth. Here are five reasons why you should get started today:

✔ **The rewards of cause marketing are available to just about every cause.** All types of causes can benefit from cause marketing. Flutie Flakes (Figure 2-7), with former Boston College hero, Heisman Trophy winner, and NFL quarterback Doug Flutie on the box, has raised millions for the Doug Flutie, Jr. Foundation for Autism. Another one of our favorites is Share Our Strength, a national anti-hunger organization based in Washington, D. C., which works with all types of businesses, but especially restaurants. Yet another is Boston-based Jumpstart, a childhood literacy group, which for several years received tens of thousands of dollars from Leprechaun Lattes sold at Starbucks. We've also seen great cause marketing programs that supported animals of all kinds, seniors, and victims of domestic violence. Okay, not every single cause can do cause marketing (someone once asked me about cause marketing for convicts . . . hmmm . . .), but nine out of ten causes seems reasonable.

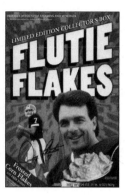

Figure 2-7:
Flutie Flakes
raised
millions for
the Doug
Flutie, Jr.
Foundation
for Autism.

✔ **You already have a corporate partner.** Most of cause marketing success comes from having a great partner to work with, regardless of your cause. When you have a partner that is committed to finding a way to work with your cause, it doesn't matter if you're a well-known national health organization or a neighborhood nonprofit that wants to strip the streets of litter. A partner in hand is better than two you hope to meet next week.

We think about this every time we go into Marshalls, a discount retail chain that's part of the TJX family of companies, and see their cause marketing campaigns for domestic violence awareness (see Figure 2-8). It must not have been easy for Marshalls to support such a painful cause. But TJX, Marshalls' parent company, is committed, and that's what made the campaign a reality. So if you have a good company to work with, what's stopping you?

✔ **Consumers will give generously to most causes.** If you can get your cause marketing program to the point that a cashier is asking a shopper to support it, it doesn't really matter what your cause is; people will donate. Even though 75 percent of the people our nonprofit serves live in that area in and around Boston called Suffolk County, some of our best cause marketing partners are retailers with stores in Rhode Island, Connecticut, New Hampshire, Maine, and even Florida. Yep, you heard us right on that last one: We said Florida! Donors are generous and give to causes that are doing good work, regardless of where they're located. If the issue has an emotional pull and the ask is sincere, consumers will give.

Look no further than the success of St. Jude Children's Research Hospital. Despite being just a 70-bed hospital in Memphis, Tennessee, St. Jude raises tens of millions of dollars across the country.

Figure 2-8:
Marshalls
Shop 'til
It Stops
program
benefits the
National
Domestic
Violence
Hotline.

✔ **Your cause targets a different demographic than women.** Businesses love working with cancer causes because they can support a great cause that has a large, loyal following of women. But aren't there other causes and key demographics? Men, teens, seniors? Take Ben & Jerry's Hubby Hubby cause marketing campaign in support of gay rights and marriage equality. There's no ribbon on the ice cream container, and this cause promotion wasn't just for women.

✔ **Shoppers are sick of pink.** We tell ourselves that pink products may have jumped the shark and oversaturated the marketplace. Businesses are looking for new causes to support and new opportunities to differentiate themselves. Make sure they find you.

Don't apologize for not being a cancer charity: Celebrate it!

Choosing your Famous Last Words

Every cause marketing program needs *Famous Last Words* (FLW). Famous Last Words is the phrase you want the consumer to remember above all else. Despite what comes before or after it, these are the words they recall and respond to.

"Would you like to make a difference in the life of a sick child?"

"Can you help feed a hungry family this holiday season?"

> *"50 cents from the sale of this pet food will help find good homes for rescued puppies and kittens in the Los Angeles area."*

All these cause marketing messages are concise, powerful, emotional, and memorable. These examples alone are reason enough to hone your cause marketing message down to a single, memorable sentence. But here's another: People don't have time for a longer pitch, especially when their hands are full with diapers, milk, and cotton swabs. Shoppers want you to get to the point.

Connect with consumers emotionally and immediately and tell them what you want. Then let them go about their day. If you've done your job well, your Famous Last Words will motivate them to give.

Messaging does not always equal mission

The challenge when choosing your Famous Last Words is that causes want to include everything in that one sentence, instead of focusing on that one thing that will blow consumers away. That's why your cause marketing message doesn't always have to reflect the full mission of your organization.

For example, our hospital serves a diverse population of lower-income residents in the Boston area. We obviously serve every age, gender, and minority group in the city. But when it comes to cause marketing, we focus (depending on the program) on one of three emotional hot-buttons: sick children, poor women, and anyone with cancer. We chose these three focus areas because the hospital deals with these three issues every day, and consumers can easily and powerfully relate to them.

Going with your best horse isn't something new or crazy. As marketing genius Al Ries, coauthor of the classic *22 Immutable Laws of Marketing*, explained in *Ad Age* (http://adage.com/article/al-ries/understanding-marketing-psychology-halo-effect/108676), Apple built its early empire by promoting the iPod and iTunes. The success of those two products trickled down to their entire product line:

> *"Focusing your marketing message on a single word or concept has been our mantra for years. But taking this idea one step further can also produce dramatic results. To cut through the clutter in today's overcommunicated society, place your marketing dollars on your best horse. Then let that product or service serve as a halo effect for the rest of the line."*

> — Al Ries

A cause that leads with its strongest hand is The Jimmy Fund, which raises money for the world-renowned Dana-Farber Cancer Institute. While the goal of The Jimmy Fund is to raise money to fight cancer in children and adults, their Famous Last Words are focused on the children they are aiding in their fight against cancer. Indeed, the enduring image of The Jimmy Fund is courageous bald-headed children stricken by cancer.

Some could argue that The Jimmy Fund mission is not just about children, and its cause marketing should include the faces of the adults they help. But by focusing on children — the *halo,* the best horse — everyone is served, including adults. We highlight in greater detail some successful Jimmy Fund programs in Chapters 13 and 15.

Your message is about marketing *and* mission. And while both should be included, you should be clear on what comes first. Pick that piece of your mission that will resonate most with consumers and make that the centerpiece of your marketing.

Keeping things simple

The best cause marketing messages are ultimately very simple ones. They're brief, compelling, emotive, persuasive, and memorable. Keep these pointers in mind when you turn your cause's mission into a cause marketing message.

- ✔ Don't be intimidated that your cause isn't the household name some causes are. With the right partner (see Chapter 3) or event (see Chapters 4 and 15) and the right message, anyone can do cause marketing.

- ✔ Think like a consumer and ask yourself what about your cause would motivate you to support it. Share it with people you know and don't know! Get their feedback and revise it until you have refined your Famous Last Words.

- ✔ Don't feel guilty if your Famous Last Words don't reflect everything your cause does. Trust that the halo it will give you in the marketplace will ultimately illuminate everything you do as consumers learn more about your organization and add other forms of giving to support your cause. At the very least, the money you raise from cause marketing may fund other important initiatives.

Moving from Transactional to Transformative Cause Marketing

Any cause or business can do cause marketing. If you have the right partner and a good message, you can raise money and build favorability with the tactics we cover in this book.

Transactional cause marketing is something businesses and causes do every day. It's an easy way to give back to a cause and generate some foot traffic for a business.

For example, once a month, a cafe near our hospital donates 5 percent of the day's receipts to a pediatric program at the hospital. It's great way to give back, and since they're so close to the hospital, it drives hungry customers, including our own employees, to their doors.

But *transformative cause marketing,* the kind of cause marketing that deeply changes your business or cause financially, culturally, and operationally, requires more than just a good partner and message. It takes a powerful, magnetic identity.

On this subject, we highly recommend Jocelyne Daw and Carol Cone's *Breakthrough Nonprofit Branding: Seven Principles to Power Extraordinary Results* (Wiley, 2010).

In this section, we look at why branding is so important to your success and the balancing act all brands face. The challenge of balancing philanthropy, marketing, and business isn't easy, but it is achievable.

Why branding is key

Local nonprofits and businesses frequently wonder how they can have a successful cause marketing program or build upon the one they have. The answer is simple. It's actually three things: Brand. Brand. Brand.

Powerful cause brands are like magnets. They do good things, and good things are in turn attracted to them. Take national causes like Feeding America, Product (RED) (see Figure 2-9), UNICEF, and Children's Miracle Network. They do great work, and companies flock to partner with them (just as causes flock to powerful business brands like New Balance, Starbucks, and Walmart and flood them with requests and proposals).

You've probably witnessed the brand power of certain causes and companies from afar because your nonprofit doesn't have the same magnetic pull. Your mission may be just as worthy as any other cause, but it's hidden by a cloak and anonymity and irrelevance that's deadly to causes.

Branding is what you experience — what you feel —when you come into contact with someone's product or service. For example, when I see a Zipcar (a car sharing company), my thoughts turn to urban-eco-hipsters. When I buy the latest Apple iPhone, I feel like a trendy geek.

Figure 2-9:
Product (RED) has raised over $150 million for the Global Fund HIV and AIDS programs through cause marketing since 2006.

Good brands, whether for-profit or nonprofit, generate strong, visceral energy that's as strong and addictive as any coffee. With a stronger brand, you'll have a better and bigger cause marketing program. Plenty of causes that raise a lot of money without cause marketing don't have well-known brands. But we don't know of any causes that are successful with large-scale cause marketing initiatives that aren't also well-known brands. We bet you don't either. Great brands do great cause marketing, and great cause marketing goes hand in hand with great brands.

How do you create that brand? Jeff Brooks of the *Future Fundraising Now* blog has a suggestion:

> *"Instead of a look-at-me brand, it's a look-at-you brand. It recognizes that donors give to make good things happen, not to support an organization. Instead of promising to be the coolest charity on the block, it promises a fulfilling, information-rich experience that will maximize the donor's impact."*

The advantages of such an approach are two-fold. First, as a cause you'll have a lot more impact. Second, supporters will see the difference you're making clearly and dramatically.

Jeff's suggestion is a great one for causes as it addresses the need to create and communicate a powerful experience for the donor that generates an equally powerful response.

Is slick what makes great brands tick?

Branding is key for long-term success in cause marketing. But what if your branding efforts go too far?

Cause branding that is over the top or too slick won't stick. Most people have radar for branding that's gone too far or doesn't match the brand.

Of course, what's slick really lies in the eyes of the beholder. What's appropriate for a teenager may turn off a retiree.

The Pepsi Refresh Project with its online submission of worthy projects and vote-getting to choose winners strikes home with a younger digital audience interested in engagement and power. Conversely, a retiree may prefer a more traditional form of giving, which a teen would find like . . . duh . . . dumb.

Slick is of keen interest to cause marketers because we often teeter on the brink of it. After all, we are marketers!

Komen's Bucket for the Cure program with Kentucky Fried Chicken went too far for many consumers and was widely criticized (see Chapter 13). But a hamburger and onion-scented candle sold by White Castle (shown in Figure 2-10) with proceeds going to Autism Speaks was a big hit with consumers, with all 10,000 candles selling in less than 48 hours.

Figure 2-10:
White Castle's hamburger and onion-scented candle was a hit with customers and raised $50,000 for Autism Speaks.

Here's how White Castle and Autism Speaks kept the spark in their program without igniting the controversy Buckets for the Cure got:

- ✔ **Think different.** Instead of raising money for Autism Speaks with their fast-food menu, which may have led to the same type of criticism KFC got, White Castle chose a nonfood item, a candle, as the centerpiece of its cause marketing promotion.

- ✔ **Focus on the social good.** Critics complained that Buckets for the Cure encouraged consumers to eat unhealthy food that could lead to obesity and illness — not to mention the KFC advertising efforts to bring pink supporters into the chicken coop with their fried and fatty Double Down sandwich. Conversely, the White Castle promotion was directed at loyalists who loved the smell of White Castle's onion-covered hamburgers. White Castle was simply giving its most loyal customers a chance to support a good cause without asking them to eat another hamburger — or even go into a restaurant, as most sales happened at its online store.

- ✔ **Keep things taut.** Great marketing, and great cause marketing in particular, has a certain tension to it. When cause marketing is provocative without being disingenuous, people remember it more, and it's more effective. While Buckets for a Cure was a much bigger cause marketing campaign, it ultimately had a negative impact for KFC and Komen (see Figure 2-11).

Figure 2-11:
Kentucky
Fried
Chicken
raised over
$4M for
Komen for
the Cure
with its
Buckets for
the Cure.
But many
consumers
felt that KFC
and Komen
put money
and fried
chicken
before
breast
cancer
awareness.

While we don't all enjoy the smell of a hamburger and onion-scented candle, White Castle's effort had one scent we could all enjoy: the sweet smell of cause marketing success.

Striking the Right Balance of Philanthropy, Marketing, and Business

While U2's Bono is best known for his cause marketing success with Product (RED), another venture with his wife, Ali Hewson, during the launch of a fashion line with clothes made in sub-Saharan Africa had a rougher start.

Bono and Hewson's noble intentions unfortunately didn't get enough consumers to pay $800 for a jacket. Design and fit mattered more.

"We focused too much on the mission in the beginning," explained Hewson. "It's the clothes, it's the product. It's a fashion company. That needs to be first and foremost."

The lesson here for cause marketers is that you have to carefully balance philanthropy, marketing, and business in the programs you create.

- ✔ **If you overemphasize philanthropy,** you may miss the powerful opportunity consumerism can deliver. Just think what would have happened if Bono had been focused on philanthropy when he first solicited companies to support Product (RED). He would have accepted their checks, which many offered, instead of signing cause marketing pacts, which raised millions more and established (RED) as a leading cause brand in just a few short years.

- ✔ **If you underweigh philanthropy,** you run the risk of putting marketing first and turning consumers off because they'll see the company's efforts as insincere and cursory. This is the chord Urban Outfitters struck with its branded National Public Radio tee that sold on NPR's and Urban Outfitters' online stores. The same tee sold in both stores, but only those sold at the NPR's store benefited public radio. Someone should have told Urban Outfitters that tees are supposed to be light. Giving isn't.

- ✔ **If you overemphasize marketing and business,** you blind yourself to the greater good. Even when the philanthropy is in the millions and the marketing even more, and seemingly well intentioned, people see it for what it is: a dumb ploy to sell more stuff.

Is cause marketing really a disaster after disasters?

No sooner had the ground stopped shaking in Japan earlier this year, and people were already shaking their fists calling for a moratorium on cause marketing. It happens after every disaster (the last being after the earthquake in Haiti).

We're not saying that these calls for pause weren't uncalled for. We're just wondering whether cause marketing is really a disaster after disasters, or are people just being overly sensitive?

Of course, post-disaster is no time for marketing ploys. This begs the question if there is ever a good time or a good way to use cause marketing for good in the wake of a disaster.

We think the answer is yes thanks to a great online cause marketing program from Zynga, the gaming company behind Mafia Wars, Farmville, and a host of other games. (Speaking of Farmville, social games are fertile ground for cause marketing. eMarketer estimates that 68 million Americans will be playing *social games* — online games in which you play with people across the street or around the world — by 2012.)

Following the earthquake in Japan, Zynga approached Direct Relief International in hopes of repeating what it did after the Haiti earthquake when it raised $1.5 million for the victims. While a violent video game such as Mafia Wars is an unlikely partner for a humanitarian aid organization, Direct Relief decided to move forward and never looked back.

Zynga created a virtual fan that players of the game could buy for $5, 100 percent of which went to Direct Relief. In a matter of weeks, Zynga raised $600,000 for Japan. Moreover, the company raised more online awareness for Direct Relief than ever before, leading Direct Relief to be listed in Charity Navigator's Top Ten Most Viewed Charities. This is impressive considering Direct Relief spends a fraction of what the other nonprofits on the list spend on marketing and advertising.

What a fantastic cause marketing program. A few key takeaways for cause marketers, which we emphasize throughout the book:

✔ **With cause marketing, the money is in the customer, not in the company.** Zynga could have just written a check to charity after the Japan earthquake, but it most likely wouldn't have been for $600,000. Zynga was smart and responsible to leverage its business model and give players a chance to support victims in Japan.

✔ **Brand matters.** Zynga sought out a well-known and respected organization to partner with in Direct Relief International. Good cause brands are like magnets that attract money, partnerships, and opportunity. If you want to succeed in cause marketing, build your brand, and companies will come.

✔ **Cause marketing can work after disasters.** Zynga didn't try to profit from the disaster or their players' support for victims. It simply chose an easy and powerful way to involve its business and customers in disaster relief.

✔ **Even killers have a soft spot.** You'll want to steer clear of offline businesses involving the Mafia, but working with nontraditional or somewhat unpopular partners is okay. While Komen had its missteps with Kentucky Fried Chicken and *Buckets for the Cure* as we discuss in this chapter and again in Chapter 13, fast-food chains can be responsible and excellent cause marketing partners.

But like in Mafia Wars you need to proceed with caution and care, or your reputation will get whacked.

Chapter 3

What a Beautiful Couple You Make! Finding the Right Partner

In This Chapter

▶ Identifying cause marketing partners that share your goals

▶ Leveraging your assets to identify new partners

▶ Keeping partners organized with CRM

Cause marketing is like a marriage: You need a partner. But choosing that special someone is never easy. Compatibility is important, but you also want a good provider. No one wants to wake up one morning and realize they picked the wrong partner!

You have to size up prospects and decide whether they're worth your time, attention, and, yes, a commitment. That's a lot of responsibility. Thankfully, you've come to cause marketing relationship experts.

This chapter looks at how to choose the right partner and what to look for. You discover that sometimes you don't have to look very far: Good partners are often closer than you think.

Defining What a Partner Is in Cause Marketing

Cause marketing is a partnership between a nonprofit and a company for mutual benefit (see Chapter 1). The company wants to enhance its reputation with customers and drive sales. The cause wants to generate awareness for its mission and raise money. Cause marketing is win-win. It's no wonder Joe named his blog Selfish Giving!

Cause marketing can't happen without two players. Some people think that when a cause that clothes the poor opens its own for-profit used clothing store, it's cause marketing. It's not, because there's no for-profit partner — it's just a nonprofit undertaking a for-profit activity.

On the other hand, a business that just gives money to a cause without working strategically with one can't be called cause marketing, either. There's another name for it: corporate philanthropy.

Cause marketing can take many shapes, but it all starts with a partnership between a cause and a company. Let the courtship begin.

Managing Prospects through a Circle Strategy

Where to find partners is a constant challenge. Our strategy for finding them will have you going in circles, but we promise you won't feel like a hamster! Whether you're a cause or a company, employing a *circle strategy* in which you plot your prospects on a target and move from your strongest leads in the bull's-eye to the weakest ones in the outer circles will help you focus on your best prospects first.

A target will help you plot your best relationships and opportunities. Figure 3-1 shows what a circle strategy looks like with three concentric circles.

Figure 3-1: A circle strategy is your best first step in finding a partner.

✔ The innermost circle of the target (the bull's-eye!) is where your closest relationships lie. These causes and companies are the people you know and with whom you already have a relationship. They're like friends: familiar, committed, and trustworthy. If you had the choice between working with a stranger and working with a friend, whom would you choose? As we like to say, go first where you are known and loved!

Our closest relationships at our nonprofit are with two New England retailers, iParty and Ocean State Job Lot. Their CEOs supported our organization and were very engaged with our cause, which made them excellent prospects for cause marketing.

✔ The second outer circle represents familiar but more distant connections. For a cause, this connection may be a business that is aware of your work but has never supported you. If you're a business, we're talking causes introduced to you by customers, friends, and employees. While they don't have a direct connection with you, their mission or link to someone you do know has earned your attention.

At our hospital, vendors that provided the hospital with goods and services fell directly in this circle. They knew us, did business with us, but hadn't supported our mission directly. Nevertheless, they had great potential. A business relationship with Staples led to a cause marketing program at 100 of its stores in New England.

✔ The outermost circle includes companies and causes that are unknown to you and you to them. The last circle is like the edge of a solar system, as these distant objects are not the hot leads of the two inner circles. But they're also not planets stuck in a fixed orbit. Today's distant orb can be tomorrow's red-hot prospect.

For example, Valvoline Instant Oil Change and Finagle-A-Bagel were neither donors nor vendors. They were prospects that we began cold-calling many years earlier. Despite not being familiar with our organization, over time they grew to admire our nonprofit's mission and recognize the benefits of cause marketing. Both have raised tens of thousands of dollars for our cause.

As you can see, we had success within each circle, but it didn't happen all at once. It began with the inner circle, which started a ripple. Success in the inner circle created opportunity at the second circle as we approached existing contacts with creative and proven ideas. Activity in the second circle led to success as prospects began to learn about our successes and respond to our calls to work together. This ultimately fed the inner circle as we had new friends and supporters that started the process anew.

Researching a company for your cause

Using the circle strategy, you may be able to start plotting a few causes on the three rings. If you're lucky, you can already see a couple bull's-eyes on the target!

But before you even think about asking a company to support your cause, ask the following questions about each one. Answering these questions first will save you time, a lot of frustration, and maybe even embarrassment.

- ✔ **Does the company support other causes?** You may think you want a company that's never worked with another cause. You'll have them all to yourself! But that company may not support causes for some very good reasons. Maybe it doesn't want to. Maybe it tried and failed. But when a company already works with one or more causes, it's a good sign they are community-minded and philanthropic. Oftentimes, a company that supports one cause will support more, especially when you're bringing a business opportunity like cause marketing to the table. The company that has never supported a cause may not be open to your ideas. Go where you're wanted and expected.

- ✔ **Is the company a "good" business?** Nonprofits use cause marketing to support their missions, not to hurt them. But aligning your cause with a company that has a poor reputation in the community, or questionable business practices, can hurt your cause. Research potential partners with your nonprofit board, local Chamber of Commerce, and the Better Business Bureau. Your cause needs cause marketing, not crisis communication.

- ✔ **Does your cause and the business share a natural connection?** What's a better fit for a toy store? A cause that supports children with HIV/AIDS or a local historical preservation group?

  When a cause and company's mission intersect, we call it *Garanimal cause marketing* because it's a natural match, sometimes too much in our opinion. We like when cause and company have distinctive identities that don't blend beyond consumer recognition. Yes, like those perfectly matched but predictable Garanimal clothes we used to wear. (Do you remember Garanimal children's clothes? They had different animals on the tags so it was easy for kids — and, face it, parents — to match pants and tops by finding the tags with giraffes or monkeys, and so on.) You can see what Garanimal cause marketing looks like in Figure 3-2.

  While the historical preservation wasn't a good match for the toy store, that doesn't mean they can't do cause marketing. How about partnering with a hardware store or paint company? There's a business for just about every cause. You just need to find the right match.

- ✔ **Are the company's customers your supporters?** The largest causes and companies that practice cause marketing put a good deal of thought and research into what nonprofits and businesses will resonate with donors. You should examine this as well. Here are examples of two nonprofits that wisely put customers before cause:

  - Komen, the breast cancer giant best known for its pink cause marketing products, targets companies that make products for women, such as footwear-maker New Balance and the hearty family meals from Campbell's Soups.

- Share Our Strength, a national anti-hunger organization based in Washington, D.C. targets companies that serve the restaurant community, as many of their fundraising events are run and supported by chefs and other food service workers.

These are just a few ideas to help you begin profiling the right companies for cause marketing. You'll probably have more questions before you ever contact a company. But if the company you're targeting has a history of supporting good causes, a good reputation in the community, a connection in either mission or customers with your cause, you may just have a good prospect.

Identifying the right cause for your company

Some of the things that apply to a nonprofit finding a good company (see preceding section) are also applicable to a company finding a good cause:

✔ Choose a cause with a good reputation.

✔ Identify a cause that has a natural connection with the product or mission of your company (for example, a bedding company that works with local shelters to give mattresses to clients moving into new apartments).

✔ Determine whether the cause's donors fit the demographic of your company's customers and prospects.

Figure 3-2:
A natural match helps establish a new relationship with a business.

However, businesses should also use its own criteria when choosing a cause. We've spent many years working with companies on cause marketing pacts. If we ran our own business and wanted to partner with a cause, here's what we would look for:

- ✔ **A cause that gets cause marketing:** Just as it's difficult to work with a business that's never worked with a cause, the opposite is true, too. That's why a cause should have a grasp of public relations, and some experience with the marketing of causes, corporate philanthropy, and sponsorship also helps. Couple these qualities with lots of enthusiasm and creativity, and your cause marketing campaign is positioned for success. If your partner needs brushing up on cause marketing, you can lend them this book!

- ✔ **A cause that understands technology and social media:** If you discover anything from this book, it will be that the mobile web and social media will play a key role in the future of cause marketing (see Chapters 9 and 10). Fortunately, many nonprofits have been avid first adopters of social media. Still, many smaller nonprofits are just getting started with social media. To make the most of the advice in this book and to increase the chances of success for your cause marketing program, you should ideally partner with a nonprofit that is comfortable with technology and social media.

- ✔ **A cause that isn't cause-centric:** We find it strange how causes are all about helping others, but all they can do is talk about themselves. A clear sign that a cause isn't a good partner is when they show little or no interest in your business or in helping you. They'll happily share every detail of their cause and pick up a check when you have one for them, but they don't view your partnership . . . well, as a partnership! If you find a nonprofit that acts this way, do yourself a favor and look elsewhere.

- ✔ **A cause that has some assets:** Given the choice between two causes that you admire equally, choose the one that already works with partners and has several established, well-attended annual events and a social media presence. Assets are like money in a marriage: You always wish you had some when the honeymoon is over.

Zeroing in on the best companies

The circle strategy isn't just for finding prospects. (See the section "Managing Prospects through a Circle Strategy," earlier in this chapter.) It also tells you where to look for them.

Start by working with your innermost circle and contact your current supporters and donors. Because they know you better than anyone else, they can open doors to other prospects. They are your No. 1 resource!

Here are the best ways to work with your supporters:

- **You need to know your supporters' contacts as well as they do.** A common mistake is showing up at a board meeting and asking attendees to write down everyone they know that could help you. Besides having a poor memory, people will leave out the contacts they are even the slightest bit hesitant about contacting on your behalf. A better approach is to continuously research your supporters and know who their best contacts are so that you can speak to them directly about helping you. "I know that you do a fair amount of business with XYZ Corporation. Do you think you could introduce us to the CEO so we could talk to her about cause marketing?"

- **Make it easy for your supporters to help you.** We're convinced that most people are sincere in their desire to help, but if you ask too much of them, they won't. While the level of help you'll need from your supporters will vary depending on the prospect, the goal should be to have them just open doors. Once they see how easy it is to help you and how well you represent your cause and your supporters, they'll be more inclined to do it again.

Educating your supporters on what cause marketing is is critical. Make sure that they know you're not just asking them to call their friends to make a donation. Cause marketing isn't philanthropy. Cause marketing is win-win. It helps the cause and the business. Be sure that they're clear on how cause marketing is different from giving.

After you contact your supporters, move on to your second circle and reconnect with your past business contacts and/or vendors. We like to say that regardless of whether a company is a partner or not, a good cause marketing prospect is a good prospect forever. That's why we keep in touch with our former partners, especially when we have new cause marketing programs on the horizon. If you work for a big hospital or organization like we do, you have vendors you can contact. They understand your mission better than anyone and benefit if your organization continues to grow.

Vendors (companies that a company or your organization buys its supplies or services from) can include the vendors of your current supporters and donors, too, so don't hesitate to work their circles as well.

Also, remember to explore your outer circle through social media and traditional means. You've worked hard to keep up on Twitter, Facebook, and LinkedIn. Make sure that you're using them to connect with prospects when possible.

For example, we've developed some great relationships by connecting with prospects on Twitter, hands down our favorite social media tool. A connection with the head of a marketing agency here in Boston started with sharing links to interesting articles and even banter on local sports teams. Staying top of mind with this contact paid off for us. When a restaurant client of his was looking for a nonprofit partner to benefit from an upcoming charity event, he thought of us.

It can also be helpful to attend networking events, read business journals and pay attention to who's advertising in your local newspaper and on television and radio. Companies that value getting people to notice them will appreciate the awareness that cause marketing offers.

Keeping your partners organized with customer relationship management (CRM)

The circle strategy can help you identify cause marketing prospects. But remembering all those contacts and your conversations with them isn't easy. That's why you need a place to store and retrieve this information, record activities related to your outreach, and update their status when things change. A Customer Relationship Management (CRM) tool helps you record and track your contacts.

There are many good CRM options to choose from, including online solutions that link with social media. Which solution you choose is up to you. We've used Sage ACT!, shown in Figure 3-3, more than any other CRM solution. Though not free, we like how flexible the contact, task, and calendar management is and how it integrates with Outlook. Sage ACT! costs about $200 for ten people sharing the same database.

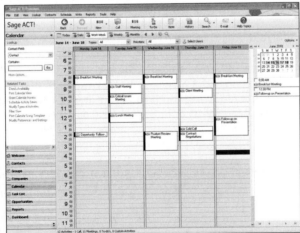

Figure 3-3:
Sage ACT!
is just
one of the
affordable,
effective,
and out-
of-the-box
solutions
available
to manage
your
prospects.

Free or affordable online CRM options to consider

If you're hesitant about committing yourself to one product and buying software you need to install on your computer, you can try one of the growing number of free online CRM solutions available.

✔ **Less Annoying Software** (www.less annoyingsoftware.com) has a free 30-day trial and afterwards is $10 a month.

✔ **Simple Sales Tracking** (www.simple salestracking.com) is free as long as you stay under 50 contacts. If you're a small nonprofit, the free version of it may be plenty. If not, a full account is $15 a month.

✔ **Zoho CRM** (www.zoho.com/crm) is free, with space for up to 100,000 records

(try to fill that!) and access for up to three users from the same organization. A professional edition offers more space and unlimited users for $12 a month.

✔ If you want an online version of Sage ACT!, subscription-based **Sage Connected Services** might be a good choice for you with access levels ranging from free to $54.95 per user, per month.

✔ **Gist** (www.gist.com) is the CRM solution of choice for social media enthusiasts. It pulls all your contact information from your address book but also from your inbox, Twitter, Facebook, and LinkedIn. Gist is currently available for free.

Here's how to make the most out of your CRM solution:

1. **Give each contact a designation that shows its place in the circle strategy.**

   For example, we would label a business in the bull's-eye a *Prospect* +; a business in the second circle, a *Prospect;* and one in the outer circle, a *Prospect TBA.*

   These are just suggested labels. Come up with your own. Just make sure that you understand what makes a *Prospect* + different from a *Prospect TBA.*

2. **Record everything.**

   Any communication with the prospect or any bit of intelligence gathered needs to be recorded. Did you leave the prospect a voicemail today? Record it. Have you read a recent news story about a prospective company's new product line? Paste the story or link into the prospect's record. This string of information may help you direct your efforts with this prospect or lead you to another prospect entirely.

3. **Let the software do the work.**

   Reminders, calendar updates, to-dos, and institutional memory should not be your worries. Allow the software to do these tedious tasks on your behalf.

4. Track your progress.

Most contact management software programs have dashboards that allow you to track your team's progress toward a goal, both in terms of activities and revenue. Every day you can get a quick snapshot of where you stand, determine what needs to be done, and generate a report for your boss. See Figure 3-4 for an example of a dashboard from Sage ACT!

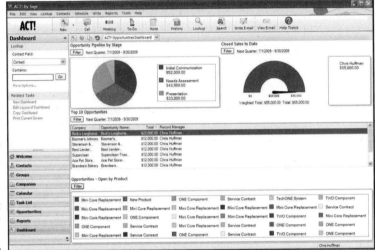

Figure 3-4: Dashboards give you a snapshot of your progress.

Weighing National versus Local Companies

Ideally, you want to find a way to work with both national and local companies. But you need to know the pros and cons of each type.

If you're working with national retailer, you may face these challenges:

- ✔ **A longer decision-making process:** The local manager doesn't always have the final say; the corporate office does. And that office may be halfway across the country or halfway around the world.

- ✔ **A disconnect with your cause in different parts of the country:** If you are a Seattle-based nonprofit that serves the Pacific Northwest, will shoppers in Florida support your cause? Will you have to customize your cause marketing materials for different regions? Figure 3-5 shows how nonprofits from different areas can work together to raise money with cause marketing.

Laws govern interstate cause marketing. Be sure that you know the laws for your state and for any state you plan to launch a program in. Just because you're doing something for a good cause doesn't give you cause to break the law.

✔ **Difficulty coordinating program kick off:** It might not be in the budget to fly to a dozen cities to kick-off a pinup program. You will most likely rely on the district managers in those cities to execute the program on your behalf. Are you prepared to hand over the reins of your success to someone else? You probably won't have to worry about these issues with local companies, but they have their own unique challenges. Here are three common ones:

- **Local businesses are late-comers to cause marketing.** While many national companies have been doing cause marketing for years, local businesses are just now gearing up to participate. So while you don't have a chain of command to climb like you do at national companies, you do face a longer learning curve.

- **They don't have the footprint national companies do.** In the next section, you discover that your success hinges largely on the number of locations and the foot traffic at those stores. You can do cause marketing with companies of any size, but the best opportunities are found by partnering with the largest local companies in your area.

- **They don't always have the operational infrastructure to ensure a smooth program.** Years ago all the supplies for a cause marketing campaign were delivered in person and cashiers kept track of donations by putting them in an envelope under the register drawer. Now cause marketing materials are drop-shipped and scanned into stores like any other store item.

Still, some local businesses will expect you to drop off pinups, and they'll keep track of donations in an envelope. This type of old school program can work, but logistical demands must be weighed carefully.

Your goal is to work with both national and local companies that will help you execute successful cause marketing programs. We've worked well with national and local companies for years. So can you.

Figure 3-5:
This pinup
was sold in
Florida.

Managing lots of locations

Most successful cause marketing campaigns involve businesses with multiple locations. For example, Chili's Grill & Bar raised $6.2 million for St. Jude Children's Research Hospital in 2008. This is an impressive total that wouldn't have been accomplished if Chili's didn't have 1,400 locations in the United States and Canada.

Even our experience with local cause marketing in Boston has pointed to an undisputable fact: the more storefronts a company has, the more money your cause is likely to raise. It's no surprise that our most successful cause marketing partner is also the retailer with the most stores (100).

When reaching out to companies with multiple locations in your area, consider the following:

- ✔ **Company-owned stores are the best to work with.** If you're lucky enough to connect with the CEO of a company with multiple stores you've got a top-down bullhorn to everyone else in the company. Even if you work with someone else in the company, you'll benefit from the close hierarchy within the organization and their ability to get things done.

- ✔ **Regionally franchised stores offer the best of both worlds.** These businesses present a great opportunity because they are national companies that have been segmented geographically and sold as franchises to investors. It's worth finding out if there are any of these companies in your community because they have the advantages of national companies (for example, brand, infrastructure, lots of locations), but they're locally owned.

- ✔ **Franchised stores present some unique challenges.** These stores are individually owned so in addition to working with a regional representative from the parent company, you have to work closely with individual store owners. It's hard work, but it can be done. As franchised stores are the most challenging, consider the following tips when dealing with them:

  - • Make sure that you have access to the franchisees. No one will explain the program to them better than you can.

  - • While you want to work directly with the franchisees, there's frequently a middleperson between them and the parent company. You should keep her informed of your work and involved in the process.

- You don't have to work with all franchisees for the program to be successful. Recruit those store owners that are committed and enthusiastic. Focusing on anyone else will cost you time and money.

- Start exploring early on how to deal with the costly drop shipping of the pinups to each individual location, a common scenario for a program with a franchise. Perhaps the company can help you either with labor or cost. Consider limiting your program — especially first-year efforts — to a specific area of franchised stores.

Shooting for lots of foot traffic

Not long ago we were doing research on a national chain of vitamin and health food stores and visited a store near us to see how a newly launched pinup program was progressing.

It was a perfect program on paper. The company was committed to the cause, the two brands were perfectly matched. The company had hundreds of stores across the country. It had the potential to be a very successful program.

But there was one problem that was very clear the moment we walked into the store: the store had barely any foot traffic. And it showed in the number of pinups they sold in the first few days: just 8!

You can have all the ingredients of a successful cause marketing program, but if you don't have foot traffic in the store(s) where the program is happening, it won't work.

We talk later in this chapter about some factors that can offset low foot traffic, but your primary focus should be on targeting businesses with high foot traffic. Figure 3-6 shows a list of businesses with the kind of foot traffic you need to be successful. These should be at the top of your prospect list.

Dealing with fewer companies than you think

You now know why you should target companies that have multiple locations with strong traffic. Your next step is to combine this with the circle strategy discussed earlier in this chapter to come up with your prospect pool.

The circle strategy consists of a target with three rings. In the bull's-eye are the companies you know best. The second ring is where prospects that are connections but not supporters are found. The third ring is for cold calls: people who don't know you and whom you don't know.

You can probably understand that the number of qualified prospects for cause marketing diminishes very quickly. There just aren't many businesses that have lots of locations and lots of foot traffic! This is reflected in the form of the ever-evolving target (refer to Figure 3-1). For example, in Boston (where we are based), there are roughly 50 good cause marketing prospects. And the area has thousands of businesses!

Figure 3-6:
These businesses serve lots of customers every day and should top your prospect list.

- QUICK SERVE RESTAURANTS
- SUPERMARKETS
- DEPARTMENT STORES
- COFFEE SHOPS
- CONVENIENCE STORES

- GAS STATIONS
- QUICK LUBES
- CHAIN RESTAURANTS
- DRUG STORES
- HARDWARE STORES

Of course, this doesn't mean you can't do cause marketing with smaller businesses or with companies with fewer locations. Programs with smaller businesses can help you get started and hone your skills. But if you're interested in making six-figures or more in cause marketing, locations and foot traffic are key. Numbers matter!

Cause Marketing Isn't for Everyone

Sigh. We hate to say it, but cause marketing won't work for everyone. We've experienced every combination of ups and downs with cause marketing: stores with lots of foot traffic, but unmotivated employees; companies with hundreds of stores, but unsuccessful, passive campaigns; trained and motivated employees, but terrible foot traffic.

W.C. Fields once said, "If at first you don't succeed, try, try again." Sometimes a first program flops and then you do a second cause marketing program and it soars! Other times, it flops like the first. That's why Fields added that if you don't succeed after trying again and again, you should quit! "No use being a damn fool about it," he concluded.

If a program isn't working, despite your best efforts, it may be time to turn your attention elsewhere.

When in doubt focus on the return on investment. And take a moment to review what cause marketing can and can't do.

What cause marketing can do

Here are some of the things we've learned about cause marketing through the years and in our current positions.

- ✔ **Cause marketing is a good fundraiser (kind of).** Cause marketing can be an effective fundraiser. In late 2010 we raised close to $300,000 in less than a month with a point-of-sale program with a local retailer. Not bad for a local nonprofit! But this represents just a small amount of what we raise every year with other types of fundraising. We advise nonprofits to expect to raise between 5 to 15 percent of their annual revenue from cause marketing. If you're hoping to hit the lottery with cause marketing, try something else.

- ✔ **Cause marketing is a good way to build awareness (we think).** We say "we think" because we have only anecdotal evidence to support this assertion. One bit of research we did do was on how cause marketing could help promote special events. Survey results from 400 attendees of our annual Halloween fundraiser showed that 1 in 5 persons that attended the event learned of it from a cause marketing promotion. We learned that cause marketing is a great way to promote events.

- ✔ **Cause marketing is good at deepening bonds with partners.** Our cause marketing programs frequently brought us closer to corporate donors and spurred additional giving. CEOs or business owners that had personally supported the hospital deepened their engagement by linking their businesses and employees through a cause marketing campaign.

- ✔ **Cause marketing is a no-brainer, if you already have a partner.** The most important asset after understanding what cause marketing is and how it works is a partner to execute a program. We always said that with a committed partner all is possible. A partner is one thing every cause marketing program needs, but once had will bring you to the very edge of success. If you a have a partner to work with on a cause marketing promotion, we suggest you get moving today.

What cause marketing can't do

Here are some of the things we've learned that cause marketing can't do:

- ✓ **Cause marketing doesn't build brand.** This was clearly our most difficult lesson. A brand, of course, is what people experience when they come into contact with your cause. The more powerful and positive the experience, the stronger the brand. Cause marketing is a brand enhancer at best. Take the successes of St. Jude Children's Research Hospital since it launched *Thanks and Giving*, a cause marketing initiative, in 2006. Cause marketing has enhanced St. Jude's brand — and raised tens of millions — but the brand itself was built long before cause marketing arrived. Cause marketing stood on the shoulders of a giant with a brand that already meant something to millions of people across the country and around the world.

- ✓ **Cause marketing isn't for the indifferent.** Anyone that ever started a cause marketing program hopes that it will lead to many, many partnerships. We did, but we had six full-time staff people dedicated to the effort. You'll have to settle for modest success unless you make a serious commitment.

- ✓ **Cause marketing partnerships can be transactional and fleeting.** Of the partners you do recruit for cause marketing, you should expect high turnover. Our experience was that a few key partners were deeply committed to our mission and the partnership. But the majority of corporate partners would come and go based on their marketing objectives, support (or lack of it) from senior management, or economic conditions.

- ✓ **Cause marketing is more about marketing than mission.** Businesses especially are interested in attracting and keeping customers, and cause marketing is a way to achieve that. This isn't a bad thing, but it is a reality you'll need to accept.

Making the choice

Of course, we think most causes and companies should consider cause marketing and focus on the positive things we discuss in "What cause marketing can do," earlier in this chapter.

Remember these key things when considering cause marketing.

- ✔ **Be happy if you raise some money.** Cause marketing can accomplish a lot of great things, but money is something you can see, count, and use. While cause marketing can enhance brand, build awareness, promote events, and boost employee and customer loyalty, measuring these outcomes is difficult and beyond the expertise of most smaller companies and causes.

- ✔ **Experience and skill count.** Don't pursue a cause marketing program unless you have marketing and sales skills and a good working knowledge of how businesses or causes operate. If you lack these things, hire someone to help you create your program, pitch it to prospects, and execute it after the deal is done.

- ✔ **Educate yourself.** You can find plenty of resources to learn about cause marketing (see Chapter 12). One of the best is the Cause Marketing Forum website, which contains examples and case studies. Cause Marketing Forum also has an annual conference where you can meet and learn from experienced cause marketers.

- ✔ **Start with cause marketing. Grow it into a program.** Doing cause marketing and having a cause marketing program are two different things. A homeless shelter down the street from our hospital had an annual cause marketing promotion with a restaurant chain that raised thousands of dollars. The restaurant did cause marketing — once a year — but didn't commit to a cause marketing program to which it would have to devote more time, staff, and money. Many causes have existing corporate relationships that could easily be turned into cause marketing promotions. We frequently point out easy wins to other causes. But before organizations commit to a full-fledged program, they need to reflect on their will and skills. Most should think twice before making a major commitment.

- ✔ **Understand the ethical and legal side of cause marketing.** Cause marketing is an evolving field that is moving toward more transparent, tangible programs that assure donors that monies raised are going to causes and making a difference for causes. Cause marketing is also getting more attention from lawmakers. Laws impacting cause marketing vary from state to state. Be sure to consult the laws in your state before proceeding.

- ✔ **Don't be arrogant.** We all like to think we work for wonderfully unique organizations with huge potential. I'm sure yours really does, but your bright future still may not include cause marketing. Stop believing your own public relations. Wasting money and resources on cause marketing based on a heady, misguided belief that you could launch the next Starbucks/Product (RED) is neither smart nor responsible.

Chapter 4

Making Your Best Qualities Work for You

In This Chapter

▶ Comparing partnering options

▶ Achieving success with training, motivation and incentives

*B*efore you can start marketing and selling your cause marketing program, you need to understand which partnering options are available to you and which factors truly drive the success of your program.

In this chapter, we also discuss the importance of being flexible and creative with smaller partners as a natural part of cause marketing. While smaller companies won't generate the big dollars that huge national chains do, large companies comprise only a small percentage of the companies in your area and are constantly under siege from causes. Also, working with large partners can pose its own set of challenges. You should be aware of these challenges as you embark on this journey.

Analyzing Your Assets

Driving the expressway to downtown Boston, advertising executive Peter Brown saw something that everyone else had missed. The tower above the Pine Street Inn (see Figure 4-1), a well-known homeless shelter in Boston's South End, was a premium piece of advertising real estate.

Mr. Brown convinced the Pine Street Inn to seize this unique opportunity. Soon after hearing from Peter, they decided to renovate the tower and, while doing so, sell billboards on the scaffolding. It turned out to be a great decision. The shelter raised more than $2 million, which was used to pay for these much-needed repairs.

Figure 4-1:
This nonprofit's "Tower of Power" looks brand-new after the creative use of an asset raised over $2 million to repair it.

Every cause has assets that can be useful to their cause marketing program. In the case of the Pine Street Inn, it was the tower right above their heads on which corporate partners were willing to advertise. Luckily, an angel pointed the opportunity out to them!

Recognizing assets requires savvy and smarts: the savvy to see them and the smarts to use them.

Leveraging what you've got

Businesses also have assets, which are usually related to the products or services they offer. As a cause marketing partner of One Warm Coat — a national effort to provide any person in need of a warm coat with one free of charge — retailer Burlington Coat Factory supported the charity with 8,000 coats in 2010 alone. Coats are obviously a natural asset for Burlington Coat Factory, and an asset of great value to any cause that clothe the needy.

Here are some steps you can take to help your business leverage its assets for a cause marketing campaign.

1. **Identify your assets.**

   Can your business provide clothes, food, or medical supplies to a cause in need? Do you have more than one asset that you can bundle for additional impact? A food pantry doesn't live by bread alone. They need many things to make their mission a reality. Pick one.

2. **Determine whether your assets are of value to a cause.**

   Your company makes hairspray, but how does that product help a hospital? It may if it's a cancer hospital with patients who need products and tips to care for their wigs.

3. **Analyze or survey your customers.**

   Would your customers respond favorably to a connection between your business and a particular cause? Clorox thought it found its perfect cause marketing match when it partnered with The Sierra Club for its new line of Green Works Natural Cleaners. However, both organizations faced heavy criticism from environmentalists who complained that the logic of a green group partnering with a manufacturer of toxic products was not as clear as a mountain stream.

As asset is only an asset when cause, company, and consumer agree that its of value. Review your assets carefully so that they don't become liabilities.

Using your events to land new partners

Most causes have fundraising events, but they don't view them as the assets they are. To many, cause marketing is one type of fundraising, and special events is another, without ever thinking to combine the two.

Many causes host large, well-attended and successful events that can be easily leveraged to recruit cause marketing partners. Take the example of the Bachmann-Strauss Dystonia & Parkinson (BSDP) Foundation in New York and its annual bike ride in honor of one of its special young clients, Jake Silverman. This event raises hundreds of thousands of dollars.

Eager to add cause marketing to the mix, BSDP event manager Beth Pfeil used the ride to recruit Garden of Eden (a small grocery chain with several locations in New York and New Jersey) as a cause marketing partner. Cause marketing helped Beth close the partnership deal with Garden of Eden in two important ways:

✔ **It increased the number of ways the grocery chain could make a difference for the charity.** Not only would Garden of Eden raise money for the cause at the register through a pinup program (see Figure 4-2), but it planned to promote the ride to boost rider participation. Garden of Eden liked the fact that its program had the potential to make a bigger impact for the cause than a sponsorship would.

✔ **Combining events and cause marketing increased the exposure for the grocery store chain.** Part of the partnership agreement included signage at the bike ride that would promote Garden of Eden's involvement, all at no extra cost. The added benefit of having visibility at the event — and not just a point-of-sale program that targeted existing customers — increased the value of the promotion to the grocer.

Figure 4-2:
Tying cause
marketing
to an event
raised this
charity an
extra $6,000.

Jake's Ride
For Dystonia Research

$1 $2 $5

(Dystonia) A debilitating neurological movement disorder affecting 500,000 people in this country, one-third of them children. The 2nd Annual Jake's Ride for Dystonia Research will take place on Sunday, October 4, 2009 at Glenwood Elementary School, Short Hills, NJ. To register visit www.jakesride.org or call 212-682-9900. Jake's Ride will benefit The Bachmann-Strauss Dystonia & Parkinson Foundation's mission to find better treatments and cures for the movement disorders dystonia and Parkinson's disease, and to provide medical and patient information.

THE BACHMANN-STRAUSS
Dystonia & Parkinson Foundation, Inc.

Perhaps more than anything else, causes are known for their fundraising events. It's time for causes to expand the value of these fundraisers by super-charging them with cause marketing.

Leapfrogging your way to success

Success breeds success. We both clearly remember in 2004 when we had only two corporate partners: iParty, a local party retailer and Ocean State Job Lot, a discount retailer. (See Chapter 3 for more on finding partners through a circle strategy.) The CEOs of both companies had supported our cause personally, but our two organizations weren't linked through cause marketing.

After we had executed successful cause marketing programs with these two founding stores, iParty and Ocean State Job Lot, we used our experience and success to approach new partners. We also leveraged any contacts or relationships they had to approach new prospects. (Think of the circle strategy — see Chapter 3.)

Our cause marketing success with iParty, for example, motivated a fast-lube chain to join for our next program, which also involved iParty. Having two great partners opened more doors with still more companies.

By October 2009, we had grown one cause marketing program to 38 corporate partners. Leapfrogging from partner to partner to partner works. But like the game, it doesn't work unless you have someone to start with, and the longer you can keep jumping, the more successful — and fun — it is.

Capitalizing on Qualitative Factors

Motivating and training employees can pay big dividends to a cause marketing program. Research conducted in 2010 by Cone LLC, a leading cause marketing agency based in Boston, showed that 70 percent of Americans said they're more likely to make a donation to a cause if an employee at the store at which they're shopping recommends it.

Cone's research supports everything cause marketers have learned in the field over the past decade:

- ✔ Employees that are motivated to support the cause are more enthusiastic fundraisers.

- ✔ Employees that are better trained, not just in the program but as professionals in general, can better communicate the program to consumers and secure more gifts.

- ✔ Incentives can boost employee motivation, but they need to be used sparingly and strategically.

Motivating

Highly motivated consumers and employees can make a big difference in the success of your cause marketing program. Motivation is especially important for local programs because they generally involve smaller businesses with fewer locations and less foot traffic. In short, you need to maximize the return on every store.

We've seen many motivated businesses succeed with cause marketing. iParty, a New England-based party retailer with more than 50 stores and great foot traffic, consistently raises $1,000 per store with cause marketing pinups.

iParty succeeds in motivating their customers and employees in several important ways.

- ✔ Their commitment to our cause is top-down and bottom-up. They support what we do at every level and know how important our mission is. They've earned their halo, and the glow from it is something everyone sees, even when you're new to the company.

- ✔ iParty has mastered executing cause marketing in their stores, making the programs easy for customers and employees. iParty plans its campaigns for busy times of year when the pinups are easy to sell. Their employees know just what to ask shoppers, and customers are incentivized with coupons to thank them for their gift.

✔ iParty motivates its employees with incentives, too. iParty encourages a competition among its stores to see who can raise the most money. The top four stores receive prizes, which the employees love!

An example of motivation at work at a retailer with less foot traffic is craft store chain A.C. Moore's partnership with Easter Seals (see Figure 4-3). At A.C. Moore's 136 stores, cashiers asked customers to donate a dollar to Easter Seal's *Act for Autism* campaign and raised over $141,000. This is an impressive figure considering that A.C. Moore stores aren't as crowded as a Target or Walmart. While stores averaged over $1,000 in donations, locations in the Philadelphia and Wilmington, Delaware region collected more than half of the total funds, with the Wilmington store earning the top fundraising spot.

Another factor contributing to the success of the campaign may have been the cause itself. Autism has broad appeal with Americans due to a large spike in the number of children affected. We all know someone who has been impacted by autism, which motivates us to give.

Finally, A.C. Moore deepened consumer engagement with the campaign by hosting an in-store crafting event at which kids created a jigsaw puzzle for autism awareness.

Figure 4-3:
A.C. Moore got creative and added an in-store jigsaw puzzle crafting event to a traditional register program with Easter Seals.

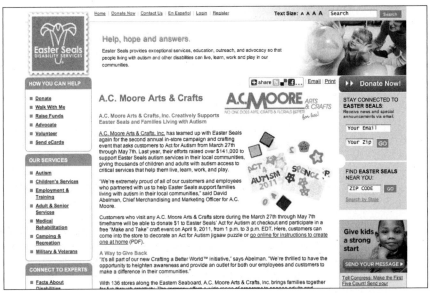

The money raised overall, and particularly from three key mid-Atlantic stores, speaks to how motivated the A.C. Moore employees were at these stores! Motivation is a key quality in every cause marketing program, big or small. But if you want to raise money at lower traffic stores, you need motivated employees that can convince nearly every shopper to give.

Finding chains with lots of foot traffic and lots of locations is a key to success. However, A.C. Moore illustrates that employee and customer energy and drive can transcend stores and foot traffic and make a cause marketing program successful. The human element of every program can never be dismissed. We truly are more than the sum of individual parts.

Training

Well-trained employees can play a big role in the success of your cause marketing program. Not only should your employees be well trained in how to execute the program, but it also helps if they're well-trained by the company in selling and servicing the customer.

Some businesses do a better job training their front-line employees than others. Certainly, most of us have been asked if we want to supersize our order or if we need batteries when we buy our kids' electronics.

For example, fast-lube businesses that can change your oil and quickly perform a host of other services on your car train their front-line employees in upselling customers on additional services. "We also have a special on a radiator flush. Would you like us to do that as well? It will take only ten more minutes."

So when it comes to asking customers to support a cause, these employees have an edge because they're asking customers to buy other things all the time. These employees will raise more money for your cause!

Having well-trained employees (see Figure 4-4) is especially important when you're weighing a program with a low foot traffic business. We've had first-hand experience with this with Valvoline Instant Oil Change, a fast-lube franchise with 40 locations in our area. After we met with the company, we learned that it ran a successful business with around 50 customer visits a day per store. (Just 50! In comparison, think about how many customers your local supermarket sees every day. The number is easily in the hundreds.)

Nevertheless, thanks to their expert staff who made a major commitment to the program and were confident they could sell the pinup for $3 instead of $1, we raised over $65,000 over three years.

Figure 4-4: Quick lubes, such as Valvoline Instant Oil Change, have highly trained staff who know how to sell.

Our success with a fast-lube franchise isn't unique.

- ✔ Jiffy Lube has raised millions for American Heart Association's *Go Red for Women* program.
- ✔ Midas has donated $5 of every $34.95 oil change purchased to Make-A-Wish.

Look for businesses that hire good employees and take the time to train them. Their expertise in selling and servicing customers will pay dividends for you.

Incentivizing

A lot of businesses reward their employees for performance, so it's no surprise we're often asked, "Should we offer employees incentives for hitting specific fundraising goals?"

This good question doesn't have a simple answer. We had high hopes for incentives when we first started running point-of-sale programs, such as pinups. Surely employees will respond to gift certificates, electronics, T-shirts, and food, we thought. But the reality was very different. Here's what we discovered:

- ✔ **Unmotivated employees stay unmotivated.** Even with incentives unmotivated employees won't push the program. Indeed, their lack of motivation seemed to extend to just about every part of their lives!

- ✔ **Motivated employees don't need incentives.** These employees support the program because they want to and because they're told to. They're more motivated and disciplined and listen to their manager.

- ✔ **Motivated employees can be marginally motivated with incentives.** Incentives can give motivated employees an extra boost to push the program. But you don't need to give them much; $5 gift cards to Starbucks or Dunkin' Donuts can do the trick. So does a pizza party for the winning store at the end of the program. In the past, we've given away more expensive incentives, but we never felt like they made a difference. In short, they were expensive giveaways, not incentives.

You should also know three more things about incentives:

- ✔ **You don't need to pay for incentives.** Getting incentives donated by various companies is easier than you think. We even recruit a pizza sponsor every year that gets a full sponsorship at one of our events in exchange for a supply of pizzas for incentives for our cause marketing partners. It's worth it!

- ✔ **If this is your first program with a business, wait to offer incentives.** See what happens. If the program does well, add the incentives to the next program to build on your success.

- ✔ **Sometimes the best incentive for store employees is an easy-to-execute program.** Cashiers have enough to do at the register and are already asking customers if they need batteries, want to apply for a credit card, and so on. The last thing they want is a complicated cause marketing program to sell. Give them a simple, one-line pitch like "Would you like to donate a dollar to help a sick child?" If you can add coupons to the pinup to give consumers an extra incentive to donate a dollar, even better. Also consider a barcode on the back of the pinup so that the cashier can simply scan it into the register like any other item in the store. Removing obstacles and making things easy is an incentive employees will appreciate. And they'll show their thanks by supporting your program.

Incentives work. You just need to know when to use them and with whom.

Part II

Promoting Your Cause Marketing Plan

The 5th Wave   By Rich Tennant

"Get ready, I think they're starting to drift."

In this part . . .

Part II teaches you two important skills: how to sell and close cause marketing programs. We give you guidance on your initial outreach, how to deal with gate-keepers, what to bring to the meeting, and how best to hone your presentation skills. We also show you how to close the deal by adopting a selling style that fits with your prospect, making it easier to address and overcome objections.

Chapter 5

Selling Cause Marketing Programs

*Y*ou may be like us and view yourself less as a fundraiser and more as a salesperson. You're in the minority in the nonprofit world, which views selling as crass and associates it with cheesy used car salesmen, bad ties, and low, low prices.

But not us. We agree with businessman Jim Barksdale, the man behind Netscape, that "Nothing happens until somebody sells something." Selling is the thing that makes things happen in the world! Selling is also the thing that will turn your cause marketing idea into a promotion with a real cause or business.

Are you still looking down your nose at selling? Don't, because if you want to be a successful cause marketer, you need to know how to sell.

In this chapter, we explore the pre-selling process of connecting and staying top of mind with prospects and how to best prepare for that first meeting.

Reaching Out to Prospects

Before trying to communicate with a prospect, take a minute to consider how you plan to connect with her about cause marketing. No, we're not talking about using a phone or sending an e-mail. That's the subject of the next section. We're talking about how you plan to identify with the needs of the prospect because that's how cause marketing — and everything else — gets sold.

Persuasion occurs through identification. The more you can align your message with the needs, beliefs, attitudes, and expectations of your prospects, the more likely they are to support you. Businesses support causes they can relate to and that meet their needs.

Here are a few tips for building that special connection:

- ✔ **Don't sell to the hard ones; sell to the easy ones.** Target businesses that are geographically and emotionally connected to your cause. Look for the intersection of location and experience with a mission. For example, if your organization is like ours and serves a poor population a good prospect may be a local business owner who grew up poor and maybe even benefited from your nonprofit's services. It's more likely he will be open to your appeals than someone who runs a business outside your area and grew up well-off. The circle strategy we discuss in Chapter 3 applies here, too. In the inner circles are companies that are geographically connected to your nonprofit's mission. They're the easy ones.

- ✔ **Play your strongest card.** What is it about your mission or your cause marketing program that is most compelling? Is it that your organization has excellent brand recognition in your area? Or do you have a partnership with a great company that everyone wants to work with? When Joe started his career at the Muscular Dystrophy Association, the juggernaut was the annual Jerry Lewis Telethon. Even then a tradition for decades, Telethon had a national reach, celebrities, and a local television broadcast. Whenever Joe met with prospects, he always led with the Telethon, because that's what got everyone's attention. A few years later, when Joe was selling underwriting for public television to local companies, the strongest card was the affluent, influential, sophisticated viewer that businesses could reach by underwriting PBS. But Joe had one other card to play with companies: public TV's award-winning children's programming. If the prospect had kids, characters like Elmo, Arthur, and Cookie Monster made for an easy, friendly, and mutual connection. We all don't have Elmo to talk about, but you do have a strong card to play. Don't leave it sitting in the deck.

- ✔ **But don't overdo it.** You should have a whole hand of cards to show your prospect. With Halloween Town, we had lots of other things to talk about in addition to the crowd. We had a month-long promotion leading up to the event and cross-promotions with participating companies.

- ✔ **Building a connection takes time.** We like to say that persuasion is incremental. People generally don't accept new ideas quickly or easily, so you need to be realistic about what you can accomplish with each interaction. Start today, but build in lots of extra time so that you can reach your goals.

Calling or e-mailing as the first step

Your first interaction with a cause marketing prospect probably won't be in person. It will be over the phone or e-mail.

Getting your prospect talking

Meeting with a prospect isn't like a poker match with opponents eyeing each other waiting for someone to make the wrong move. The more you get your prospects talking, the better the chance you'll discover their interests, problems, or challenges and how you're part of the answer, and not just contributing to the problem by wasting their time.

Here are some open-ended questions to get them talking:

✔ Your competitor, X, works with ABC cause. They've both benefited a lot from the partnership. Have you considered cause marketing?

✔ How does your business currently market itself?

✔ Favorability and credibility are so important for companies these days. How do you think your customers would rate you in this area?

✔ What causes do you (or the CEO) support personally? Why? Do you share your interest in these causes with your employees?

✔ What do you think are some of the favorite causes of your customers?

✔ How do you show your customers your support for the community?

It's interesting that even on our own cause marketing team there's a schism about the best way to initially connect with prospects: phone or e-mail.

Dialers, as we call them at my work, argue that the phone is more personal, builds a relationship sooner, and is overall more effective. *Technologists* counter that e-mail is instant, preferred, detailed, and actionable. We've used both with success: Joe prefers e-mail, and Joanna dials away on the phone!

Regardless of which channel you use, keep the following in mind:

✔ **A sale is not your goal.** You're not an inside sales position that has to close cause marketing pacts over the phone or through e-mail. Your No. 1 goal is face time — a meeting. A meeting allows you to present your pitch in person.

✔ **Make them beg for more.** Ideally, you want to give them just enough info on all the great things you can do so that they'll meet with you and take the meeting serious enough to include the right decision makers. Okay, maybe we've never had a prospect begging for more. But we have hung up the phone with a prospect knowing that she was eager to hear more and was looking forward to the meeting.

The best way to excite a prospect about working with you is to address their needs and to relate to their interests, concerns, and goals.

✔ **Get them talking — a lot.** You should be listening for clues on what their needs might be and how you can best address them. (For more on getting them talking, see the nearby sidebar.)

✔ **Get the lay of the land.** Whether it's by phone or e-mail, use the time to find out the decision-making process. Can the vice president of marketing really make the decision, or does he have to run everything by the CEO? Will you have to meet with three people at once to get a decision? Or meet with one person three times? It's never too early to make sure that you're talking to the right person and begin counting the steps to success.

✔ **Know when to shut up.** Your goal is to speak strategically so that you land a meeting with the right decision maker. If you drone on, you risk giving the prospect too much information, and he can make a decision without ever meeting you! That's why you should never talk for too long. E-mails should be short and never, ever include attachments. People say they open them, but they rarely do.

Opening with an offer

We've always heeded the advice of famed trial lawyer Clarence Darrow when it came to speaking to an audience. You have to engage a listener immediately, he advised, or everything you say afterwards will be a failure.

We learned this years ago when the two of us worked together at a local Chamber of Commerce and had to recruit new members for the organization. The sales strategy then was to call businesses and ask them whether they wanted to join the Chamber. It wasn't the most compelling sales pitch in the world, and the membership numbers proved it.

We took a different approach. The Chamber was known for its high-profile programs on everything from legislative affairs to leading business issues. So when we spoke to businesses, we invited them to attend a program as our guest:

> *"Hi, Jim. Joe Waters calling from the Chamber. I read in the paper that you're one of the people involved in the new hotel project downtown. We're having a special briefing from the mayor's office on new building codes in the city. Would you like to attend as our guest?"*

I wasn't selling the prospect anything. I was offering them something — something that introduced him to the benefits of my organization instead of just saying, "Would you like to join?" (We called this strategy of inviting prospects to our programs and events "selling in the showroom." Any car salesperson will tell you that getting a prospective buyer in the showroom where the cars are is half the battle. Car dealerships don't sell a lot cars across the street or down the block — just as we didn't sell a lot of Chamber memberships over the phone.)

Stop selling and start offering something to your prospective partner.

Say that you're calling a prospect regarding a cause marketing program. The gimme call goes like this:

> *"Hi Jim, Joanna MacDonald calling from The Cause. We have lots of disadvantaged people that need your help, so I'm hoping our two organizations can execute a cause marketing program together. We would really appreciate your support. When can I come in and see you?"*

Umm, never.

You're too busy talking about what you need. Not about what Jim needs and what you could accomplish together. Make him an offer he can't resist or one that at least gets his attention!

Consider this approach instead:

> *"Hi, Jim. Joanna MacDonald calling from The Cause. I want to share some results from a recent program we did with a company like yours. It involved a cause marketing cross-promotion with two other companies where each partner saw significant redemption of coupons and increased sales totaling $400,000. Best of all, 10,000 kids got fed. Could we get together so I could explain how these three companies accomplished so much, and all at no direct cost to them?"*

You're not asking Jim to do anything except let you share the results of a program that

- ✔ Succeeded at a company similar to his.
- ✔ Generated foot traffic and sales for the companies involved.
- ✔ Helped a good cause.
- ✔ Can be replicated at no cost.

Always think about how you can begin with some kind of offer, some incentive to get the prospect's attention and to keep her engaged.

Here are other ways you can build offers into your calls and e-mails:

- ✔ **Invite the prospect to an event as your guest.** We make a point throughout the year to invite prospects to our events so that they can see our work firsthand, even if they're not a good prospect for that particular program. With our Halloween Town event, we created a special R.I.P (Really Important Person!) reception for prospects. Inviting prospects and their families to such a great event made calling them easy. "I'm not calling you to ask for anything. (I bet they could see my Cheshire cat smile through the phone!) I just want to invite you and your family to attend an event as our special guests." We know for a fact that those calls were appreciated and led to business.

✔ **Send them an article of interest.** We both do a ton of reading, so we're always seeing things that are applicable for clients and prospects. We usually send these articles along with a short note letting the prospect know that we were "just thinking of them."

✔ **Invite them to sign up for your e-mail newsletter.** If you get a favorable response from the prospect on what you sent her, ask her whether you can sign her up for your cause marketing newsletter (which we talk about more in Chapter 9), which is a great tool to stay top of mind with the prospect. There are many e-mail marketing services that you can use for your newsletter. Joe uses Constant Contact (see Figure 5-1) for his, but he also likes Aweber.

✔ **Add value on an unrelated issue.** We always say we're problem solvers, and we really don't care what the problem is. It doesn't have to be related to cause marketing. Not long ago, Joe shared some advice he had gotten from an expert in the restaurant industry with a cafe partner that was struggling with laptop-toting customers that were hogging up seating during lunch hours. Adding value in any way shows the prospect just how helpful you can be and keeps you top of mind, the importance of which we can't stress enough. Out of sight, out of mind means out of business.

By showing prospects that you're useful in many ways, they'll come around to recognize your worth in the one way you want them to value you most: as a cause marketing partner!

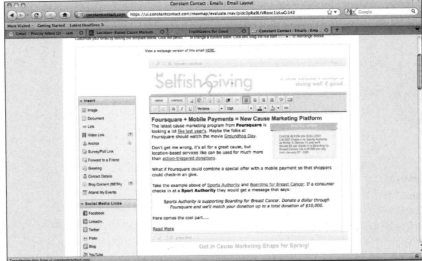

Figure 5-1: Constant Contact is an easy and inexpensive e-mail marketing service to help you create a professional newsletter for prospects.

Positioning cause marketing as win-win-win

When communicating by phone or e-mail, it's critical that you position cause marketing as win-win-win. A win for the company. A win for the customer. A win for the cause.

Here are some suggestions for things to say about the positive impact of cause marketing for company, customer, and cause.

A win for the company

You'll notice in the following list that we're not talking about how great our cause is. No, we're focusing on the client and his needs. This is a language many causes don't speak. It may sound foreign, but it's just what you need to say:

✔ **"Other forms of marketing increase your visibility. Cause marketing enhances your favorability."** When you advertise on radio, TV, or print, the sales representatives in those industries will tell you all about the number of eyeballs you'll get by running your ad in the Sunday newspaper or airing your commercial during primetime. Cause marketing is different in that it actually enhances your favorability, not just your visibility, with your target audience.

According to the 2010 Cone Cause Evolution Study, 85 percent of Americans believe that when a company supports a cause they care about, they have a more positive image of the company (see Figure 5-2). That is something you'll never get from advertising in your local newspaper.

✔ **"Cause marketing gives you a competitive edge that goes beyond product and price."** Again, according to Cone, 1 in 5 consumers will pay more for a cause-related product. A cause will prompt 61 percent to try a product they've never heard of. And a whopping 80 percent of consumers would switch to a brand that supports a cause when price and quality are equal.

Figure 5-2:
The 2010
Cone Cause
Evolution
Study.

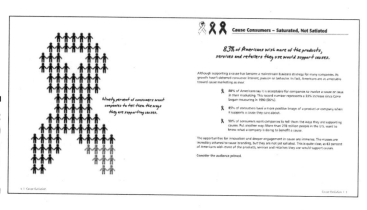

A win for the consumer

Businesses really like two things: getting customers and keeping customers. Here's how cause marketing does both:

- ✔ **"Consumers overwhelmingly think that cause marketing is acceptable (88 percent; Cone) and more (83 percent; Cone) wish the products, services, and retailers they used would support causes."** Consumers want and expect companies and causes to work together on cause marketing. If nearly 100 percent of your shoppers were clamoring for you to carry a new product in your store, would you stock it? Of course you would. That's why every business should stock cause marketing!

- ✔ **"Women are the natural target audience for cause marketing, but so are Millennials and men."** *Millennials,* Americans between ages 18 and 24, respond very positively to cause messages. Causes are not just important when they shop, they're important to their lives. That's why these people represent a significant growth opportunity for companies that care and aren't shy about showing it.

  Research by Kansas City-based Barkley Public Relations in 2010 shows that cause marketing is no longer gender based. Eighty-eight percent of men said that it was important for brands to support a cause, while 55 percent said that they would pay more for a brand or product that supported a cause they cared about. Two-thirds said they would try a new brand because of a cause.

A win for the cause

Causes are big winners as cause marketing does something that other types of fundraising can't do:

- ✔ **"Cause marketing raises money and awareness for the cause."** Cause marketing is a new way to raise money that's different from traditional fundraising (foundations, major gifts, special events, and so on) and corporate fundraising (employee and corporate giving, sponsorships, corporate grants). The new revenue cause marketing can generate is surpassed only by its potential to build visibility and awareness for the cause.

- ✔ **"Cause marketing can build something that causes could never afford to buy."** While St. Jude Children's Research Hospital opened in 1962 and was a well-known cause for many years, it wasn't until 2004 that it launched its *Thanks and Giving* cause marketing program with national retailers. Just six years after launching *Thanks and Giving*, consumers chose St. Jude third among causes they planned to support over the holiday season. That's impressive, considering the top two causes, The Salvation Army and Toys for Tots, have together been serving the needy for more than 180 years.

Dealing with gatekeepers

Gatekeepers, employees who stand between you and a decision maker, are an inescapable part of sales. Your goal is not to avoid or demonize gatekeepers, but to get them to join your team. Gatekeepers are, after all, just doing their jobs — limiting and protecting a decision maker as needed and instructed. That said we both know firsthand just how frustrating gatekeepers can be to work with!

Gatekeepers can be a powerful ally behind the scenes helping you close a cause marketing agreement. Here's how you can earn their allegiance:

- ✔ **Build rapport.** It's unfortunate and shortsighted when sales people look past gatekeepers, sometimes as if they're not there or if they are not very important. We think this is a big mistake. Gatekeepers are people, too! Learn about them, their lives, and their place within the organization. These details are an important first step to building a connection and creating an ally.

- ✔ **Be sincere.** Gatekeepers deal with salespeople (and that means you!) all the time and know when you're just sweet talking them to gain access to their boss. Talk to them as a person and forget the canned "getting to know you" questions.

- ✔ **Show respect.** Tell the gatekeepers a bit about your program (not too much because you don't want them to turn into a messenger!) and ask a few questions about the company. Your interest in their feedback shows them they're part of the process.

- ✔ **Play by their rules.** Every gatekeeper has a way that he wants to work with outsiders. (Keep in mind that these rules come straight from the boss.) He may want all communications with his boss to go through him. Maybe he just wants you to cc him on any e-mails. Whatever process the gatekeeper wants you to follow, do it! You'll build comfort and trust, and you won't risk him blocking or limiting your contact with his boss.

- ✔ **Find out what they want.** Everyone has needs, desires, and aspirations. Gatekeepers are no exception. What do they want, and how can you help? Does he want his boss to see he can handle more important work? Maybe your cause marketing program would be a good project for him. Selling is about solving problems, addressing needs, and giving people something better than what they have. Do this, and your gatekeeper will become a gate opener.

Like everything you do with cause marketing, you need a strategy with gatekeepers. You truly have only one chance to make a first impression.

Staying Top of Mind

"Men more frequently require to be reminded than informed."

Samuel Johnson, the 18th century founder of the modern dictionary, undoubtedly chose his words carefully. You should, too, when following up with prospects about your cause marketing program and scheduling a meeting.

Cause marketing isn't a complicated topic like tax law or rocket science, so it's unlikely that you'll need to keep informing the prospect about what it is and how it works.

More likely, you'll need to gently remind the prospect of the value of cause marketing and your willingness to meet with her to discuss the opportunity. For this, we rely on regular communication with the prospect via phone or voicemail to nudge them. We also have a blog that updates them on our progress and successes. Finally, we avoid any sense of finality with the prospect; we always keep the window of opportunity to work with each other fully open.

Leaving messages — two perspectives

To leave a message, or not leave a message — that is the question.

Like using the phone or e-mail to contact prospects, our cause marketing team has always been evenly split on whether or not to leave a phone message. In one corner is our senior sales representative, Holt Murray, who rarely leaves a message. He will call repeatedly on different days and at different times until the prospect picks up. He thinks leaving a message gives the prospect a reason not to pick up her phone the next time she sees your number. Also, he believes if you leave too detailed a message, the prospect may feel informed enough to make a decision about your program without calling you back, which he won't because his answer is no.

In the other corner are salespeople like Joe who actually prefer to leave a voicemail with a prospect before he speaks to them. Joe's aware of the liabilities of voicemail, which is why he leaves a short, strategic message designed to whet the prospect's appetite. Instead of ignoring your calls, the prospect may look forward to them and be inclined to hear more.

What Joe likes best about leaving a message is that subsequent calls aren't cold calls because you've already called to introduce yourself and shared some of the best points about your proposal. "Yes, I remember your message from yesterday. When was the start date of your next program?"

Using a blog to stay relevant

Calling and e-mailing a prospect isn't the only way to stay top of mind. Another great way is a blog. A *blog* is an online journal that is regularly updated with the most recent entry, or post, at the top of the main page. Like everything we share with you in this book, we have our own perspective on blogging because we've done that too.

Joe started his blog *Selfish Giving* (see Figure 5-3) in December 2004 in part because he was tired of clipping and e-mailing all the news and stories he was finding on cause marketing. Putting it into a blog was a more effective way to share it with everyone.

Figure 5-3: Joe started Selfish Giving in 2004 in part as a marketing tool to promote our nonprofit's cause marketing program.

To read Joe's blog, scan the QR code to the left with your smartphone or visit `http://selfishgiving.com`.

In addition to making sharing easier, a blog has other advantages:

- ✔ **A blog enhances your credibility.** If your blog is well-written, has a good design, and has regular entries, you'll impress your prospect with your leadership, creativity, and discipline.

✔ **Prospects may find you without your ever asking them to look.** Search engines, such as Google and Bing, love blogs! Because blogs are frequently updated with fresh content and earn links from other active bloggers, your posts may rank higher than other types of web content. In short, if your prospect is searching the web looking for information on cause marketing, they may find you first!

✔ **Blogging plays well with other online tools.** If your prospect is active on Twitter, you can share links to your most recent blog posts. Same with Facebook and LinkedIn.

For those prospects that weren't regular blog readers, we started an e-mail newsletter that gave summaries of recent posts with links back to the blog. Whatever online outpost you use, drive them back to your home base, your blog.

Twitter, Facebook, LinkedIn, and so on are outposts, places you hang out, but are not yours. Their purpose is to feed traffic to your home base. But they can't do that if you don't have a blog!

Avoiding finality, unless it's a yes

During the course of a sales cycle with a prospect, you'll surely have many conversations, but there's one word you never want to hear: No, as in, "No, we have no interest in working with you."

A verbal no will trigger a defensiveness in the prospect that can be very difficult to overcome. That's why you never want to cross that bridge. Your goal with a good prospect is to keep the lines of communication open so that you can work together some day.

There are many good ways to avoid the dreaded no. How you go about it depends a lot on what you have to say:

"Let's wait until next month when you have all the information you need."

"I'll sign you up for our e-mail newsletter so that you can get regular updates on the progress and success of our programs."

"How about our next program in March? It has many of the same things you liked about this program, but the timeframe is better for you. I'll call you in February."

Always try to keep the door open, even if it's just a little bit. Because a closed door might just never open again.

Preparing for the Meeting

Congratulations! You've landed a meeting! A meeting is a big step toward closing a cause marketing deal. Prospects are busy and generally don't give their time to meet with just anyone. A meeting means a prospect sees some promise in what you have to offer. Don't let poor preparation be your undoing.

To prepare for a successful meeting, you want to make sure that you include the right people from your team, set clear expectations of what you hope to accomplish, avoid presenting anything with sponsorship levels, plan all your questions, and think twice about the big PowerPoint deck you had planned to bring.

So what should you bring to the meeting?

- ✔ A blank notepad to capture any possible ideas, options, and next steps.

- ✔ Two ears that you plan to use to listen for what the prospect needs from the program to call it a success. Remember, the ears are for listening to others, not to hear the sound of your own voice!

- ✔ A full inventory of everything you could offer your prospect as a cause marketing partner. This way, you can build a program à la carte based on their level of potential support and their needs. It also means you can pitch them on another program if the one you had in mind for them flops.

Leaving your boss at the office

If you have a choice about whether to bring your boss, a board member, or your president to a meeting, do everyone a favor and leave them back at the office — at least for the first meeting.

Your goal in the meeting is to position cause marketing as a win-win strategy and to find out as much from the prospect as you can about his business and how you might work successfully together.

That's not your boss's objectives for the meeting (and in all fairness, she probably hasn't been taught to have a different goal). Your boss wants to talk about your organization's fabulous mission and all the great things the prospect could do to support it. Your boss probably thinks like a traditional fundraiser: She's cause-centric. It's about the mission (her mission). Such a conversation does have its place in philanthropy. But not when you're talking about cause marketing, which is a win-win partnership between cause and company.

However, if your boss insists on going to a meeting, here are a few suggestions for turning her into an asset:

- ✔ **Educate your boss on cause marketing.** Educating your boss is something you should be doing anyway, but before a meeting, it becomes critical. Share with her the latest research from Cone, Edelman, and Barkley. Point her to case studies involving national players like Pepsi, Dairy Queen, and Target on the for-profit side and causes like Children's Miracle Network, Make-A-Wish, and Feeding America. Refer her to Cause Marketing Forum's website (see Figure 5-4) or better yet, convert her to an active reader, which is easy if she signs up for CMF's regular newsletter. It may take time, but reading about the success that others are having with cause marketing will convert her into a true believer and an advocate for your efforts.

- ✔ **Be clear that this meeting is about mission and margin.** Make sure that your boss understands that there is a time and place to talk about your cause and the wonderful work it does. But this meeting is about mutual benefit for both partners, so you have to be equally focused on the rewards for your prospective partner.

- ✔ **Have an agenda and give your boss a role.** Beforehand, set an agenda for the meeting on which you and your boss agree. It should include a clearly defined role for your boss that's useful and not counterproductive to the real mission.

Figure 5-4:
The website Cause Marketing Forum has plenty of cause marketing case studies to share with your boss.

Setting expectations

Just like you have to be realistic about what one phone call can accomplish, you have to be equally clear on where one meeting will get you.

Persuasion is incremental. It takes time. People don't generally change their minds quickly or easily, so you need to be realistic about what you can accomplish with each interaction. In addition to putting the building blocks of persuasion in place, build in lots of extra time to achieve your goals, too. You may need it.

Postponing levels for later

Cause marketing is not sponsorship. While sponsorship and cause marketing are both win-win, they're different in several important ways. One is how sponsorship programs frequently have levels of support (for example, $5,000, $10,000, $25,000) with corresponding benefits. If you invest in the $10,000 level, for example, you get your banner at the event, your logo on T-shirts, a booth to distribute product or info, and so on.

Some people think that cause marketing is like sponsorship, and they should prepare something with levels for the prospect. We're going to level with you: Forget using levels.

Here are two good reasons not to deal with levels in your meeting:

- ✔ **It limits the conversation.** Anything with levels invariably limits your ability to explore different opportunities because you're too busy trying to make things fit in a level, instead of talking about what the prospect needs and what you have to offer.

- ✔ **It may hurt your fundraising.** With sponsorship, the corporate partner writes a check for the sponsorship level they want, and then you, the nonprofit, fulfills the benefits. But with cause marketing, the money generally comes from the consumer via register programs or product purchase, not from the company. The amount you raise varies depending on the company, time of year, and so on. So if you sell cause marketing by levels, you might give too much for too little or have a partner that raises their goal amount too quickly and stops fundraising. This is the last thing you want!

Bringing your questions

Yes, looking and sounding smart are important to your success in meetings, but it's crucial that you understand the prospect's needs and goals and ask smart questions, too.

Here are 15 questions that always come up in our meetings and lead to productive conversations. Plan to ask some of these questions and be ready to answer them if they're asked of you:

✔ How much do you know about cause marketing?

✔ Do you currently work with any causes? If so, who and how?

✔ Why do you feel passionate about the work of my cause?

✔ If you do work with causes, how do you feel you benefit from the partnership?

✔ Do you share with your customers that you support causes or try to involve them in any way?

✔ How would you describe your customers?

✔ Who are your competitors? How do they work with causes?

✔ Have you ever rewarded shoppers at the register for their purchase or their loyalty?

✔ What are your goals for the next six months? The next year?

✔ How do you currently market your business?

✔ What do you consider your best marketing promotion?

✔ How motivated are your employees to support a cause?

✔ What are some of the ways you communicate with your customers — for example, e-mail marketing, Twitter, Facebook, blog, and so on?

✔ If you had a choice, what types of businesses would you like to work with on a cross-promotion?

✔ Have you experimented with location-based services like Foursquare, SCVNGR, or Facebook Places?

Packing punch to your PowerPoint

The story of PowerPoint is as old and familiar as any other creature comfort people have ever invented.

> *The civilized man has built a coach, but has lost the use of his feet. He is supported on crutches, but lacks so much support of muscle. He has a fine Geneva watch, but he fails of the skill to tell the hour by the sun. A Greenwich nautical almanac he has, and so being sure of the information when he wants it, the man in the street does not know a star in the sky.*
>
> — Ralph Waldo Emerson, 1841

With PowerPoint, we've gained the ability to share our presentations on a screen or in a handout. But as was true with so many other advancements, we've given up something powerful in exchange.

Instead of developing and using our skills as presenters, we rely on PowerPoint to reduce our role at meetings. But what we really do is reduce our effectiveness. Prospects don't buy from PowerPoint decks. They buy from people.

PowerPoint can be useful in a meeting. But like any technology, it makes a good servant, but a poor master. Here's how to keep PowerPoint firmly under foot:

✔ **Use PowerPoint for what can't be said or explained in words.** PowerPoint isn't meant to record every word of your presentation. Use PowerPoint when you find yourself saying, "I wish I could show this to you!" That's the moment to include a slide to show the prospect exactly what you're talking about. Or if cause marketing is completely foreign to your audience, a very simple visual can replace ten minutes of your trying to explain it to them (see Figure 5-5). Now you can make your point in about 20 seconds. PowerPoint, when used well, is a tool to break down the walls of misunderstanding and ambiguity between you and the prospect.

✔ **Limit one idea to each slide.** Many PowerPoint slides have too much information on them. It's better to communicate a single idea simply, directly, and powerfully (see Figure 5-6). You may never get the chance to say everything you want to say, but your prospect will never forget that one thing you did say.

Figure 5-5:
We use a slide to visually illustrate how cause marketing works. The program flows from cause to company to consumer, and the benefits return to company and cause.

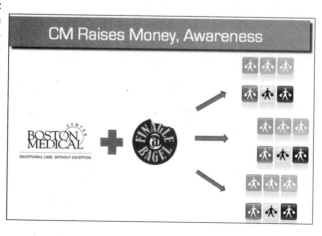

✔ **Don't use PowerPoint to share your agenda.** Your PowerPoint is not your meeting agenda. They're two different things. Your agenda, if you have one, is something you bring to a meeting and share with your prospect on a separate sheet of paper. It guides your meeting. Your PowerPoint is part of your presentation to your prospect. It clarifies and magnifies your message. As the name implies, don't forget the power in your points when sharing a presentation with a prospect.

Figure 5-6:
Your slides
need to
have less
information
on them, not
more. Limit
yourself to
one idea
and a few
keywords.

Chapter 6

Closing the Deal

· ·

In This Chapter

▶ Getting to know the person who can say yes

▶ Overcoming objections

▶ Making selling easier

· ·

*I*n sales, there's a simple difference between meeting with prospects and getting them to sign on the dotted line. The latter is selling; the former is not.

In this chapter, we look at the types of decision makers, examine several strategies for getting to yes, and get advice on making the numbers from someone who's been in the sales trenches for many years. Our goal is simple: We want you closing sales the moment the door opens.

Knowing the Three Types of Decision Makers

Closing the deal is when you have a commitment between a company and a cause to execute a cause marketing program. Most people don't close deals very well because they view closing as more of an act than a process. Yes, we say that we *closed a deal* when a deal is done. But closing begins the moment we meet a prospect.

Over the course of selling cause marketing programs, we've concluded that three types of decision makers exist:

 ✔ Thinkers

 ✔ Feelers

 ✔ Deferrers

No decision maker is ever just one type. It's never that simple. Everyone is a mixture of all three types to some degree. But one type dominates, and that's where you need to focus your efforts to be successful.

Just the facts, ma'am: Thinkers

The mainstays of thinkers are facts, figures, and logical arguments. These folks pour over numbers, analyze graphs, ask how you collect your data, and are most interested in the bottom-line return cause marketing has to offer. Thinkers are also the first to cry foul if your arguments aren't passing the smell test.

A lot of marketing directors are thinkers, which isn't surprising. They constantly have to show their bosses how a campaign has achieved a particular goal, driven sales, or met a particular return-on-investment.

The overriding question you may need to answer for a thinker, although they may never ask you directly, is "Does cause marketing make sense for my business?"

Here are three suggestions for making yourself crystal clear to thinkers:

- ✔ **Present your arguments logically.** A thinker isn't the right person to have a wide-ranging discussion of ideas. It's best to let them clearly understand the progression of your argument. Rely either on a point-by-point approach (for example, "Our first point is that cause marketing should be an important part of your marketing mix . . .") or a problem-solution approach that first addresses an agreed upon issue (for example, building a stronger connection with customers) and how cause marketing can solve it.

- ✔ **Present evidence from sources they know and respect.** An added edge in giving a thinker the facts and figures they want is obtaining them from a credible source. How do you find out who a thinker respects? The authoritative trade publications within her industry are a good start. Try Googling her to see whether she's quoted in the media or has her presentations up on YouTube or SlideShare. You can also check social media sites like LinkedIn and Twitter (see Figure 6-1), which would allow you to check out her followers and give you clues to her business connections. Depending on the person, you might just want to ask her who she respects.

Persuasion occurs through identification. When you can identify with the needs, experiences, beliefs, and attitudes of the prospects, you're more likely to ignite the spark that leads to closing a deal.

Figure 6-1: Twitter is a great tool for thought leadership, both for sharing and learning. It's just one of the resources to find out more about decision makers.

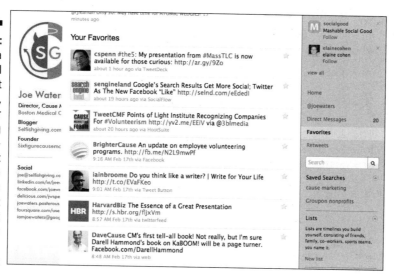

✔ **Present your arguments with creativity and passion.** Don't forget to balance logic with other appeals. For example, during our first year selling our signature Halloween event, an agency bidding on the project presented their proposal to us inside a *Book of Spells,* shown in Figure 6-2, which they had hand-delivered by the Grim Reaper himself. (Okay, maybe someone dressed up like the reaper!) While the agency knew they were dealing with thinkers that were ultimately interested in their ability to get the job done, their creativity and obvious passion for Halloween gave them an edge and eventually the business.

This feels right: Feelers

Feelers are driven by their emotions. They don't fixate on the graphs and charts and numbers. They focus on the pictures, watch the videos, and listen to the stories you have to share as they emotionally try to connect with your mission and the opportunity for their company. It doesn't have to make sense, but it does have to *feel right* for their business.

Because causes are no strangers to emotional appeals, dealing with feelers is easy for most nonprofits. However, you should take care to avoid a few hazards:

✔ **Don't overdo it.** Even with feelers, an overly emotional pitch can be a big turn-off. Emotions are like explosives. A little bit of dynamite can pack a lot of punch. Think twice about how much you use.

Figure 6-2:
The Book of Spells turned a dry proposal into a creative symbol of the potential inside. We used it for subsequent meetings with prospective partners to share our passion for Halloween and our event.

✔ **Balance emotion with other appeals.** Go for both the head and the heart. You can balance the two by using figures and facts to appeal to the prospect's logical side and then drill down deeper for an emotional connection. Saying that your food pantry served 75,000 people last year is important, but so, too, is your story of one local family that benefited from your pantry. Talk about their hardship and how the pantry helped turn their lives around. Don't ever let the prospect forget that you're dealing with an issue that impacts real people.

✔ **Stay positive.** Research on fear appeals shows that when they are overused, people will shut down and tune you out. Have you ever felt this way when a fundraising appeal overdid fear, anger, guilt, or shame? What's more effective is to focus on hope, joy, love, respect, and other positive emotions. People want to feel good about supporting a cause. Don't deprive them of that feeling, or they'll deprive you of their support.

However, fear can have its place as an appeal. The *Not Even Once* ad campaign from the Montana Meth Project is a great example of successful fear marketing. These powerful spots are prescribed in high doses that are appropriate for the teens they aim to sway. The ads wouldn't resonate with other audiences, nor will they remain forever effective with their target audience before the Meth Project will have to adopt a different approach. To watch the ads from the Montana Meth Project, scan the QR code to the left with your smartphone or visit `http://bit.ly/H4wV4`.

It's all about trust: Deferrers

Of the three types of decision makers, deferrers fascinate us the most because they're people of compliance, trust, and faith. Deferrers don't linger over the pictures like a feeler or pour over the stats like a thinker. No, what interests them is who else is involved, who else has already signed on as a partner.

Deferrers are not first adopters. They prefer to follow the lead of others. If a deferrer admires ABC Company and they've already signed on for a program, there's a good chance the deferrer will, too. Getting Mr. Smith from XYZ Company to put in a call to the deferrer may go a long way in sealing a deal.

Deferrers aren't patsies, mind you, but credibility, reputation, and prestige (like hobnobbing with a celebrity; see Figure 6-3) mean a lot to them when it comes to making a decision — certainly more than it does to thinkers and feelers.

Once we recruit a well-known business for a cause marketing program, we then call our prospective deferrers first to see whether they are interested in working with them.

> *"Hey, Jen, guess who we just signed on for our next cause marketing program? They have 100 stores, and they plan to use advertising, which you know is significant, to promote their participation and that of any cross-promotional partners. I know this is a company you respect and admire. Can we count you in as a partner in this program?"*

Figure 6-3:
Celebrity involvement in a cause marketing promotion can motivate a deferrer to join your ranks. Deferrers like being starstruck and rubbing elbows with people they know, admire, and respect.

Sometimes the deferrer defers to *you!* Deferrers want to work with people they admire, respect, and trust. And it's not enough for you to bring the tidings from others. Just as deferrers are trustworthy, you must be trustworthy. Just as they're competent, you must be competent. And just as deferrers are professional, articulate, and polished, you must be those things, too.

You are a surrogate for the great men and women deferrers to look to for their decisions. The king's messenger just doesn't carry his seal; he, too, is finely dressed and well spoken. Be the king's man.

Getting to Yes

Getting to yes and closing the deal is never easy, even when you know the type of decision maker with whom you're dealing. You need a value proposition that is irresistible, undeniable, and meaningful. In this section, we look at how free is a powerful way to sell cause marketing, ways to stop sabotaging yourself, ways to build a stronger connection with prospects, and ways to close the deal.

Free is for me

If you can't sell something, try giving it away. That's what King Gillette, the inventor of the Gillette disposable razor concluded. Giving away his razors is how he grew demand for his new invention when at first he couldn't sell it.

Free has changed all sorts of businesses — Web, software, newspapers, video games — and it can make your cause marketing efforts more successful. We can give you two good reasons that you should follow Gillette's lead and give away your cause marketing programs, instead of selling them:

- **Finding a buyer isn't always easy.** It's tough to sell cause marketing because a lot of the companies either don't know a lot about cause marketing or don't really believe it works. (Don't be insulted. Be comforted knowing that most of the paid advertising companies do *really* doesn't work!) Given the choice between buying traditional advertising or investing in cause marketing, businesses will choose advertising nine out of ten times for no other reason than they would rather stick with something that doesn't work than try something new that's been proven to work. That's why so many of the nonprofits that jump on the cause marketing bandwagon end up abandoning it. Like King Gillette when he first tried selling his razors, they can't find any buyers but don't think of giving their programs away to build demand.

- **The company is the rainbow TO the pot of gold.** You wouldn't want to take a corporate check for the same reason U2's Bono didn't when he was pitching Product (RED) to companies like Armani, Gap, and Apple. He knew the real money in cause marketing was not in the company checkbook, but in the wallets of the millions of customers who would buy these products and services. That's why Bono insisted on a cause product from which Product (RED) would benefit. Today, Bono has well over 160 million reasons why he was right.

You can be the Bono, the rock star of your cause. Stop viewing cause marketing as something that needs to be sold and start presenting it as something that only requires free activation. Whenever we talk to a business about cause marketing, they're almost always attentive but also share the same question: "How much?" We have a standard response: "Nothing."

If you're dealing with a Thinker, he might respond to this simple equation we sometimes use with prospects:

Value + Free – Risk = Great Opportunity

We haven't met a business yet that wasn't interested in a high value, low-risk, *free* opportunity.

For your program to succeed, it must be free.

Product (RED)

While Product (RED) is aptly named for the victims of HIV/AIDS with infected blood, it also covers the two reactions people generally have to the cause. Either they're red-faced from gushing over its marketing prowess and success or are seeing red from what they view as a marketing scheme that profits big corporate brands.

U2 front man Bono and Kennedy scion, Bobby Shriver, started Product (RED)'s portion of sales cause marketing program (see Chapter 10) in 2006 to help AIDS-ravaged Africa. Consumers buy items from Product (RED) partners like the Gap, Apple, Nike, and others, and a portion of the proceeds go to buying the medicine Africans with HIV/AIDS need to stay alive (see figure).

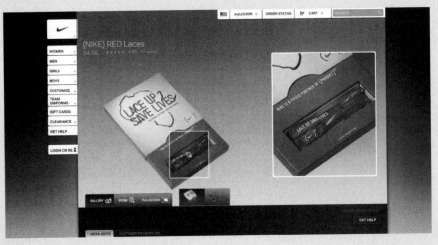

To date Product (RED) has raised more than $160 million — an impressive amount in such a short time.

Product (RED) is pure play cause marketing. It was founded to develop cause marketing programs with retailers to raise money and fight HIV/AIDS in Africa.

Yes, Product (RED) is heaven on earth for cause marketers!

But Product (RED) is not without its critics who complain that retailers are cashing in on the cause. This bubbled over in 2007 when it was revealed that (RED) partners like the Gap had spent tens of millions of dollars on marketing (RED). In some cases, spending had exceeded what companies had raised for the cause.

But what Product (RED) has gained is undeniable. Since 2006, it has received millions of dollars in donations as promised. And the promotion, which came at no cost to (RED), has helped position it as a top philanthropic brand in perhaps the shortest time period in history. (Consider that top cause brands like the Salvation Army have been at it for over a hundred years and St. Jude Children's Research Hospital for nearly 50.)

Product (RED) highlights an important distinction about cause marketing, which we discuss in Chapter 1. Both Product (RED) and its partners are focused on mutual profit. While the goals of cause marketing are charitable, it's not charity. Cause marketing is a business.

But even free won't persuade some prospects. Not surprisingly, people value the things they get for free less than the things they pay for. It's an attitude that's common from less committed partners who signed on for a cause marketing program but then let it flop because they had nothing to lose or no "skin in the game."

You also have to be careful because free does have costs. YouTube loses hundreds of millions of dollars each year giving away its service in hopes of one day turning a profit by selling ads and other services on its site. Cause marketing has its own expenses. Pinups, for example, have design, printing, and shipping expenses to cover, just to name a few.

The lesson? Screen your partners carefully to make sure that they recognize the real, valuable benefits of the program — for both partners — and are committed to its success.

Avoiding excuses to say no

Are you getting prospects closer to yes, or are you just giving them an excuse to say no at every turn? Here are just some of the ways causes sabotage themselves:

- ✔ Repeatedly calling the wrong person at a business about the wrong opportunity. The word will spread quickly that you're the wrong person to talk to.

- ✔ Mailing prospects reams of information and details about your cause marketing proposal. Thus giving the prospect all the info they need to make a decision without you (almost always a no, by the way). And they know just how to get rid of you: "Send me some information, and I'll get back to you."

- ✔ Not calling prospects back when they ask you to. Would you do a potential six-figure cause marketing program with someone who can't even get back to you?

- ✔ Not being flexible to adjust your cause marketing proposal to the needs and interests of the prospects. Just exactly who needs whom here? Act accordingly.

- ✔ Allowing a prospect to give you a flat-out no. Psychologically, saying no is an important threshold for a decision maker to cross. When a decision maker says no, he generally means it.

- ✔ Wasting a prospect's time with a meeting or presentation that's poorly planned, lacks focus, and has no value proposition. You can scratch that prospect off your list for life.

✔ Failing to demonstrate a good understanding of cause marketing, its benefits and the implications for causes and businesses. There's no excuse for not knowing your own business — or your prospect's, for that matter.

Increasing the number of touchpoints

In working with a company, you always want to find ways to make it less transactional and more meaningful. That's where touchpoints come in handy. *Touchpoints* are the intersections of where your company and cause overlap, eliciting a positive response.

For example, a powerful touchpoint is to invite a prospect to tour your non-profit (or sometimes the company may invite you to tour their operation) so that they can see firsthand the incredible work you're doing. This touchpoint certainly increases your chances of getting to yes with a prospect.

But immersing a potential partner into your cause is just one of the touchpoints you can leverage. Some others include

✔ **Building a connection between a prospect and a board member or other supporter whom the prospect may already know or respect.** This approach gives you another ally in the sales process.

✔ **Targeting businesses that work directly with your organization.** The waters can be tricky to navigate because of the conflict of interest business partners pose, but unlike most businesses, they probably truly understand and appreciate what your organization does. That's a touchpoint you want to leverage.

✔ **Offer to be helpful in any way — and not just in a way that benefits you.** Knowing that we have expertise in social media, a potential partner will often contact us to ask questions about Twitter or Facebook. We're happy to assist as this kind of situation builds a stronger bond and relationship with the prospect and demonstrates our aptitude for online marketing.

Recently, a cause marketing partner of ours was interested in switching its loyalty program from a card-based program to one using location-based services like Foursquare. We offered to help in any way we could, even if it didn't involve our cause. Working with the company was a great opportunity to build a better bond that would lead to stronger cause marketing ties down the road.

Making the Numbers

As cause marketers, we call ourselves development officers, fundraisers, and marketers. But none of these names describes what we do as well as "salesperson" does. Face it, we all have sales goals, and just like salespeople, we have to "make the numbers."

Joe began his nonprofit career with the Muscular Dystrophy Association in 1993. At a regional training seminar his first year, he met a trainer, Jack Falvey, who would shape Joe's approach to selling for years to come.

Even back then, Jack had been "carrying a bag" for a generation and was teaching some of the best sales people in the country how to sell better.

Jack's advice that day stuck with Joe. Jack understood the essence of selling, regardless of what industry you worked in. Jack was a kind of Socrates of sales, and Joe was determined not to go wandering by him in the marketplace, but to stop and listen and learn.

Accepting selling as the key to your success

Joe remembers Jack repeating a quote he's heard many times since they met: "Nothing happens in this world until somebody sells something." The world is driven by sales. And the profession you're in really doesn't matter. In some way, we're all in sales!

Accepting the fact that we're all in sales is tough for some cause professionals to stomach because they see themselves as "fundraisers" or in "development." Call yourself what you want, but whenever you're trying to convince another person to do something they're not inclined to do on their own, you're selling. If it makes you feel better substitute "persuading" for selling! Maybe you'll be a director or vice president of "persuading" some day!

When Jack told Joe and all the fundraisers with him in 1994 that they were all in sales, Joe breathed a sigh of relief and opened himself to becoming a nonprofit salesperson.

Your ability to close cause marketing partnerships will depend greatly on your sales skills. Don't sabotage your success as a cause marketer just because sales advice reminds you of a bad experience you had at your local used car lot.

Knowing, seeing, selling

Jack's prescription for selling success is a simple four-step process.

- ✔ **Know your product.** Understanding cause marketing is key, but so is your ability to present cause marketing simply and compellingly to your prospect. You should be clear on what cause marketing can and can't do and how it's unique from other forms of marketing.

- ✔ **Know your customer.** With the amount of information available on the Internet, you have no excuse not to know about your prospect. From the Internet, you can explore needs and goals via your own personal network of contacts. You can dig further in phone calls and meetings with the prospect. The information is out there. You need to be adept at finding and collecting it.

- ✔ **See a lot of people.** Here's a strange fact about selling: Most people say no. In order to get some people to say yes, you'll have to hear a lot of people say no. Plan accordingly. See as many people as you can to improve your closing average.

- ✔ **Ask all to buy.** If you're not asking people to buy, you're in customer service, not sales. Sales isn't just about information, telling prospects about your organization and the benefits of cause marketing. That approach works only to a point. At some point, you have to ask the prospect to join you. Don't be shy. It's unlikely the prospect will ask you to marry him first.

Getting over the ones that got away

A lot of people will say no. It's a fact of selling anything, including cause marketing.

There's a big difference between a prospect that says, "No, not right now" and "No, I can never see us ever working with your organization." You arrive at the former by addressing as closely as you can the needs, interests, and values of the prospect.

To help deal with the prospects that got away, Jack gave Joe a simple formula to remember:

$$SW(3) = N$$

Translation: Some will. Some won't. So what. Next!

Jack followed up his advice with this story about two business people on the golf course. One was older and had been successful. The other was young, just starting out and struggling with rejection. The older man counseled him to soldier on. "I've spent 95 percent of my life hearing people say no to me. But I've built a successful career on the other 5 percent that said yes."

Building your cause marketing program is like growing a business. Like selling any business, you'll get more than your share of no's. The key is to keep selling, and you'll close your 5 percent, maybe even more.

As Jack Falvey taught Joe, making the numbers requires dedication to your craft, a laser-like focus on closing business, and a can-do attitude that rejection can't undo.

You can learn from Jack just as Joe did. When you visit his website, `http://MakingTheNumbers.com` (see Figure 6-4), you can sign up to receive a free sales tip of the day. Joe still receives his tip daily, and it helps guide his selling every day.

Figure 6-4: When you sign up for a sales tip, you get a free daily e-mail on topics like this one.

Preparing Winning Proposals

Most prospects like to see some type of proposal when you pitch them on a cause marketing program. But consider yourself warned: Proposals are a crutch for seller and prospect alike. The seller uses them so that they can avoid selling to the prospect, which is uncomfortable to them. Prospects ask for proposals so that they can appear to have given your offer much thought.

But the real reason is so they can say no to your proposal without hurting your feelings, which is uncomfortable to them. Proposals are not effective for communicating your message or closing business. Proposals don't close deals; people do.

But not bringing a proposal to a meeting is like showing up as a guest for Thanksgiving dinner empty-handed. People will be surprised and maybe just a bit insulted. So bring a proposal. But use it strategically and realistically:

- **Know when to use them. Proposals are not for first meetings.** We greet prospects with pen and paper in hand, but it's blank. It's time to listen and explore. We save our proposals for later after we have a better idea of their objectives.

- **The proposal isn't about you.** Save that for the agreement. It's about converting a prospect into a partner. So make sure to include the examples, the metrics, and the benefits a partner needs to make an educated decision about working with you.

- **Be clear on what the company has to do — and just how much you will do.** Everyone wants to know just how much time, effort, and resources executing a cause marketing program will involve. We always make sure that partners have a short checklist to work from. It generally has must-do items that only they can execute, such as monitoring and helping to motivate cashiers to execute point-of-sale programs. We make it clear that we handle the rest.

- **Be clear on money.** This is critical. How will they raise money? Put it in the proposal. Have you agreed on an amount? Put it in the proposal. What if they don't reach the agreed on amount? Put it in the proposal. How long after the promotion ends will you have to wait to receive the money? Do you get the point?

- **Have Legal review it.** That's easy to do if your cause has a legal department. But if your cause doesn't, perhaps a lawyer on your board could be helpful, or you could invest in one for just this purpose. It may seem like overkill, but it's worth it, especially when you're new to cause marketing.

- **Proposals don't close deals; you do.** Causes too often think if they wallpaper their business contacts with proposals, they'll eventually land a partner. This never works. Your physical presence and role in the outreach is the most important part of closing a deal. The proposal is just a nail — and just one at that. You're the hammer.

Part III
Implementing Your Cause Marketing Program

The 5th Wave　　　　By Rich Tennant

"Does the check writing pen go above the dessert spoon or next to the salad fork?"

In this part . . .

*P*art III fills you in on the details of implementing a successful cause marketing program. We explain point-of-sale cause marketing and how to create a simple, powerful ask for your campaign. We also offer strategies for working with key stakeholders: stores managers and frontline employees. We talk about purchase or action-triggered donations and offer some helpful examples of successful programs. We also keep you on the straight and narrow with advice on staying on the good side of consumers and the right side of the law.

Chapter 7

Implementing Your Point-of-Sale Program

. . . .

In This Chapter

▶ Ensuring the success of your point-of-sale program with a simple, emotional ask

▶ Using managers and incentives to motivate front-line employees

▶ Printing and shipping tips that will get you started and save you money

. . . .

We have simple reasons for recommending point-of-sale pinups to causes and companies. They're lucrative, easy to execute, and relatively inexpensive, and you can combine them with other tools, such as events and social media.

In this chapter, we offer specific guidelines for implementing a pinup program, beginning with the basics of creating a compelling message and adding value for consumers. We look at two key drivers behind pinup programs: managers and incentives. Finally, we offer our tips for producing pinups so that you raise the most money for your cause with the least expense.

Your No. 1 Weapon: Pinups

We call them pinups. But you may have heard them called something else: paper icons, mobiles, paper plaques, scannables (because of the barcodes on the back of pinups so that they can be easily scanned at the register).

Regardless of what you call them, pinups are an important cause marketing tool, which is why they are a key focus of this book. They should be on your shortlist of programs for many reasons:

> ✔ **Pinups are easy.** Well, pinups are easy when compared to other tactics, such as planning a walk, coordinating a gala, or organizing a golf tournament. After you have a partner aboard, you design and print a pinup and then deliver it to the retailer who sells it at checkout. Now you may go back to the store to deliver more pinups if the program is really successful. Or visit again to pick up your check. This is the kind of work you'll like doing!

✔ **Pinups are lucrative.** Some of the most successful cause marketing campaigns are pinup programs. St. Jude Children's Research Hospital's Thanks and Giving program raises millions with its green, round pinup. The Jimmy Fund in Boston boasts a very successful pinup program with supermarket chain Stop & Shop that has raised more than $50 million since 1991. Pinups have been a big part of our success, too. One of our partners, Ocean State Job Lot, a discount retailer with 100 locations in New England, hit the million-dollar mark in 2011 for dollars raised through pinups over seven years.

✔ **Pinups are cost-effective.** Pinups aren't free, but they're not expensive either. Our pinups, depending on design and printing, have ranged from just a few pennies per pinup to up to 13 cents for ones that were die-cut and included coupons.

✔ **Pinups play well with others.** Pinups are very versatile. They go well with events, co-marketing partnerships, and social media. In short, we're always finding new ways to work with pinups to create better cause marketing partnerships.

✔ **Pinups are great promotion.** The visual display of pinups hanging at the front of the store is a powerful sign of both the business and the consumer's commitment to the cause (see Figure 7-1). Individual pinups can include sponsor or event information that can be torn off and given to the customer with their donation.

Figure 7-1:
The visual display pinups create in a business is powerful and gratifying.

Keeping Your Message Simple

Cashiers asking customers to support your cause is critical to the success of your pinup program. If there is no ask, your chances of success drop sharply.

But even when cashiers are asking shoppers to support a cause, it's important that the ask be simple, powerful, and actionable. For us, this means

- ✔ **Keeping your message to one compelling sentence:** As generals of old used to advise, mass your forces. Defeat your shopper's inclination to say no with a devastatingly disarming question. That doesn't mean subsequent volleys can't follow. But the first ask will do most of the work for you.

- ✔ **Leading with the emotional:** People want to give from deep within themselves. Win their hearts first, and their heads will follow.

- ✔ **Focusing on your issue:** This is especially true if consumers are not familiar with your nonprofit. For example, our hospital isn't as well known as some hospitals in Boston. Most people still call it "city hospital," a name associated with marginal care and urban decay, which didn't have the best reputation. To avoid giving shoppers an excuse not to give a gift (for example, "Huh? I've never heard of that charity"), we instead focus on the issues they do know and care about (for example, sick kids, cancer, women's issues, and so on).

Here are some of the good asks we've heard from cashiers soliciting support from shoppers.

"Would you like to donate a dollar to help a sick child?"

"We're trying to raise enough money today to feed a family of four for a week. Can you help?"

"We're raising money so that no child has to live without their mother because of cancer. Can you donate a dollar today?"

Honing in on the Power of One

"If I look at the mass, I will never act. If I look at the one, I will."

— Mother Theresa

Human beings have a basic flight-or-fight response to imminent danger, which forces our primitive minds to limit its choices and, interestingly, our *humanity.*

For example, a problem like AIDS in Africa that affects millions and millions of people can short-circuit our humanity because we can't wrap our minds around that level of suffering. However, the waves of individual stories of tragedy that follow a disaster, like the Japan earthquake, evoke a knee-jerk humanitarian response.

The lesson here for cause marketers isn't new, but it is worth repeating. Numbers are "human beings with the tears dried off" and don't move donors to give. Urgent, emotional, and personal images and language do. This advice is true whether you're communicating with a donor in person or through a pinup sold at a store register.

You can whet your appetite for crafting a personal, emotional appeal by scanning the QR code to the left and watching the video "Strong as Iron" from The Jimmy Fund, the fundraising arm of the Dana-Farber Cancer Institute. You can also watch the video by visiting `http://bit.ly/1JsYM6`.

Setting Limits Will Raise More Money

Seth Godin, the marketing guru and author of such classics as *The Purple Cow* (Portfolio Hardcover), is a big fan of setting limits for consumers, lest they opt out all together. For Seth, it's all about telling people where the end lies and how much is enough. He goes on to say that this advice is true whether you're trying to persuade people to join a gym or go on a diet, among other things.

If donors don't feel their support will make a difference or make them feel good, they will "avert their eyes." Seth contends that fewer people will turn away and a new class of donors could rise if they have a ceiling set for them. That's why limits are key to your success in cause marketing.

Keep these two things in mind:

- ✔ **Cause marketing isn't blue-blooded philanthropy.** It's red-blooded. It's fundraising for the masses that either asks shoppers for a small donation when they checkout or a company makes a donation to their favorite causes when they purchase a product.

- ✔ **Cause marketing asks should always have a ceiling.** Donate a buck, two bucks. That's it. Buy a coffee, and a dime goes to Haiti or Africa. Consumers want to know what they can do and how their donation is making a real difference.

So, you should make sure to set a limit — generally $1 to $5 for point-of-sale programs — of how much you want shoppers to contribute.

We had only one retailer that worked outside a limit. Ocean State Job Lot, a Rhode Island–based retailer with 100 New England stores, sold a $1 pinup but then encouraged shoppers to give more. It wasn't a bad strategy. The company raised a lot of money. But our research indicated that most of their customers chose the dollar limit. Thanks to the polite but persistent efforts of Job Lot employees, some generous shoppers gave more. But others may have given less or not at all because there were no limits.

Experiment for yourself and see what happens. Don't forget to share your results with us!

Getting Results with Active and Passive Cause Marketing

Active cause marketing (ACM) is when a cashier asks a customer to support a cause: "Would you like to donate a dollar to help *(insert your favorite cause or issue)?*" Proactive upselling isn't reserved for causes. It happens all the time at the register. (For more on how point-of-sale programs work, see Chapter 1.)

> *"Do you need batteries for that?"*
>
> *"Would you like to try Via, our new instant coffee?"*
>
> *"Would you like to supersize your meal?"*

Businesses learned long ago that shoppers respond more favorably to an ask than to a sign or bag stuffer. McDonald's learned years ago that if it asked a customer if he "Would like fries with that?" the answer was usually yes.

The same is true for active cause marketing, and that's why the most successful cause marketing programs in the country are active cause marketing promotions, like the one between St. Jude and Chili's that has raised tens of millions of dollars, mostly from point-of-sale transactions. This campaign takes place during September during National Childhood Cancer Awareness month. Throughout the Create-A-Pepper campaign, guests at locations nationwide and in Puerto Rico can help support the lifesaving work of St. Jude Children's Research Hospital through several in-restaurant, digital, and interactive promotions (see Figure 7-2). Guests are asked to make a donation to St. Jude and receive a Create-A-Pepper chili pepper coloring sheet. Decorated sheets are then displayed in restaurants throughout September.

Other in-store components of the program include the option to buy merchandise, which also benefits St. Jude Children's Research Hospital. During the annual Donate Profits Day, historically the last Monday of the month, participating restaurants donate 100 percent of their profits to St. Jude. While these two programs are best described as purchase-triggered donation programs, when combined with the coloring sheets, it's a great example of how two types of cause marketing promotions can work side by side.

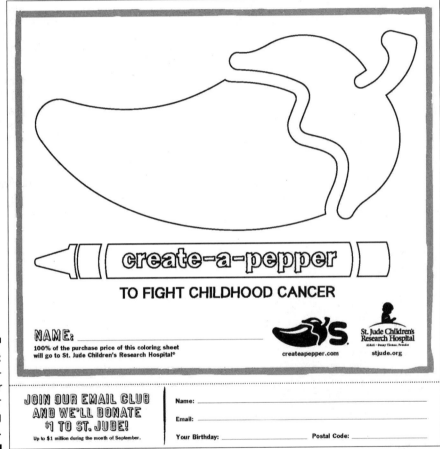

Figure 7-2:
Create-A-Pepper chili pepper coloring sheet (front).

Not every business likes asking customers for donations. Some view it as pestering, while others don't think it fits with their business. In a down economy especially, businesses tend to avoid programs that may dissatisfy customers.

An alternative to ACM is *passive cause marketing* (PCM). Passive cause marketing is less intrusive because it doesn't involve an ask from the cashier.

The request comes from either a sign or a tear-off flyer that ideally is in a visible location at the register where shoppers can decide for themselves if they want to contribute to the cause.

Active cause marketing is your best point-of-sale option, but passive cause marketing can produce good results.

Whole Foods is a national supermarket chain that executes passive cause marketing very well. Just about every month, Whole Foods has a different cause, mostly local organizations, that shoppers can support. For example, we came across a passive cause marketing program for autism at a local Whole Foods near Boston (see Figure 7-3). The ask was in a great location — in direct line of sight on the credit card machine where consumers couldn't miss it.

To support the cause, the shopper simply had to choose her donation and hand one of the laminated cards to the cashier. (We've also seen this as a tear-off pad.) The card has a barcode on it, which the cashier scans and is recorded like every other product in the store. The shopper pays for the donation with the rest of her groceries, and the cashier returns the donation card to the register sign for the next shopper in line.

There is no verbal ask from the cashier. The shopper simply decides whether she wants to give, chooses the corresponding card, and pays her shopping bill, which includes the donation.

Figure 7-3:
A passive cause marketing program for autism at Whole Foods gave shoppers the choice of donating $2 or $5.

A passive cause marketing campaign will rarely raise as much money as an active cause marketing campaign. (Would automakers really sell more cars if they didn't have salespeople and relied instead on window stickers to persuade shoppers? We think not. Humans make the difference.) But Whole Foods' passive cause marketing is tops among other programs. We've seen many others that are not in a good spot for shoppers to see or even hidden behind a gum display in aisle 3!

Why does a passive cause marketing program work at Whole Foods? The demographics of its customers certainly help. The average Whole Foods shopper is affluent, educated, and sophisticated, which makes them more open and progressive about seeking out and supporting causes they care about. Whole Foods also chooses causes that fit its healthy, organic mission, another selling point with shoppers.

While this particular program was for autism, other passive cause marketing programs we've seen at Whole Foods' registers are for food pantries, homeless shelters, and green causes — right in line with the interests and concerns of its shoppers' attitudes, concerns, and beliefs.

In short, passive cause marketing is probably a good fit for Whole Foods. But it may not work so well at a traditional supermarket chain.

Choose active cause marketing programs over passive. Active cause marketing will work better for more businesses, and you'll raise more money. Passive cause marketing is a good second choice, but it's important to learn from the Whole Foods model: The shopper needs to be an active giver, and placement of the ask is critical.

Consumers are bombarded by messages and distractions at checkout. Make sure that your cause marketing ask doesn't get left at the bottom of the cart.

Avoiding Unnecessary Signage

With point-of-sale, the ask at the register is everything. With active cause marketing (see preceding section), the ask is articulated by the cashier. "Would you like to donate a dollar to . . .?" With passive cause marketing, the ask comes in the form of a register sign, usually in clear site of the shopper (for example, on a credit card machine).

With any cause marketing promotion, there's a temptation to produce additional signage and materials to promote the program. Resist it. They don't work. Posters, fliers, and buttons are fodder for failure because shoppers will ignore them, and employees will use them as excuses to skip asking the consumer to support the program (thinking the button on their shirt will do the asking for them).

However, we're realists about promotional materials and know that many businesses will insist on something in-store to promote the program. We've found that the best and cheapest promotional tool after a committed employee is a simple register sign, such as the one in Figure 7-4.

We've learned to focus our efforts on developing a dedicated and motivated employee that will drive the program. But when businesses ask for something more, we give them register signs.

Register signs are cheap and highly visible to shoppers. And they just might make a difference. Just don't make the mistake of thinking that people will give because of a sign. People give to other people.

Figure 7-4:
Register
sign.

Adding Value with Coupons

We almost always include coupons on our pinups (see Figure 7-5). They have an immediate value at the register when cashiers are asking shoppers to support our cause.

Figure 7-5:
Coupons add value for donors and help you recruit more partners.

"Would you like to donate a dollar to help sick kids? As a thank you, you get these coupons that have $50 in savings."

Here are four more reasons your cause marketing program should have coupons.

- ✔ **Coupons open the door to cross-promotional partners.** We learned early on that some retailers would partner with us if they could comarket with another business. Landing one partner meant you could potentially recruit many more.

- ✔ **Coupons are hot!** According to *Ad Age,* in 2009, redemption of coupons that go through clearinghouses surged 23 percent to 3.2 billion coupons (and up 30 percent to $3.5 billion in value) in the United States, the first gain in 17 consecutive years. Through the first nine months of 2010, coupon redemption was up another 5.3 percent to 2.5 billion versus the year-ago period, with the value of coupons redeemed up 7.7 percent to $2.8 billion. Consumers are looking for more coupons, which is great for cause marketers like us that add coupons to pinups.

- ✔ **Coupons are overwhelmingly clipped, not downloaded.** The surprising news is that consumers of all ages aren't getting their coupons from the Internet. They're getting them the old-fashioned way: They're clipping them. More than 2 billion coupon redemptions in 2009 came from print inserts. Internet coupons account for just 1 percent of distributions. So if you think adding coupons to your pinups seems a bit old school, think again. Consumers are eager to use coupons, and they're getting them almost exclusively offline. And what better place for them to get their coupons than from your pinups after supporting a great cause?

✔ **Coupons prove that cause marketing works.** Coupon redemption during or after a campaign is an excellent way to demonstrate that cause marketing works and is driving traffic for partners. After helping your cause, this result is just what a business wants. One of our partners was thrilled when a pinup program brought in 1,100 coupon-bearing customers from cross-partner stores. These coupons generated an additional $400,000 in revenue for this retailer.

Pizza chain uses coupon booklet to raise funds for causes

For 33 years, New England–based Papa Gino's and its sister company D'Angelo have been raising money a buck at a time for two causes: Easter Seals and The Genesis Fund (see figure). What's always distinguished this point-of-sale program from others is that Papa Gino's and D'Angelo didn't use a traditional pinup. They used a coupon book. It's worked well as over $3.3 million has been raised!

We've been buying the coupon books for years, and it's always had money-saving coupons for the two restaurants. This year, the pizza and sub chain added coupons from other businesses: a national chain of movie theaters, a local party-supply retailer, two from local sports teams (the Boston Red Sox and New England Revolution), and several from local tourist attractions and sites.

Adding comarketing partners to the coupon adds value for the consumer. They get to help a cause and save money.

What Papa Gino's and D'Angelo didn't do that you can do is ask the other partners in the coupon book to sell the book in their stores (see figure). Getting a discount from these partners is great. But taking it one step further and having them join you in raising money is what comarketing with cause marketing is all about.

Coupons give your cause marketing program a one-two punch, open the door to additional partners, and provide the paper trail that cause marketing works. You also have the wind at your back. Coupons are in high demand, and consumers get them offline, so why not through a pinup?

Why *wouldn't* you want to include coupons in your next cause marketing program?

Focusing on Managers Is Key

Nothing will determine the success of your point-of-sale program more than store managers. Their commitment to the program will keep front-line employees engaged and asking customers to give.

Think of store employees like soldiers at the front. Individually, there are always examples of heroism and bravery. But to be truly successful, soldiers have to be properly trained and led by their commander. In a company, this responsibility falls to the role of the manager.

Here are some ways to get and keep managers focused on victory:

- ✔ **Meet with them individually or as a group.** Before the start of a cause marketing promotion, we make a point to connect with each store manager to introduce ourselves, talk about our mission, and pledge our support in any way to make the program just as turnkey and successful as possible. It's important to assure managers that you're an ally, not an adversary or coward who will run away when it's time to charge ahead.

- ✔ **Make sure that they understand the incentives you're offering.** These rewards will help them in their efforts to motivate employees. Share with managers both the material incentives you're offering employees and the intangible incentives of helping a great cause and how easy it is for them to activate the program.

- ✔ **Encourage them to visit your nonprofit.** By visiting, managers can see firsthand the work you do and the difference you're making in the community (see Figure 7-6). For example, seeing all the dogs and cats your nonprofit saves will strike a chord with managers and motivate them to push the program in their stores and make it more than just another promotion from corporate.

- ✔ **Educate them on the win-win benefits of cause marketing.** Managers may not be aware of the bottom-line benefits of cause marketing to their company. Educate them on how the halo earned from cause marketing can mean more sales at the cash register, and bigger bonuses and profit sharing for them.

Figure 7-6:
These managers from Boston's Finagle-A-Bagel visited our hospital and saw firsthand the incredible work we do.

Using Incentives as Motivation

We talk a lot about incentives in Chapter 4 and whether or not they work. The short story is that incentives do work — if you know how to use them.

If you're launching a point-of-sale program with a new partner, follow these tips:

- **Don't offer any incentives.** See what happens. If the program goes well, you'll know you're working with a great group of employees. You can always offer incentives in the next program.

- **Remember our mantra: Focus on managers.** A manager staying on top of cashiers reminding them to ask customers to donate a dollar is worth his weight in gold.

- **Identify the employees who will benefit from incentives.** Highly trained employees that upsell with skill are great candidates for incentives.

- **The best incentive is an easy program.** Cashiers have enough to do at the register and are frequently upselling customers on a variety of items: "Do you need any batteries today?" "Apply for our credit card and save 10 percent." "Are your children a member of our kids club?" The last thing they want or need is a complicated cause marketing program to execute. Give them a simple, one-line pitch like, "Would you like to donate a dollar to help a sick child?" If you can add an incentive for the consumer, like a coupon, the pitch is even easier. And don't forget the barcode for easy scanning!

Incentives can work. You just need to know how and when to use them, and with whom.

Using weekly versus monthly incentives

When working with incentives, you need to decide when to distribute them. You can wait until the end of the campaign as a grand finale to the program, or you can distribute them weekly to keep motivation high. Or you can do both!

During a four-week point-of-sale program, we've been known to incorporate weekly and monthly incentives, as well as secret shoppers. The weekly incentives are usually gift cards to use in drawings for the employees at top-performing stores for that week. At the end of the month, the stores that have raised the most over the course of the entire program receive prizes for all their employees — and then there can be bonus drawings. The program we offer depends on what items we've been able to get for free. (We discuss tactics for getting free stuff in the next section.)

Finding free incentive prizes

We never pay for incentive prizes. Neither should you! There are too many easy and good places to get them for free.

Here are our strategies:

- ✔ **Ask local companies to give them to you.** We're always amazed by what people will give you if you just ask them. But you'll never know if you don't ask. Try it. You may be surprised. In exchange, you may be able to offer them some promotion in the stores selling your pinup.

- ✔ **Recruit an incentive partner.** We did this with a local pizza chain. The pizza chain wanted its coupon on our pinup, but it didn't want to pay to be on it or sell it at its restaurants. Joanna came up with the idea of the chain compensating with pizzas! This trade was win-win because they got their coupon on our pinup, and we got free pizzas we could use as incentives with our other partners.

- ✔ **Nonprofits of all sizes can tap the points on their company credit cards for incentives.** You could also ask donors to exchange their credit card points for incentive items that could be used for a program.

- ✔ **Ask the company you're partnering with to support your program with incentive prizes for their employees.** Even better, if your program includes co-marketing with other businesses, exchange prizes so that employees get something different, and the company gets access to a new audience of potential customers. An employee in a coffee shop doesn't want a coupon for a free coffee. But the employee at the sub shop across town may love a free latte and may become a new regular customer.

A sample incentive program

Here's an example of an incentive program we've used with a partner. This retailer divided their stores into four groups so that stores were competing against other stores of equal size and foot traffic.

Incentive #1 (upon completion of the program)

For the top store in each of the four groups:

Each employee will be rewarded with a Halloween Town family four-pack, which includes tickets to the event, t-shirts, and a cool pumpkin bag.

Bonus raffle: One employee from each store will win a $100 gift certificate to LL Bean.

Grand prize: One employee from this pool of four stores will win a vacation.

Incentive #2 (upon completion of the program)

Pizza party for each of the top four stores.

Incentive #3 (weekly)

One employee from each of the top four stores will be entered to win a $25 gift certificate to one of the following: LL Bean, Williams-Sonoma, or Sharper Image.

Incentive #4 (throughout the program)

Throughout October, secret shoppers will regularly visit stores. If a cashier asks the secret shopper to support the program, he will receive a prize, such as movie passes, coupons for partner freebies, ice cream parties and other exciting rewards!

Using secret shoppers

A great way to keep cashiers on their toes and asking shoppers to support your cause at the register is *secret shoppers*. You've probably heard of secret shoppers. These hired guns masquerade as everyday shoppers to find out more about what a business is doing well and what needs improvement.

Some of the companies we work with already have secret shoppers that we can use to monitor our program. Other times, we've used really good volunteers or our own staff.

If you use staff or volunteers, here's a suggestion to make it more fun for the employees they're scrutinizing. Arm your secret shoppers with small prizes and gifts for the cashiers that are doing a great job asking shoppers to support your cause.

Our secret shoppers get in checkout lines like any other shopper, but when the cashiers ask them to donate to our cause, they inform them who they are. They thank the cashiers for their support and give them a small reward, such as a t-shirt or a $5 gift card to a coffee shop.

This reward is your way of saying thank you! Make a big deal of it, letting the cashiers around them know they're being rewarded for their efforts. Also, tell their manager that they're doing a great job selling the program.

Of course, not every cashier will ask the secret shopper to support the cause. You have a couple options if they aren't asked:

✔ Tell them they just missed out on a chance to win a great prize! Then take a moment to tell the cashier about your cause and how important this program is to your mission.

Above all, stay positive. Shaming and humiliating the employee won't work. It will have the opposite effect. Don't give the employee a really good reason *not* to support the program.

✔ Your secret shopper could pass through the checkout line without saying anything and then make a beeline for the manager to talk about getting employees to solicit shoppers. Remember, managers are key. If you had a particularly bad experience with a cashier, share it with the manager, not the employee. The manager is in a position to be critical of his staff, if needed. You're not. Again, even with the manager, stay positive and don't harp on him about his staff's performance.

These managers and cashiers are volunteering their effort and support for your program. Regardless of what corporate is telling them, they have a choice of whether to give it their full effort, or a half-hearted one.

Do you want your influence to be positive or negative? As the saying goes, you'll catch more flies with honey than vinegar.

Addressing Pinup Fatigue

If you've done a good job working with stores, you'll have no trouble getting people excited to execute the point-of-sale program and getting it off to a great start.

Employee enthusiasm is contagious! And shoppers will embrace the program with their support.

But how long can the fire burn? We've executed programs anywhere from a week to two months, and there's definitely a saturation point when employees and customers begin to lose interest and can even become angry or hostile toward the promotion (see Figure 7-7).

Figure 7-7:
This employee from iParty, one of our key cause marketing partners, is eager to share the program with customers. If you let your program run too long, that enthusiasm will fade.

The ideal length of a point-of-sale program is two to four weeks. However, some exceptions do justify a longer program:

- ✔ **You're working with seasoned and enthusiastic employees.** Enthusiasm goes a long way in keeping employees engaged in a longer-than-usual point-of-sale program. One way to keep energy high is to arrange visits for employees to your nonprofit during the course of the program. That way, they can see firsthand how their efforts are making a difference.

- ✔ **Your partner's customers are infrequent shoppers.** This is critical because they won't be asked repeatedly to give to a campaign they've either already supported or chosen not to. Take the customers of national quick lube chains, such as Jiffy Lube or Valvoline Instant Oil Change. Most drivers change their motor oil about every three months or 3,000 miles, whichever comes first. In the quick lube business, customers visit less frequently. It's not like the donut shop where regulars congregate daily. Shopping habits justify a longer program of a couple of months, so more customers can be included in the promotion.

Ten signs that you overstayed your welcome with cause marketing

Some people don't always get the hint that their cause marketing efforts have gone too far or on for too long. Here are ten signals to watch for.

1. When you visit a partner's store you see large stacks of pinups at the register, but no effort from cashiers to sell them.

2. Employees take out a restraining order on you so that you can't come within 25 feet of their store.

3. Stores are relocating and not notifying you.

4. Employees start complaining that previous programs with other charities didn't last so long.

5. Managers start complaining to the corporate office that they should choose a different program next year.

6. Stores aren't requesting any new supplies, and donations have slowed to a trickle.

7. Employees know your secret shoppers too well and use their visit to convince them to end the program and "stop the madness!"

8. Instead of asking customers to donate $1 for your cause, the cashier takes the time to tell customers how annoying the program is.

9. All the pinups that had previously been hung on the walls and strung along the ceiling are gone. There's no evidence the program ever existed.

10. You arrive at a partnering store, and employees and customers are stoking a large bonfire of pinups. (Suggestion: Stay in the car!)

Knowing when to stop a cause marketing program is similar to when Hemingway suggested you stop writing.

"I learned never to empty the well of my writing, but always to stop when there was still something there in the deep part of the well, and let it refill at night from the springs that fed it."

The same is true of cause marketing. If you leave your partner's employees with a good feeling about the program instead of feeling used and drained, you'll have happier, more receptive employees for the next program.

The goal is to make your cause marketing program a positive experience for employees and customers. You don't want to sour the program because you overstayed your welcome.

Working with Your Partner

It's important to work closely with your company partner throughout the point-of-sale process. You need to make sure that you work with the right people and that you have a timeline for what needs to be executed and when. You also need a plan for including a partner in the approval process.

✔ **Working with operations people.** To recruit the partner for the program, you've probably worked directly with the CEO or the marketing team. Now you need to learn to work with the operations people behind the scenes who will make your program happen. These back-office workers busy themselves with shipping and fulfillment, dealing with managers in the stores, and making sure that everything is running smoothly. These people are not minions or office help to be commanded or disregarded! They're valuable, critical people who can be important allies in motivating managers and ensuring that stores are well supplied for your program. Alienate them at your own risk!

✔ **Creating a timeline for executing your program.** A timeline is invaluable in keeping everyone on task and in the loop. Your timeline doesn't have to be anything fancy, but it should include deadlines for when materials are due, when creative design needs to be approved, when things will go to print, and when deliveries are expected. Keeping the timeline updated means keeping your partner updated on the latest changes and developments. Trust us, they'll appreciate it, and your program will be better with it.

✔ **Including partners in the approval process.** Make sure that your partner approves the design of the pinup, especially if he's including a coupon. An error on a coupon could lead to lost revenue for your partner, an expensive reprinting for you, or both! Haste really does make waste here. Give yourself, your printer, and your partner plenty of time to review the proof for the pinup before it goes to print. The key here is attention to detail and flexibility.

Printing Guidelines for Pinups

Printing is a critical step in the pinup process. If you manage it correctly, you'll maximize the money you can raise for your organization and drive down expenses. Take it from us. We've learned from trial and error.

The key is to exercise control. Control over the design. Control over your return trips to the printer. Control over perhaps the single most important item on your pinup: the barcode!

✔ **Control the design.** The design is in your hands, and no one else's. This way, you can create a pinup that is appealing but affordable. Avoid things like die-cutting, large sizes, perforations that go in multiple directions, and stapling. These things drive up costs, but don't increase sales.

✔ **Choose the best printer for the job.** We like to get three quotes. Trust, but verify. Talk to each printer about additional design elements for your pinups. Every printer is unique and has different in-house expertise. What's expensive at one may be affordable at another.

✔ **Reduce the number of trips to the printer.** Going to the printer is like going to the gas station: It will cost you every time. Ideally, you want to do one large run. A second run is almost never worth it. Most money from point-of-sale is made in the beginning of the program when motivation is high. Also, if stores do run out, you'll lose momentum and ultimately money on the second printing, which generally takes eight to ten business days to fulfill. Get it right the first time! A simpler design will be easier to reprint if you do have to make that second trip.

There is an exception to our rule — when you're working with a retailer for the first time, and they have a lot of stores. In this situation, you may want to plan for two print runs so that you don't end up tossing thousands of unsold pinups because of unseasoned, unmotivated cashiers.

✔ **Barcode.** Work with your printer to barcode the pinups (see Figure 7-8) and even the boxes they're delivered in. You need to work with your retail partners and your printer on a barcode that will work for everyone. Choosing a unified barcode is less complicated than it sounds, but it needs to be on your to-do list.

Figure 7-8:
Barcoding your boxes allows for seamless tracking, receiving, and fulfilling.

Shipping and logistics

After design and printing, shipping can be a big expense for point-of-sale programs. Here are your different options and what we suggest:

✔ **Work with warehouse fulfillment.** Working with one main distribution warehouse is the ideal shipping arrangement. But unfortunately it's the domain of the larger companies that have warehouses from which they supply their stores. Warehouse fulfillment is great for you because you can just send your pinups to one location where they're sorted by store and delivered.

✔ **Try drop shipping.** Drop shipping is the most common method for delivering pinups. Most businesses don't have a large warehouse from which they can fulfill orders. Instead, deliveries are made by UPS or FedEx directly from the manufacturer or distributor. You'll do the same thing. You'll bundle, label, and ship your pinups to each store. Some stores use a mailbag system to get smaller items and local mail to the stores, so you may be able to refill the stores with small quantities of pinups after the program gets started.

✔ **Talk with your printer about shipping.** Many printers have their own trucks that deliver. This may be a more affordable way to deliver pinups, especially for programs with stores clustered in a relatively small geographic area.

✔ **Keep it simple and avoid kitting.** Some retailers will inevitably ask you to send kits to each store. They may have seen them before as some charities still subscribe to this expensive and wasteful tactic. Each kit contains signage, buttons, donation cans, pinups, memos, and so on. Unfortunately, kitting gets costly! Besides, these things don't do anything to make the program more successful. Educate your retailers on what really makes point-of-sale programs successful: Cashiers asking shoppers to support a great cause.

Determining the quantities and fulfillment

If you print too few pinups, you could stymy your program and hurt fundraising if stores run out. Conversely, print too many pinups, and you'll waste money and resources and fill landfills with unnecessary paper.

Determining just the right number of pinups to produce is part experience, part art. And Joanna has been as prolific as Picasso with pinups!

Here are her guidelines for quantities and fulfillment:

✓ **If you're working with an experienced retailer that's done point-of-sale programs before:** Total print quantity = 20 percent of the total transactions for the period in which you plan to execute the program. For example, if a retailer has 40,000 transactions over four weeks, the same length as your program, you'd print 8,000 pinups. Distribute 12 percent of the pinups to the stores and keep 8 percent for yourself so that you can replenish the pinups as needed.

Have your printer shrink-wrap the pinups in packs of 100s or 200s. This will prevent waste so that you don't have to send out too many to any one store while also helping you to keep track of supplies.

✓ **If your retail partner is new to point-of-sale:** Lower the amount in the preceding bullet to 16 percent of transactions and distribute 10 percent to stores.

✓ **For very small, newbie point-of-sale retailers with fewer than ten locations:** Lower the amount in the first bullet to 14 percent and distribute 10 percent to stores.

Chapter 8

Working with Purchase or Action-Triggered Donation Programs

In This Chapter

▶ Including purchased or action-triggered donations in your cause marketing

▶ Seeing examples in action

▶ Making sure that your program doesn't run afoul of consumers and the law

Chapter 7 focuses on point-of-sale or register programs when a cashier either solicits shopper for a donation (active cause marketing) or signage is prominently displayed to encourage the shopper to make a gift (passive cause marketing).

In this chapter, we look at purchased and action-triggered programs, offer some examples of successful promotions, explain how to be successful, and what you can expect for results.

Getting the Inside Scoop on Purchased-Triggered Donation Programs

The concept behind *purchased* or *action-triggered donation programs* (PTD) is a simple one. The consumer buys a product or service or performs some action, and a donation is made to a cause. But who's making the actual donation. Sometimes it's the company; other times it's the consumer through the company.

When the company makes the donation

In action-triggered donation programs (ATD), the company makes a monetary — it can also be in-kind — donation to a cause in exchange for the consumer performing a specific action.

Here are three examples:

- ✔ In Yoplait yogurt's long-running "Save Lids to Save Lives" campaign consumers mail in pink lids, and Yoplait donates 10 cents for each lid to Komen for the Cure. Action: Mail in the lids. Triggers: Ten cents for each lid goes to Komen.

- ✔ Cybex, a leading exercise equipment manufacturer, teamed up with the Breast Cancer Research Foundation and offered participating athletic clubs a turnkey cause marketing program: Cybex would donate 10 cents for every mile logged on one of its customized pink treadmills. Action: Log a mile on a special pink treadmill. Triggers: Ten cents for each mile logged goes to BCRF.

- ✔ Macy's encouraged shoppers to support the Make-a-Wish Foundation by dropping letters to Santa into special letter boxes at Macy's stores. The department store promised to donate $1 for each letter received to the cause. Action: Mail your letter to Santa at Macy's. Triggers: One dollar for each letter goes to MAW.

When the consumer makes the donation

With purchased-triggered donations (PTD), a cause receives a donation when the consumer purchases a product or service. To be clear, the company is still the one making the offer, handling the money, sending the charity the check, and reaping the tax benefits. But it's the consumer that triggers the donation through his or her purchase.

Here are a few examples:

- ✔ When diners visit Chili's Bar & Grill on a designated day, 100 percent of the profits from participating restaurants go to St. Jude Children's Research Hospital.

- ✔ On World AIDS Day, Starbucks donated 5 cents for every hand-crafted beverage sold at participating stores in the United States and Canada to Product (RED).

- ✔ On National Pancake Day, IHOP gave away free short stacks of butter-milk pancakes and asked customers to donate what they would have paid to their local Children's Miracle Network hospital.

PUMA runs wicked far with action-triggered donations

Patriots Day in Massachusetts, traditionally the third Monday in April, commemorates the beginning of the American Revolutionary War at Lexington and Concord. But it's also Marathon Monday, the running of the Boston Marathon, the most famous foot race in the world (we're biased).

Marathon day always inspires fun and interesting promotions. In 2011, the footwear and apparel maker PUMA staged an action-triggered cause marketing promotion that benefited Soles4Souls, a nonprofit that provides shoes to poor people around the globe.

For three days, including Marathon Monday, runners lined up to run on the treadmill at PUMA's Newbury Street location in Boston. For each mile recorded on the in-store treadmill PUMA donated $100 and a pair of shoes to Soles4Souls.

Any company could do this promotion. You don't have to be a big international footwear company like PUMA. It's a simple action-triggered donation program that could be executed by any business that wants to help a good cause by having a "good" run on a treadmill.

Sure, a store that sells running footwear and clothes is perfect for this promotion. But the idea could work at a bank, health club, the lobby of a skyscraper, or any place gym equipment is sold.

Just because a big-name footwear company sets the pace doesn't mean you can't trod the same course.

FOR EVERY MILE RUN ON OUR TREADMILL FROM **APRIL 15 TO APRIL 18,** PUMA WILL DONATE ONE PAIR OF SHOES AND $100 TO SOLES4SOULS, **A WICKED GOOD CAUSE.**

Looking at Some Great Programs

We've seen a lot of purchased-triggered donation programs through the years, but we like three programs in particular. These three share two common qualities. First, they all have a local, hometown quality that distinguishes them from bigger, national programs. Second, each program tapped the corporate partners' unique asset, which makes the program easy, natural, and spontaneous to execute.

As we often emphasize, don't take the hard road to cause marketing success. Take the easy one. And cause marketing programs that are locally made with natural ingredients are a great way to succeed.

Leprechaun Lattes

Leprechaun Lattes, a peppermint mocha flavored beverage topped with green whipped cream, was initially sold at just one downtown Boston Starbucks the month preceding St. Patrick's Day. Twenty-five cents from each drink sold went to Jumpstart, a national children-focused literacy organization based in Boston.

Over the next five years, the program expanded to all New England stores. In February and March 2005, Starbucks sold 53,000 drinks and raised $13,000 for Jumpstart.

While Starbucks is a large international company with several equally large cause marketing programs, most notably with Product (RED), this program had a homespun, local vibe to it.

Starbucks supported the campaign with a bit of advertising in the hometown newspaper, *Boston Globe*. But most of the promotion for it was scribbled on those popular A-frame chalkboards Starbucks stores rely on to promote new products. Word of mouth in this program was key (see Figure 8-1).

Figure 8-1:
Starbucks'
New
England
stores and
Boston-
based
Jumpstart
teamed
up for
Leprechaun
Lattes.

Any business could do what Starbucks did: Choose a time period, designate a specific product or service, and donate a percentage or portion of sales to the charity of its choosing.

Warm Coats & Warm Hearts Drive

Purchase and action-triggered programs can also become *donation-triggered programs* that help a cause and reward the consumer, as in this case with Burlington Coat Factory and One Warm Coat.

Burlington Coat Factory, a national department store retail chain, works with One Warm Coat, a national nonprofit organization dedicated to providing coats to those in need, on the *Warm Coat & Warm Hearts Drive* from October through January each year.

Anyone wishing to donate gently used or new coats can use the drop box at 45 Burlington Coat Factory locations nationwide. As a thank you, donors receive a coupon for 10 percent off their purchase at Burlington Coat Factory through January.

In 2009, One Warm Coat received 220,000 coats. They warmed many hearts and bodies!

iPartinis

Our personal experience with a purchase-triggered donation program is when we teamed up with iParty, a large chain of party-supply stores in New England, and the restaurants and bars of the Glynn Hospitality Group in Boston. The goal was to unveil a martini to promote iParty and support a great cause. iParty had been selling pinups for us for some time, and now, having formed this new relationship with the Glynn Hospitality Group, iParty was ready to try something new: the iPartini.

For every iPartini sold, our cause received $2. In addition to tabletops informing customers of the promotion, wait staff of the Glynn Group eagerly shared the details of the promotion. The iPartini was a big hit and raised $10,000.

Accepting proceeds from an alcoholic product wasn't an easy decision. Fortunately, the program was well received and managed responsibly. But other purchase-triggered cause marketing programs involving unhealthy products, like the one between Kentucky Fried Chicken and Komen for the Cure in 2010, are lightning rods for criticism (see Figure 8-2).

Be sure to carefully consider from what products or services your cause receives proceeds. Though Komen for the Cure raised $4 million from its partnership with KFC, some would say it wasn't worth the negative press and damaged credibility.

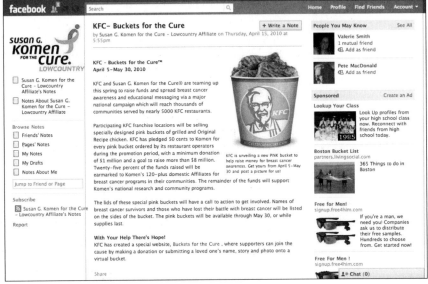

Figure 8-2:
Receiving proceeds from the sale of a controversial product or service can cost you more than you'll raise when you include the damage to your reputation.

Understanding Why Triggered Donations May Not Be as Lucrative as Point-of-Sale

Purchased-triggered donation programs are different from point-of-sale or register programs.

When a store cashier solicits a shopper to donate to a cause, we call it point-of-sale cause marketing. These programs frequently involve pinups — sometimes called paper icons, mobiles, scannables, and so on — that are frequently signed by the customer and prominently displayed in the store. The pinup in Figure 8-3 was sold in a credit union shortly after the earthquake in Haiti. Its members donated at teller windows, directly from their accounts. Before long, pinups were hanging throughout the credit union's branches, highlighting the generous support of company and customers.

While both point-of-sale and purchase-triggered donation programs can be very successful for companies and very lucrative for causes — especially for causes working with large chains, such as Gap, Chili's, or Walmart — point-of-sale is generally the better strategy for local organizations. Here's why:

✔ **Point-of-sale has a direct ask.** The choice to participate in a purchase-triggered donation program is left up to the consumer. For example, when shopping at a grocery store, customers may see lots of cause products that have triggered donations. But unlike a point-of-sale program, a cashier doesn't ask the shopper to donate. What moves you more — a table full of Girl Scout cookies with a "Please buy!" sign on it or a 7-year-old scout tugging at your coat to buy a box?

✔ **Point-of-sale applies to everyone.** Only so many consumers will want a latte topped with green foam or a stack of pancakes for breakfast or crave the concoction of liquors and juices found in an iPartini. Consumer preference for the product determines how much money a cause will raise. But with point-of-sale, you're limited only by the cashier's commitment to ask every shopper, "Would you like to make a donation to . . . ?"

✔ **Point-of-sale usually means a bigger gift.** Some PTD programs donate as little as a penny, nickel, or a dime to causes. Some donate more, like the $100 PUMA donated for every mile logged. A nickel or dime is a lot if you're working with a behemoth like Starbucks donating 5 cents for every beverage made on World AIDS Day. But the return would be much less if the promotion was executed at a local business with just a few locations. The better alternative would be a point-of-sale program. You'll raise more money.

Figure 8-3: Point-of-sale cause marketing programs generally involve pinups that are sold and hung in stores.

Choosing point-of-sale over purchase-triggered is sometimes a better choice. Here's an example from one of our best partners, Ocean State Job Lot, a Rhode Island-based discount retailer with 100 stores in New England. Job Lot raised $1 million for my nonprofit by annually selling pinups (see Figure 8-4) at its checkout twice a year, once in December and again in July.

THANK YOU FOR YOUR SUPPORT!
$1 MILLION RAISED FOR CANCER CARE SINCE 2004

A gift of hope

from

_____

to

BOSTON
MEDICAL
CENTER

EXCEPTIONAL CARE. WITHOUT EXCEPTION.

Beating cancer is tough enough....

*But what if you made minimum wage, had
no car, and no money? Wouldn't you still
want the best cancer care available for you
or your loved one?*

Visit us at www.bmc.org

*Thank you
for your gift!*

Ocean State
JOB LOT
The End Of High Prices!

**Compassionate
cancer care
for everyone**

BOSTON
MEDICAL
CENTER

Figure 8-4:
Our annual pinup program with Ocean State Job Lot has raised over a million dollars.

But what if instead we did a purchase-triggered donation program with one or more products from Job Lot stores — maybe a set of pans or a mixer? (Some of their support went to our food pantry, so those products would certainly be appropriate!) Then Job Lot could have decided what portion of the sale from that item would go to our cause. Twenty-five or 50 cents? A dollar or two? Does it really matter? Would we have ever raised $1 million from a purchase-triggered donation program on the sale of mixers and pans? Never.

Purchase-triggered donation programs are great. But unless your cause is working with the likes of Starbucks or Apple, you have to be realistic on how much they can raise. Given the choice, take our advice: Follow the money and use point-of-sale.

Paying Attention to the Fine Print

Purchase-triggered donation programs are under a lot of scrutiny right now because consumers are rightfully questioning how much of their donation and to what cause their money is going. Consumers want to be assured that gifts are being funneled to a good cause and not misused.

Here are some guidelines for ensuring that your purchase-triggered donation programs are authentic, transparent, and legal:

✔ **Strive for authentic programs.** The good of the cause needs to come before the success of the cause marketing program. Period. If you fail to put the cause first, at the very least you'll sacrifice the favorability benefits of cause marketing and reduce the program to plain old marketing. Worst case, you'll anger and alienate consumers who will hold you accountable for your inauthenticity.

✔ **Be transparent.** Always be clear on how much of the money is going to the cause and which cause it's going to. It's unacceptable to slap a sticker on a cause product that says, "A portion of proceeds will go to animal rights organizations." We need to be clear and specific, as Dannon is on its yogurt label (see Figure 8-5). The company clearly states that 10 cents will be donated to the National Breast Cancer Foundation every time someone logs on to the Cups of Hope website and enters the code found under their yogurt lid. Hold yourself to a higher ideal, or consumers will do it for you.

According to the Cone 2010 Cause Evolution Study, only 45 percent of Americans believe companies are providing enough details about their cause marketing efforts.

✔ **Know the law.** Laws vary by state and country, and an in-depth discussion on cause marketing law is beyond the scope of this book. But remember that most jurisdictions do have legal requirements pertaining to cause partnerships. Be sure to familiarize yourself with local regulations. Two good places to start your research are Cause Marketing Forum and Las Vegas attorney Ed Chansky. Cause Marketing Forum frequently has sessions on cause marketing law that are informative, specific, and enlightening. Attorney Ed Chansky is a frequent contributor to the forum and an expert on cause marketing law. He's worth looking up on Google if you have more specific concerns or questions.

✔ **Expect to be held accountable.** Weigh the worst-case scenario. What if a consumer or the attorney general's office in your state questioned your cause marketing practices? Could you defend them? Or are you hoping they'll never call?

Figure 8-5:
Here's an example of a transparent cause marketing disclosure.

Photo taken by Paul Jones from Alden Keene & Associates.

Rating Your PTD Program

Writing in *PhilanthropyAction.com*, Editor-in-Chief Tim Ogden proposed a cause marketing rating system for businesses and causes to follow and for consumers to use when they evaluate cause promotions.

Try applying Ogden's standards to your next cause marketing program:

✔ **First standard:** *The program says exactly what charity will receive the funds, with enough information for a person to find and investigate the charity on their own.* No more "A portion of the proceeds from this product will support cancer research." Tell us which organization(s) the donation will benefit so that we can explore its efforts ourselves.

✔ **Second standard:** *The program says exactly how much money the charity will receive (either in total or from each purchase with a projection of the total and any minimum or maximums built-in). Note that percentages, especially such nebulous percentages as "2 percent of the profits," do not meet this standard. Tell me the money.* Tell us in plain English what the donation will be! A penny? A dime? A buck for each item sold? Or will a flat donation of a fixed amount be made at the end of the program?

✔ **Third standard:** *The program says when the charity will receive the funds.* Having a date when the promotion concludes and when the money will be delivered to the cause shows consumers that you're committed to ethical, transparent, and impactful giving.

✔ **Fourth standard:** *The program says what the funds will be used for or if there are any restrictions on the use of funds. This is especially important when brands link up to very large charities that do lots of things in lots of places (for example, Save the Children, United Way, World Wildlife Fund). This isn't about the good or bad of restricted funds; it's just asking for full disclosure on the terms of the funds and what they will be used for.* Will the money be *unrestricted* (can be used for anything the cause chooses) or *restricted* (limited to a specific program or type of expenditure, such as food, equipment, or medicine). Be specific on where the money is going and how it will be used.

✔ **Fifth standard:** *The program says why the charity was chosen. I don't expect any program to meet this criteria, but I think it's important to push corporations with charitable programs to using the resources at their disposal to help the general public find good charities. Corporations invest millions of dollars in these cause marketing campaigns. The least they could do is spend some of that money doing due diligence on the charities and telling the public what they find.* Causes would be foolish to leave out this storytelling component. As Tim indicates, this is less a standard and more a reminder for companies and causes to share their stories and the impact they had on each other.

To see these standards in action, see the sidebar "Rating a recent cause marketing program."

Rating a recent cause marketing program

When we first read Tim Ogden's standards we liked every one of them. So we put them to the test with a recent cause marketing program (see figure) we ran with our longtime partner, iParty. As Tim suggested, we gave each standard a full star (*) using a scale up to 5 stars so that we could measure our success.

Thank you for your pumpkin purchase and for supporting the Kids Fund at Halloween Fest Boston!

The Kids Fund provides a variety of necessity items — from eyeglasses to home medical equipment — for the hospital's pediatric patients. More than 25,000 children receive care at BMC, and they are among the needest population in the Boston area.
The fund also supports other BMC programs including the Preventive Food Pantry and Demonstration Kitchen, the Medical-Legal Partnership for Children and the Children and the Child Witness to Violence Project.

Standard 1: Plenty of information here on our hospital and The Kids Fund, the program within the hospital that provides nonmedical items to children like coats, food, and eyeglasses. But we didn't include a website so that consumers could get more information. Bad, Joe and Joanna. ***

Standard 2: Nope, nothing. We thank shoppers for their support, but never specifically say that 100 percent goes to The Kids Fund. I think point-of-sale is different in that people expect all the money to go to the cause because no product is involved. But that's not enough. We should assure consumers that all funds go to The Kids Fund and assume nothing. *

Standard 3: No mention of when my charity will receive the funds. Rats. No star.

Standard 4: Yes (phew) the pinup mentions what the funds will be used for. It goes on to mention other programs the funds will support. *****

Standard 5: No, the pinup doesn't say why the charity was chosen, but iParty has a longstanding commitment to our cause and has gone to great lengths to share with their employees and customers why they support our organization.*

Total Score: 3 out of 5 Stars

Clearly, we have some work to do, but at least we know *what* we should be doing. That's why an easy, practical cause marketing rating systems like Tim's is so useful.

Part IV
Taking Your Cause Marketing Program Online

The 5th Wave   By Rich Tennant

"I know you're passionate about your fundraising, but I wish you wouldn't refer to my family as your donor-in-laws."

In this part . . .

*P*art IV enters the virtual world of online cause marketing with social media and location-based services.
We explore how to use online resources as varied as
group-buying sites and Facebook Likes for cause marketing. We also show you how to build awareness for your
cause marketing program using blogs, Twitter, and
Facebook.

Feeling good about your hard earned social media
prowess? Put your skills to work competing in an online
contest. We talk about a new, exciting area of cause marketing: location-based services. We take you through the
different services, show you how to create a program, and
introduce QR codes, a new digital tool to deepen consumer engagement with your cause.

Chapter 9

Taking Your Cause Marketing Program Online

***

In This Chapter

▶ Using the Internet and social media to raise money and build awareness

▶ Attracting attention to your cause marketing program with social media

▶ Leveraging your social media prowess to compete in online contests

***

*T*he web and technology are ubiquitous parts of people's lives, and many of the things we used to do offline we now do online.

Instead of going to the bank, we move assets from one account to another with the click of a button. A trip to the department store for holiday gifts and a visit with Santa Claus has been replaced with online shopping and chats with Old Saint Nick on Twitter!

The evolution of cause marketing online has been similar to other industries — slow but steady. As consumers have become more comfortable with online commerce, online giving has increased steadily. According to Blackbaud's 2010 Online Giving Report, online giving grew 35 percent in 2010 and accounted for 8 percent of all fundraising.

In this chapter, we look at how companies and causes can work together to raise money and build awareness through group-buying sites, Facebook Likes, and Twitter hashtags. We also look at the importance of promoting your cause marketing through blogging, Facebook, Twitter, and Quora and how to get started. Finally, we discuss how you can put your social media skills and followers to work competing in and maybe winning online contests.

Harnessing the Power of Group-Buying Sites

You've probably heard of or even bought a discounted product or service from Groupon or Living Social. They are the two best known names in *group buying,* which is when a specified number of people agree to purchase a discounted offer. If the minimum number of purchasers is not met, no one gets the deal. As you can see in Figure 9-1, this small, local restaurant's offer is basically 50 percent off for everyone who bids on the deal *if* the minimum number of bids is met. In this case, the minimum of 100 bids was greatly exceeded, and, in fact, at least 797 people are getting the deal.

Businesses love group-buying sites because of the sales promotion and the quantity discounts. Consumers love them because of the deep discounts they get, generally 50 percent or more.

Figure 9-1: A Groupon deal-of-the-day.

But group-buying sites aren't just for products and services. They've also been shown to work for causes. In 2010, Groupon teamed up with DonorsChoose.org for a deal and raised $162,000 for classrooms in need.

The nonprofit group used a grant from Pershing Square Foundation to match money that Groupon users spent on charitable gift cards to DonorsChoose.org. If a Groupon user paid $25, the foundation doubled the gift to $50 to fund education projects on the DonorsChoose.org website.

Nearly 1,500 coupons were sold, many of them to people unfamiliar with DonorsChoose.org, according to the organization.

Groupon also worked with National Public Radio in Los Angeles. The station sold $50 memberships at a discounted rate of $25 using Groupon. After the 50 percent cut that Groupon takes — a common percentage for group-buying sites, but it's sometimes waived for causes — this Groupon deal raised nearly $11,000 dollars (see Figure 9-2).

Figure 9-2: This Groupon deal-of-the-day for KCRW public radio in Los Angeles raised more than $11,000.

Group-buying site Living Social has also raised money for causes, including Donorschoose.org and Global Giving. Through the *12 Days of Giving,* which gave 1 percent of every Daily Deal purchased during the 12 days leading up to Christmas, Living Social raised $130,000 for DonorChoose.org and GlobalGiving.

Picking the best group-buying site for your program

Not all group-buying sites are created equal or are suitable for your cause marketing program. Use this criteria when choosing one:

✔ **Look for a site that allows you to run customized deals.** Most group-buying sites solicit businesses to offer discounts, which is great and you can probably take advantage of this feature, but you're a cause marketer, and you can land your own deals. You just need the right group-buying platform to bring commerce and cause together. Say that you're working with a restaurant that wants to help you raise money through a group buying program. What you really need is a service that allows you to offer the deal and maybe keep track of purchases and help with distribution.

> ✔ **You want a group-buying site that you can regularly access — not one that picks you or one that votes you in.** This site is part of your cause marketing business plan, not a one-off.
>
> ✔ **Ideally, the group-buying site allows you access to a variety of consumer databases to maximize outreach.** It's great that you can use your own database, but wouldn't it be even better if the site had its own list of potential buyers to e-mail?

So what's the best group-buying site that fits these three important criteria?

Groupon and Living Social don't. They manage the deals from businesses. Causes are treated like businesses, which means they usually only get one shot at the daily deal. It works (or doesn't), and then it's on to the next deal. Finally, the deal goes out to their databases, which is admittedly very large, but you can't use more targeted e-mail lists that might be better suited for your organization.

That might explain why Austin-based nonprofit Lights. Camera. Help, which worked with Groupon in late 2010, raised only $150. The deal was to donate $5, $10, or $25 to the charity so that it could provide video training to five area nonprofits. Groupon's database didn't do the job, at least in this instance. Another one may have, but it's not an option.

Washington, D.C.-based Deals for Deeds is a hybrid of many different types of deal buying sites. It's like Groupon and Living Social in that it has a real deal with a retailer that is appealing to discount seekers, but it always has a cause component. As you can see from Figure 9-3, the nonprofit is featured as the top of the deal of the day. The featured nonprofit receives a percentage of the money from each purchase. But you have the same problem here as with Groupon and Living Social: You don't control the group-buying platform. You're a passenger, not a captain steering the ship.

However, one group-buying site does meet all three criteria: GoodTwo.

Raising money with GoodTwo

Like other group-buying sites, GoodTwo.com has a sales team to land the deals with businesses and a platform to share the deals with users, but what's different is that causes can select the deals they think their supporters will like and purchase from a menu of products and services. As you can see from Figure 9-4, the Ellie Fund has four deals from which donors can choose. The nonprofit shares these deals with its supporters through e-mail, social media, and so on and receives a portion of the purchase price.

Figure 9-3:
Deals for
Deeds.

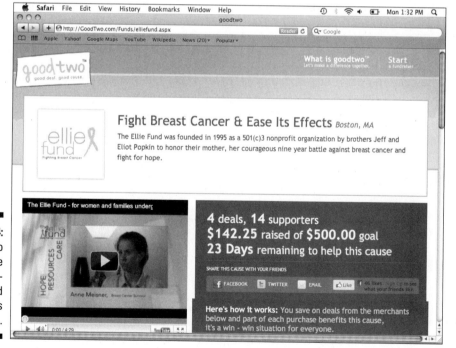

Figure 9-4:
GoodTwo
deals are
for non-
profits and
individuals
fundraisers.

GoodTwo isn't focused on building a database — unlike Groupon, which has 35 million registered users, GoodTwo is a platform that combines commerce with cause and contacts (your contacts, not theirs) to raise money.

Our favorite part about GoodTwo is that the success of your daily deal is really up to you; the site simply provides a customized solution for combining contacts with commerce — so much so that GoodTwo lets causes even submit their own deals. If you're a nonprofit with a decent e-mail list, you can solicit your own deal and use the GoodTwo platform to share it with your supporters.

You need two things to succeed with GoodTwo:

- ✔ **Businesses that will give you deals:** GoodTwo already has deals from local businesses that you can use, but the ones you can secure will probably be better and raise more money for your cause. A daily deal partnership with a business may also lead to another cause marketing opportunity.

- ✔ **A good database of contacts to send your daily deal to:** This aspect is critical as the success of your campaign will depend on the people who receive the offer. If you don't have a good-size database, you may want to use another group buying site that has a large audience to e-mail.

GoodTwo allows fundraisers to run a customized campaign with discounts of 50 percent or more at local and national businesses, hand-picked for their donor base. Every time a donor buys a deal, the fundraiser keeps half the profits. The business running the deal through the fundraiser receives an influx of new customers and a valuable cause association.

You won't receive all the money, even if you solicit your own deal. Every time a donor buys a deal, the nonprofit keeps half the profits. If a donor buys a massage at 50 percent off for $35, the nonprofit gets half the profits, $8.75. This percentage can vary based on the deal and the partners.

Raising Money and Awareness with Facebook Likes

You really can't overstate the importance of Facebook Likes to companies and causes. Likes have become the dominant symbol of social proof and popularity on the web. With one simple click, you can share your opinion with the world!

Using Facebook Likes to raise money and awareness is a digital version of the action-triggered donation programs we cover in Chapter 8.

The difference here is that instead of the customer mailing the company an item, such as a cover from a yogurt, that then triggers a donation to a cancer cause, the company agrees to make a donation for every Like it receives on its Facebook page.

This is win-win cause marketing. The cause gets the money, and the company gets new Facebook visitors. As long as the visitors continue to "like" the page, the company can market to them through Facebook. For example, in Figure 9-5, Bank Atlantic in Florida pledged a total donation of up to $5,000 to six area causes in exchange for Facebook Likes.

Facebook Like programs are easy to setup. The Like icon is already on your Facebook page. You just need to give people a great reason to click it. The key is promotion and getting the word out to stakeholders.

An interesting variation to this program is when the company rewards the cause when *the cause* gets Likes. This situation is a double-win for the cause, and the company earns its halo, in a big way. The Food Bank For New York City is just one cause that benefitted from this arrangement when Fed Ex provided five meals to the Food Bank each time someone Liked the Food Bank's Facebook page (see Figure 9-6).

Figure 9-5:
Bank Atlantic in Florida exchanged Facebook likes for donations to area causes.

Fundraising with Twitter Hashtags

You're probably familiar with Twitter, the microblogging platform that lets you send messages, or *tweets,* of up to 140 characters to followers. What you may not know is what the pound (#) sign means when it comes before a word(s) on Twitter (for example, #fundraising).

These #'s are called *hashtags,* which are kind of like bookmarks that allow people to easily find tweets around a particular issue or topic.

When tweeting about cause marketing, Joe frequently uses the hashtag #cause-marketing so that other twitterers, including those that may not follow him on Twitter, can easily find tweets of common interest (see Figure 9-7).

You can search for a hashtag in many ways, but one of the easiest methods is to type it in to Twitter search (http://search.twitter.com) and view the results (see Figure 9-8).

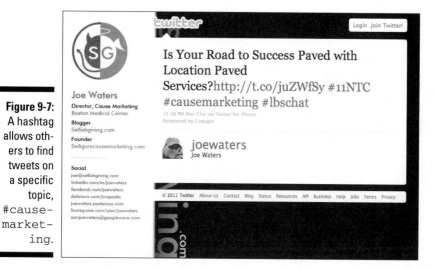

Figure 9-7:
A hashtag
allows oth-
ers to find
tweets on
a specific
topic,
#cause-
market-
ing.

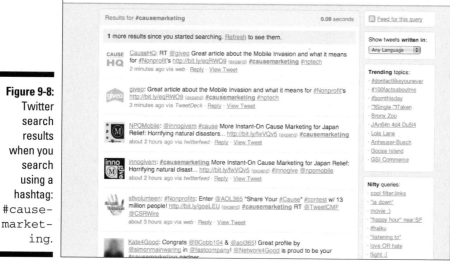

Figure 9-8:
Twitter
search
results
when you
search
using a
hashtag:
#cause-
market-
ing.

A Twitter dictionary

Twitter can be a confusing place for newbies. Since a tweet is limited to 140 characters, users pack their tweets with lingo and acronyms to keep them short and punchy. Here are some of the more common phrases, expressions, and acronyms you should know:

RT — Retweet. You see this when someone tweets someone else's tweet so that others can see it. Think of it as forwarding an e-mail.

DM — Direct message. You can send a direct, private message to someone you follow on Twitter — so long as they follow you.

 # — Hashtag. Hashtags such as #causemarketing help users organize tweets by topic so that others can more easily find them.

@[Followed by a user's handle, such as @dummies] — A reply. A response to someone else's tweet, as in @joewaters I thought Cause Marketing For Dummies was great!

OH — Overheard. Quoting someone else's remarks usually "overhead" at a conference, restaurant, and so on.

BTW — By the way. As in, BTW, the play was better than I thought it would be.

Fail Whale — There she blow! You'll see the fail whale when Twitter is overloaded or down.

U — You. Frequently seen on Twitter.

Twewbie — What you probably are: new to Twitter.

b/b4/bc — Be. Before. Because.

<3 — Text version of a heart. Aww. . . .

IMO, IMHO — In my opinion, in my humble opinion. Like in life, modesty can go a long way on Twitter.

FB — Facebook. You know, that place I spend the other half of my work day on. . . .

LOL — Laugh out loud. Boy, was that funny!

NSFW — Not safe for work. Yikes! Tweet that includes a link to a site that is not appropriate for your work computer!

Tweetup — A gathering of twitterers. (People who tweet!)

Twoser — A word Joe uses to describe a loser who isn't on Twitter — like my coauthor Joanna!

You can also use hashtags for cause marketing:

1. **A cause and company work on a campaign, and the company agrees to donate a certain dollar amount for each tweet that contains the agreed on hashtag.**

   The amount can be $.05, $.10, $1, $5, and so on. Often, a company will agree to donate up to a certain amount — for example, $1,000 or $5,000. It's important to clarify this amount right in the beginning.

2. **The partners need to agree on one hashtag that will be used for the duration of the campaign.**

   A consistent hashtag is important for branding and tracking how much is raised.

3. **Both partners need to promote the hashtag fundraiser through every promotional vehicle they have, but especially through social media (blogs, Facebook, Foursquare, and so on).**

   People who use Twitter tend to be active social media users, so engaging them on other platforms can be very effective.

4. **At the end of the program, add up the number of hashtag mentions and collect your donation from the company.**

   Also, don't forget to include and share all the great exposure you got out of the program!

One of the most successful hashtag fundraisers is #beatcancer, a partnership between PayPal and SWAGG.com to raise money for cancer charities, such as Stand Up to Cancer and Lance Armstrong Foundation. Since 2009, #beatcancer has raised nearly $100,000.

Another successful hashtag program is #teamautism from Samsung in cooperation with the Dan Marino Foundation (see Figure 9-9). Samsung agreed to donate $5 each time #teamautism was used. This donation, combined with other efforts, raised $100,000 in just 72 hours.

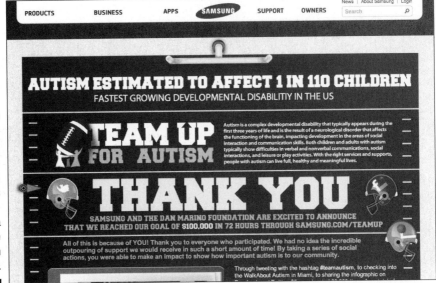

Figure 9-9:
Samsung
and the
Dan Marino
Foundation's
`#team-
autism`
helped raise
$100,000 in
three days.

Promoting Your Program with Social Media

We're passionate about the power of social media to drive your cause marketing program. Blogging, Facebook, and Twitter are new, innovative, and free ways to educate prospects about your program.

The question is not whether you should use social media, but how. That's what this section is all about.

Starting a blog

Of all the things Joe has done in his cause marketing career, he's adamant that starting his blog Selfishgiving.com in December 2004 was his best decision (see Figure 9-10).

A *blog* is a regularly updated online journal with chronologically ordered posts (most recent first). A blog isn't always written. Pictures, video, and audio are just a few of the mediums you can find on a blog. (We talk more about blogs in Chapter 5.)

Selfish Giving

a cause marketer's musings on **doing well & good.**

6-Figure Cause Marketing   About   Foursquare for Causes   What is Cause Marketing?

8 Cause Marketing Survival Rules for a Zombie World

Written on October 27, 2010 in Cause Marketing 101   2 Comments

 Like   10   18

I love zombie films.

I can't get enough of them, especially this time of year when the shadows from the leafless trees take on ominous shapes. Yikes!

While you may not share my enthusiasm for the semi-dead, you might agree with this: most of us are surrounded by these mute, will-less, dumb, sometimes evil brutes everyday.

Our zombies are the people and situations we face daily that must be avoided at all cost if we are to be successful cause marketers.

CAUTION! ZOMBIES! AHEAD!!!

GET THE NEWSLETTER

Email: [   ] GO

COMING IN JULY

Making Everything Easier!

Cause Marketing

for DUMMIES

QUICK BIO

Joe Waters is Director, Cause Marketing for a Boston hospital.

Figure 9-10: Selfish giving.com.

Joe enjoys working on his blog for a lot of personal reasons. He loves to write, learn about new trends in cause marketing, and share them with his readers.

REMEMBER

But Joe's blog has a practical benefit: It's been a great tool to promote the cause marketing program at his nonprofit. It's evolved into an online resource and sales pitch for companies that are considering working with his team.

Are you interested in how point-of-sale would work in your stores? Check out this post on a recent program that raised over $100,000 for our hospital. Are you curious on the benefits of social media for your business? Read this post on how we're working with a local retailer to link social media with cause marketing.

Joe's written more than 700 posts for his blog. The good news is that you don't have to be that prolific to promote your cause marketing program through blogging.

Picking a blogging platform

In recommending a blogging platform for you, we set a number of criteria for ourselves:

- ✔ **It had to be easy to use.** We want people spending their time blogging, not trying to figure out how to use the blogging interface.

- ✔ **It had to offer a lot of easy to use themes and options.** That way, you can make your blog look great without the aid of a professional web designer.

✔ **It had to be search engine friendly.** People browsing the web find just about everything they're looking for on search engines like Google. The platform you're using for blogging should make it easier, not harder, for people to find you on the web.

Our two top choices for your blogging platform are Posterous (www. posterous.com) and Tumblr (www.tumblr.com), shown in Figure 9-11. You can get a blog up and running in just a few minutes using these two platforms.

Figure 9-11: Posterous versus Tumblr. Whichever you choose, your blog is easy to update, looks great, and will be found on all the major search engines.

A word about search engine optimization

Throughout our discussions about blogging, Facebook, Twitter, and Quora, we mention *search engine optimization,* or SEO. SEO is the process of improving the volume or quality of traffic to a website from search engines.

SEO is an increasing area of interest to companies and causes as consumers and donors are relying more than ever on the search engines to find what they need.

Many people believe that a website is all they need to be successful with SEO. While a website is a start, a website is static. It doesn't change much, and it isn't frequently updated, which doesn't exactly make it a search-engine darling.

On the other hand, social media — especially blogs — are uniquely positioned to excel on search engines for three important reasons.

✔ Blogs, tweets, and Facebook updates are written by humans for humans. They're conversational and informal and don't have any of the corporate-speak and jargon found on websites. In short, social media is a human, reader-friendly resource that keeps people coming back.

✔ Social media sites are updated all the time. Joe updates his blog at least twice a week. More prolific bloggers update their blogs many times a day! Search engines love fresh content, and unlike websites, which are largely built and forgotten, social media delivers.

✔ Blogs have inbound and outbound links — they link to other websites, and others link to them. This web of connection gives blogs authority and further increases their search engine ranking.

Not only is social media a better way to promote your cause marketing program, but it's also a better way for it to be found.

In addition to being very easy to use and customizable to fit everyone's eye for design, Posterous (www.posterous.com) and Tumblr (www.tumblr.com) have these advantages:

✔ **Free is for me.** Both Posterous and Tumblr are 100 percent free.

✔ **You can e-mail posts right from your inbox.** You don't have to log in or learn anything. You just write your post and e-mail it to either Posterous or Tumblr. Have an image you want to include? No problem. Just copy and paste it into your e-mail or attach the image. These blogging platforms will post them, too. If you prefer a traditional web interface to enter your posts, these platforms both have them.

✔ **You're not limited to text.** You can e-mail either service pictures, video, audio — just about anything. To post a YouTube video or set of pictures from Flickr, all you need is the URL. You can talk about cause marketing any way you like.

✔ **Owning a smartphone like an iPhone or Android makes blogging even easier.** Both services have apps in the Apple store you can download that will make it even easier to capture and post pictures and videos to your blog.

✔ **When you post to one, you post to everything.** The autoposting feature on Posterous and Tumblr automatically pings Twitter, Facebook, YouTube, Delicious, Flickr, and a host of other sites. This feature is a real timesaver that keeps you connected without the demand of having to update multiple sites.

The cause marketer's smartphone

We use our smartphones for just about everything we do, including cause marketing. No computer? No problem! It's all in the palm of your hand. But a smartphone isn't much good if you don't have the right applications loaded on it.

Here's the rundown on the key apps we use for cause marketing (see figure). (We use the iPhone 4G, but many of these apps are available for other devices.)

✔ **Camera:** To quickly capture all those cause marketing programs you'll see in the marketplace, including yours!

✔ **Calendar:** To book all those cause marketing meetings you'll have lined up after you finish this book.

✔ **Safari:** Need to browse the Internet? Here you go.

✔ **Quora:** Did a shopper leave you a question on your cause marketing program? See and answer it here.

✔ **Facebook:** Keep up with the people that Like your Facebook page right from your phone.

✔ **Starbucks Mobile Card:** Cause marketing requires a lot of energy. Starbucks' mobile payment app ensures ours never flags.

✔ **QR Reader:** QR codes are turning up everywhere! Show people how easy they are to scan by having an app right at your fingertips.

✔ **Tungle:** You'll be fielding a lot of calls for meetings. Sometimes we don't have time to process all of them, so we'll ask people to visit our Tungle calendar. There, they can see when we're available and request a meeting. If we agree, Tungle syncs with Outlook, Google, and other calendars.

✔ **Evernote:** This app has many, many uses, but here's one you're going to love. When someone hands you a business card, use the Evernote app to take a picture of it and then hand the card back. How environmentally friendly is that! The text on the card is searchable on Evernote, which makes it very easy to find the next time you need it.

✔ **Dropbox:** The very best application. We describe Dropbox as having a flash drive with you all the time. You can view saved items on any device (smartphone, iPad, desktop, laptop, and so on), and any changes you make are automatically synched. You can also share files with other Dropbox users. We wrote this entire book using Dropbox!

✔ **Analytics Pro:** Get all the information on who's visiting your cause marketing blog, how often and how long, and plenty of other data from this one app.

✔ **Constant Contact:** With this app, we keep track of readers that open our newsletter and click through to posts. If you're out and about and someone says they've been meaning to sign up for your newsletter, test their sincerity by signing them up right from this app.

✔ **NotifyMe2:** A quick way to schedule alerts for key appointments. You finally get a prospect on the phone and they ask you to call them back in 20 minutes. Schedule an alert with this app, and you'll never stand up a prospect.

✔ **Remember the Milk:** A useful app for task management. You'll remember so much more than the milk with RTM! We create lists for individual campaigns and schedule tasks as needed. If you're tired of your to-do list looking like Santa's, give Remember the Milk a try.

✔ **Foursquare:** Location-based services are the future of cause marketing. Our favorite is Foursquare, but whatever yours is, you should have it on your smartphone and use it!

✔ **Google:** We find everything on Google. Don't you? That's why you should have it on your phone!

✔ **Phone, e-mail, text:** The basic tools.

✔ **Twitter:** After e-mail, Twitter is our app of choice for communicating with the outside world. Follow the right people, and it's also a great place to learn about cause marketing or get last night's sports scores. Go Red Sox!

Taking your blogging to the next level

You could easily use Tumblr or Posterous for blogging indefinitely, and many well-known bloggers do. Steve Rubel, a well-known technology and media thought leader, uses Posterous. Wine guy, business expert, and bestselling author Gary Vaynerchuk uses Tumblr. They're both great platforms. That's why we encourage you to use them!

But in the world of blogging, no platform is more used or loved than Wordpress. Joe agrees: His blog Selfishgiving.com is a Wordpress blog.

Like Posterous and Tumblr, Wordpress is free, although you can upgrade for an additional fee. The benefit of using Wordpress for your blog is flexibility. You can customize a Wordpress blog in just about any way you want. While blogs on Posterous or Tumblr are hosted by the companies, you can host your Wordpress blog wherever you like. That way, if a company's server goes down (Tumblr had technical difficulties last year that had some blogs offline for days) or they shutter the business, you don't have to worry about your blog going dark. Wordpress blogs also tend to have better plug-ins and features for SEO optimization.

The bottom-line is that if you're looking for maximum flexibility and customization and don't mind paying a little more for it, Wordpress is an excellent option.

If you're undecided, start blogging on Posterous or Tumblr and then make the move over to Wordpress when it's clear you're serious about blogging regularly. If you abandon writing your blog after a month, it won't matter what platform you're using. You'll be less disappointed if you know it didn't cost you anything to try.

Making blogging easier and more effective

If you do choose Wordpress, you should select a theme to use. A theme is kind of *skin* for your blog, but that description really doesn't capture the full extent of a theme. A skin would change only the look of your blog, whereas a theme also provides much more control over the look *and presentation* of the material on your website.

The free theme directory on Wordpress has over 1,300 themes to choose from. Joe purchased the one he uses for Selfishgiving.com from Headway Themes (`www.headwaythemes.com`).

Free or paid, Joe believes you should choose a theme that has the same advantages as Headway:

> ✔ **You don't need to know any code to change the look of your blog.**
> You can easily access a visual editor and make all the changes you want. This saves you time and money as you don't have to keep calling your designer or web master to make the changes for you. Joe has trouble

figuring out the remotes to his TV. But he's never had any difficulty using the Headway visual editor.

✔ **A theme should help search engine optimization.** Joe swears by this one. Before installing Headway, he could *never* crack the first page of Google for the search term "cause marketing." After he installed it, there hasn't been a day that Joe's blog hasn't been on the first page.

✔ **Make sure that customer service is a priority.** If you have a problem with your theme, you want someone there to address it. Before you buy or download a theme, make sure that you can get answers if you need them. Headway has great forums to answer your questions. The principals of the company, Grant and Clay Griffiths, are very responsive. Grant is very active on Twitter, and you can tweet him if you need direction. Joe has done it many times! (Grant may think Joe's a *twalker,* a stalker on Twitter — another word to add to your Twitter dictionary.)

Premium themes like Headway are easy to use, come optimized for SEO, and have loads of help if you get into trouble. No, they're not free, but you definitely get what you pay for.

Choosing the right content for your blog

Text, video, pictures, podcasts — which do you prefer? What medium you want to use is your choice. It's best to pick one you feel most comfortable and expressive.

Joe prefers text because he enjoys working with words. Gary Vaynerchuk, the famed *vlogger —* someone who blogs with videos instead of words, pictures, or podcasts — behind Wine Library TV (www.winelibrary.com), prefers video. Humanitarian photographer David duChemin (www.pixelatedimage.com/blog) likes using pictures (believe it or not!). But David also mixes it up with text and podcasts, which brings me to my final point.

Your best strategy is to use a combination of text, video, pictures, and podcasts.

Text

Text is the default medium for blogs, so you'll be in good company if you choose words (hey, they worked for Shakespeare). Joe's blog Selfishgiving.com is a text-based blog. While Joe uses pictures and sometimes video, he prefers words above all else. You may, too. When using text in your blogs, follow these guidelines:

✔ **Until you figure out what your readers prefer, keep your posts short (300 to 500 words).** Online readers want news they can use and prefer bite-size reading.

✔ **Make your posts scannable.** Use bullets and numbers to draw the reader's eye to key points. Underline and bold words that you want to emphasize. Include hyperlinks to posts, articles, and sites that expand and explain key ideas.

✔ **Write like a human being.** Use short, active sentences to make your points. Avoid jargon, big words, and long sentences. Joe likes to say, quoting Mark Twain: "If you can catch an adjective, kill it!"

Video

Video can be a fantastic option. Not only are videos very popular — YouTube is the second largest search engine on the web, and 24 hours of video are uploaded to the site every minute — but if you use it for blogging, you can call yourself a *vlogger*. How cool is that?!

Here are a few tips on how to best use video on your blog:

✔ **If you're including a video from a site like YouTube, don't just provide a link to the video.** Embed the video right into your post so that viewers can watch it on your blog instead of visiting a separate site (see Figure 9-12). You can embed a video right from YouTube. Just click Embed to get the embed video code, copy it, and paste it in your post.

✔ **If you're making your own video, don't get too caught up in the production quality of your video, especially in the beginning.** It's easy to capture cause marketing programs in stores and interviews with the video app on your iPhone or a Flip video camera (www.theflip.com), both of which we've used. Most of the time, you'll want a small, handy device you can carry with you. Your smartphone or a Flip fit in your hand perfectly, and it can even record in high definition.

✔ Like text posts, keep your videos short. Don't increase their length until you have a better feel for creating videos and your viewers are craving longer pieces.

Figure 9-12: Embed your videos on your blog.

Lights. Camera. Help.

Lights. Camera. Help. is an Austin-based non-profit cofounded by David J. Neff, coauthor of *The Future of Nonprofits* (Wiley), that is dedicated to encouraging nonprofits and cause-driven organizations to use film and video to tell their stories.

Lights. Camera. Help. does this through education and volunteer match programs, screenings, and an annual film festival.

We caught up with David and got his five non-profit film tips:

✔ **Know your story.** What are you filming today? Before you ever buy a camera, write a script, or sign up for YouTube, know what story you're trying to tell. Your story is the same thing as your elevator pitch. Is it funny, serious, light-hearted, or something else? Figure that out and write it down before you start.

✔ **Buy a good camera.** Before you haul that donated, bulky VHS camera out of the closet, ask yourself, "How do I get this footage online?" That's right. You don't. It's time for an upgrade. Invest in a Kodak Zi8. It's one of the better HD cameras on the market and is easy to use.

✔ **Buy a good microphone.** No one wants to crank up the volume on their laptop to hear your film. Make sure that you have good sound from the get-go. If you're outside, move away from noisy areas, such as busy roadways or construction sites. If you're inside, find a quiet area. If you bought the Zi8 (see preceding bullet), pick up the ECM-DS70P microphone from Sony for a killer combo!

✔ **Don't go into the light, Carol Ann.** Watch out for poor lighting. When you're filming that great interview with a volunteer or capturing the great work your executive director does so that you can share it with donors, make sure that you have good lighting. Avoid shadowy faces or faces that look green or yellow under office lighting. Don't trust your eyes. Review the footage at the scene so that you can make adjustments and reshoot, if necessary.

✔ **Buy a good editing program.** Schools and colleges in your area offer courses on film editing. You can also check out what David offers at www.lightscamera help.com. You need to know how to use film-editing software. Gone are the days of cutting film reels with razor blades. Now, everything is edited on a computer. David's suggestions for software are iMovie for Mac and Sony Vegas for PC.

Pictures

A picture is worth a thousand words, right? More than podcasts or video, pictures need to play an important role in your blog, especially if your blog is mostly text. Pictures engage, enliven, and educate your reader. Don't forget to include them.

Here's how to use pictures effectively in your blog:

✔ **Complement text posts with pictures.** You want to use pictures that grab the readers' attention, explain a point, draw their eyes down the post, and connect them emotionally to the topic.

✔ **Be careful not to use licensed pictures without permission or free pictures without noting the source.** You can buy images for as little as a dollar at iStockphoto.com, or you can get free images at Flickr's Creative Commons pool (www.flickr.com/creativecommons). You can give credit by linking the picture directly to an owner's Flickr page. That way, readers can go straight to the source, where they can see who took the photo, leave comments, and explore other photos.

✔ **In general, use pictures to say or capture something that just cannot be said in words.** Pictures can tell a powerful story. Just don't clutter your posts with random photos. Dramatize, elicit, enlighten, and educate.

Podcasting

A *podcast* is an audio (or video) file that you can listen to and download from the Internet. Podcasts generally are broken up into episodes and have a regular host. If you ever wanted to host your own show, a podcast may be your best shot!

Keep these pointers in mind when you're creating a podcast:

✔ **Choose a good mic.** Don't use the one on your computer, as it will pick up sounds from all around your room. Many good sites (www.podcasting news.com) review good microphones, even ones for under $100.

✔ **Keep your podcasts short.** Fifteen minutes is probably just about right. Conserve your extra time for equipment checks, production, planning, and good editing. Many podcasts are on the Web. Make sure that yours stands out.

Keeping your blog top of mind with an e-mail newsletter

The question on every blogger's mind is how to keep readers coming back. It's easy for readers to visit your blog once or twice and then just forget to visit it again as they move on to a new project, interest, or blog.

Samuel Johnson famously said that it's more important to be reminded than informed. Assume that your readers are still interested in the content; they just need to be reminded that it's still out there.

Enter the e-mail newsletter, which has three important benefits to bloggers:

✔ **E-mail is familiar to almost everyone.** While not everyone fully understands what a blog is or how to navigate one, nearly everyone has an e-mail address and knows how to open a new message in their inbox.

- **Readers don't have to visit your blog to read your latest posts.** It visits them! (This benefit goes back to something we've stressed throughout the book — never give people an excuse to say no.)

- **E-mail newsletters are easy to view and share.** Most e-mail newsletter services, such as Aweber and Constant Contact, offer a dedicated webpage as a backup to e-mail and social media links so that readers can quickly and easily share content (see Figure 9-13).

Extending your reach with a Facebook page

If your cause or company doesn't already have a Facebook page, you should. As we like to say, 600 million people can't be wrong. That's how many users Facebook currently has.

A Facebook page for an organization is similar to the personal profile page you may already have on Facebook. The difference is that people don't have to go through the process of friending you on a page. They can just Like it.

A Like on Facebook can trigger a chain reaction of Likes on other Facebook walls and activity at other social media sites. For example, if I Like the Facebook page for *Cause Marketing For Dummies,* my Like is recorded on my Facebook wall. If someone sees that Like and Likes my Like or visits the Dummies page and Likes it, it's recorded on his wall.

Figure 9-13: Constant Contact allows the reader to view the newsletter on a webpage and to share its content on Twitter, Facebook, and other social networks.

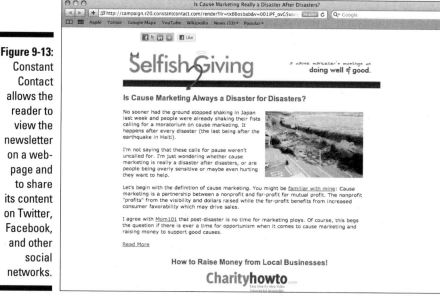

Now take it a step further and say my Facebook Like prompts a reader to post the Dummies book or page on Twitter that goes out to their followers who can forward (retweet) it to their followers, and so on.

If the Facebook Like prompts me to save the page to Delicious, a social book-marking site, or submit it to Digg or Stumbleupon, two social voting sites, the communities on these respective sites have the chance to see the story and rank it.

Yes, Facebook Likes can have a pretty far-reaching effect. And that's exactly why you want to have a Facebook page.

Not convinced? Maybe you're thinking, "You've already set me up with a blog to promote my cause marketing program. Why do I need a Facebook page? Isn't a page a bit redundant?"

Not at all. Here are a few more good reasons to Like Facebook pages.

- ✔ **Facebook is a world unto itself.** People love Facebook and spend a great deal of leisure time (and, face it, work time) updating their status, checking out the profiles of friends, and Liking the things they see. The point is that Facebook is a comfortable, familiar place, and adding a page for your company or cause and chatting up your cause marketing program makes it easier for your fans to follow your activities.

- ✔ **Facebook pages are open to everyone.** You don't need to friend some-one to access the page. In a way, a fan page is like a de facto website that, thanks to vanity URL's on Facebook (for example, `www.facebook.com/dummies`), users can visit directly and even find it indexed in search engines.

- ✔ **A Facebook page is another place to connect and converse.** It gives people another way to learn about your cause marketing program and to stay in touch with you. Again, it's about not giving people an excuse to say no.

- ✔ **A Facebook page is easy to create and maintain.** Because most people are familiar with the setup and functionality of Facebook and have their own Facebook profile to connect with family and friends, the process of creating and updating a page is simple.

- ✔ **Facebook is a great place to explain your actions when things go wrong.** Use Facebook (and Twitter) to quickly respond to comments and criticism that may arise about a cause marketing campaign. Social media was a key driver in the criticisms of Komen's Bucket for the Cure. But Komen never thought to use social media to quell the ire of even their most loyal donors.

TIP

If you're not familiar with creating a Facebook fan page, a good place to start is Facebook, which has detailed instructions in its online help center on setting up a page. You can also find out a lot by checking out other company and cause pages on Facebook (see Figures 9-14 and 9-15). Learn from example by visiting the leaders of business (Starbucks, Coca-Cola, Burt's Bees) and cause (Komen for the Cure, Share Our Strength, Best Friends Animal Society).

Small causes and companies should also visit the guru of Facebook instruction and marketing, social media advisor John Haydon (www.johnhaydon.com). John has tons of advice and videos on how to master Facebook, for pages and beyond.

Making Twitter a part of your strategy

Twitter can be an invaluable tool for promoting your cause marketing program. We can speak from experience on the value of Twitter as Joe has been very active on it since 2008.

Figure 9-14:
Looking for inspiration on what to include on your Facebook fan page?

Figure 9-15:
You can
learn from
the leaders
of business
and cause,
such as
Share Our
Strength.

Here's what Joe likes about Twitter for cause marketing.

✔ **You can learn a lot about cause marketing on Twitter.** Joe used to read three daily newspapers and a host of online sites to stay abreast of the latest cause marketing partnerships and moves. Now he just follows Twitter. Not only does he feel he gets all the news he needs on cause marketing, but the people he follows on Twitter help decide what is and isn't worth reading.

✔ **Twitter users are eager to learn about cause marketing from you.** After Google, Twitter (see Figure 9-16) ranks high on Joe's list of sites that drive traffic to his cause marketing blog. Twitter users tend to be great consumers and promoters of good content — just the kind of people you want visiting and reading your blog.

✔ **Your connection with followers on Twitter is immediate and direct.** There are no gatekeepers, no voicemails, no glad-handing at networking events. People are surprisingly upfront, responsive, and transparent. Joe says Twitter makes him feel like he has a direct line of communication to his followers so that they can talk, ask questions, get feedback, and strengthen relationships. The same dynamic just doesn't exist on a blog or even Facebook.

✔ **Twitter is truly mobile social media.** If you're out at a store and see a great cause product, and you want to share it with the world, what will you do? Whip out your iPhone and write a 300 word blog post? Your best choice is to snap a picture and attach it to a tweet! You also have the option with many Twitter smartphone applications to add your tweet to your Facebook wall.

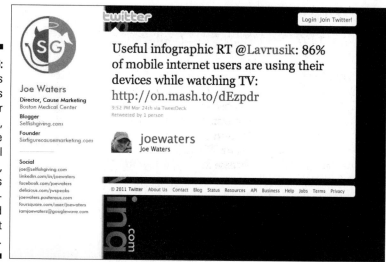

Login Join Twitter!

Useful infographic RT @Lavrusik: 86% of mobile internet users are using their devices while watching TV: http://on.mash.to/dEzpdr

9:52 PM Mar 24th via TweetDeck
Retweeted by 1 person

joewaters
Joe Waters

Joe Waters
Director, Cause Marketing
Boston Medical Center
Blogger
Selfishgiving.com
Founder
Sixfigurecausemarketing.com

Social
joe@selfishgiving.com
linkedin.com/in/joewaters
facebook.com/joewaters
delicious.com/jwspeaks
joewaters.posterous.com
foursquare.com/user/joewaters
iamjoewaters@googlewave.com

© 2011 Twitter   About Us   Contact   Blog   Status   Resources   API   Business   Help   Jobs   Terms   Privacy

Figure 9-16:
Joe's tweets promote our program, educate potential partners, get answers to questions, and share best practices.

Here's the easiest way to get signed up on Twitter, to find some key people in cause marketing to follow, and to start learning and promoting your program on Twitter!

1. **Sign up for Twitter at** www.twitter.com.

2. **Complete your Twitter bio and mention your interest in cause marketing.**

   Your bio will be visible to everyone who looks at your profile.

3. **Find people to follow.**

   Refer to Chapter 12 for a list of great people to follow on Twitter.

   Be sure to follow Joe on Twitter at @joewaters (http://twitter.com/joewaters).

4. **Check out Joe's "The 200."**

   Joe follows a small group of people on Twitter who he has dubbed "The 200." (It's your choice how many people you want to follow on Twitter. Joe just finds it easier to follow a few hundred instead of a few thousand!) These people are tops in social media, advertising, public relations, and, of course, marketing. You'll find some real gems here to follow.

5. **Add your Twitter handle to everything.**

   Include it on business cards and in your e-mail signature, among other things. You want everyone to know, especially potential partners, that Twitter is a place they can find you.

6. **Start tweeting!**

   You can tweet at Twitter.com, but better alternatives exist. We use a third-party application called Tweetdeck (www.tweetdeck.com) (see Figure 9-17). Not only does Tweetdeck allow you to see your Twitter feed, but you can see and update Facebook and LinkedIn from Tweetdeck as well!

   If you own a smartphone, visit your app store and choose a Twitter app to tweet with. (The Twitter and Tweetdeck apps for smartphones are excellent choices.) Remember, Twitter is mobile social media! You can capture cause marketing on the go!

7. **Regardless of the interface you choose for tweeting, create a search column for Cause Marketing so that you can pick up mentions of the topic and find new people to follow.**

   Alternatively, you can visit www.search.twitter.com and type "cause marketing" for the latest results.

Oh, one last thing. Don't forget to tweet. Twitter doesn't work very well if you don't.

Figure 9-17: Tweetdeck is our application of choice for tweeting.

Improving Transparency with Quora

Consumers want more information about cause marketing programs. They want to know where the money is going, to what program, how much, when the funds will be distributed, and so on. One place to answer consumer questions about your cause marketing program is the question and answer site Quora (see Figure 9-18).

Quora is a new site, and you've probably never heard of it. That doesn't mean that you shouldn't give it a try!

What we like about Quora is that it's a dedicated site to questions and answers so that you can filter out all the other noise you would get if you asked the same question on, say, Facebook or Twitter, which are used for a lot of things.

An added bonus of Quora is that while it's better than just plugging a question into Google, Quora answers are appearing on Google, which gives people another way to find information about your program.

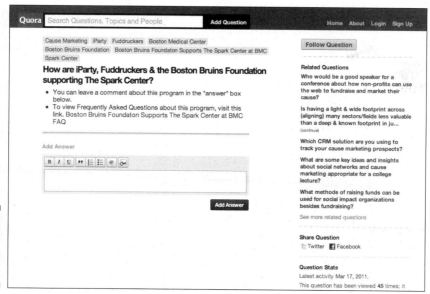

Figure 9-18:
Use Quora
to ask
questions.

Here's how you can use Quora for your next cause marketing campaign:

1. **After you signup for Quora, add a question about your cause marketing program that you think consumers would ask.**

   Don't agonize over picking just the right question. Quora's search bar provides instant results to users so that even if people input a couple of the correct words, they'll find your question.

2. **Add topics to your questions.**

   These topics will also make it easier for users to locate your question because they can search questions by topic and even person.

3. **Create one main topic for your question and let users know they can find more information about it there.**

4. **Search on the main topic, add a relevant picture, and click Create FAQ.**

5. **Create a section of frequently asked questions (see Figure 9-19) to which users can refer.**

After you've set up your Quora page, monitor it for questions so that you can answer them promptly. These questions and answers will be visible for everyone to see, creating a valuable info and disclosure page.

Most people will find your Quora page via search engines. Not enough people know about Quora yet that they'll go to it directly, but that shouldn't deter you from using it.

Figure 9-19:
Use the
FAQ page
on Quora
to answer
common
questions
about the
program.

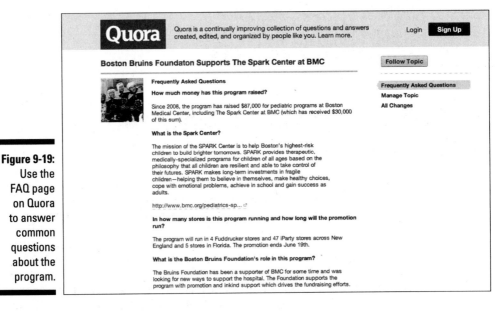

Users will type the name of your campaign or a few key search words in search engines to find it. One way to increase the chances that they do this is to include references to your Quora page in your blog, Facebook page, and Tweets, which can all increase your search engine ranking.

We used a QR code on our pinup that directed people to our Quora site, which had additional information about our nonprofit, our retail partners, and our other partner, the Boston Bruins Foundation (see Figure 9-20). Anyone who purchased this pinup for $1 at our retail partner locations could immediately use their smartphone QR reader and be directed to the Quora site we set up for this program.

Again, don't be concerned about people not knowing what Quora is. Be more concerned about Quora as a tool to ask questions and give answers. In that regard, it's a very good one.

Figure 9-20:
This pinup had a QR code on it so that consumers could scan the code with their smartphone and learn more.

Using Social Media to Compete in Online Contests

Since Pepsi announced just before the 2010 Superbowl that it was moving its advertising dollars from the big game to an online contest for nonprofits, many companies have followed suit and launched their own online competitions.

These voting contests pit one charity against another to see who can get the most votes and win the prize(s). As an example, Sam's Club launched the "Giving Made Simple" contest and gave away $4 million in prize money (see Figure 9-21). Participants could vote for their favorite charity either at Sam's Club stores or once per day at the Sam's Club Giving website.

Social media has proven to be an important way for causes to get out the vote and win contests. Online contests are another way nonprofits can flex their social media muscle.

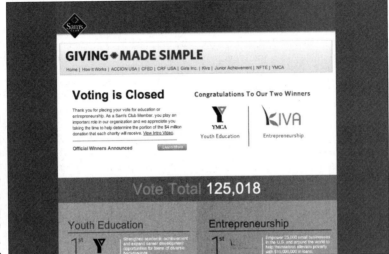

Figure 9-21:
Sam's Club is one of many companies launching online competitions.

How a computer-savvy rabbi kicked the butts of Boston's biggest charities

We've had a picture of Rabbi Chaim Wolosow hanging in our office since 2009 to remind us of what success looks like. An unassuming man with a beard, spectacles, and a black hat with a brim, Rabbi Chaim leads a small group south of Boston called The Sharon Friendship Circle. In February 2009, he and his group beat out 400 local charities to win $25,000 from Virgin America Airlines.

To promote its new service out of Boston, Virgin America created a competition among nonprofits for a modest cash prize: $25,000. The cause that got the most votes won.

Because the economy was just beginning to tank in 2009, it seemed all of Boston's nonprofits — big and small — jumped in. In fact, 400 nonprofits were vying for the prize.

And our nonprofit jumped in, too, with a simple strategy of grassroots get-out-the-vote, e-mail, and social media:

- ✔ **Grassroots:** With 5,500 employees over several city blocks in Boston, we knew we had a captive audience we could tap. Also, with our affiliation with Boston University, we had a large base of students and faculty to reach out to. And because we were hoping to win the money for the hospital's pediatric AIDS program, we reached out to AIDS organizations across the state and country and asked them to vote for us.

- ✔ **E-mail:** With thousands of e-mail addresses for donors, employees, and business partners, we galvanized them to vote for our organization.

- ✔ **Social media:** We were new to social media in 2009, but we felt strongly that Facebook and Twitter could contribute 10 percent or more to our total votes. We created an event page on Facebook and had everyone we knew post it to their walls and send invites to their friends asking them to vote and to invite their friends to join them.

For a while things went well. We even beat back the local chapter of the Girl Scouts, which came on very strong with its 45,000 local members. We led by a couple hundred votes and were feeling good as we entered the final week.

But then things changed dramatically.

Suddenly, The Friendship Circle of Sharon landed in third place. Sure, the group was still a good 1,200 votes behind BMC and 1,000 from the Girl Scouts, but it was such a big jump! Joanna remembers e-mailing the team, "Who are these people?!"

As the hours passed, The Friendship Circle gained on us. The day before the competition ended, I left the office at 5 p.m., and the Friends were 900 votes behind us. By midnight, they were leading by 200 votes. Heading to bed that night, I prepared myself for the worst. We'll be down by a thousand votes by morning, I thought.

But when I awoke that next day, we were down by only 300. Maybe we could win. But I had to understand more about what I was up against.

That's when we took some time off to learn more Rabbi Chaim's get-out-the-vote efforts. In Jewish blogs, forums, and newsletters across the country and around the world was one simple request: "Please help the Friendship Circle of Sharon." And people were responding from everywhere!

Looking at the Rabbi's efforts, I saw one possible chink in his armor, which briefly inspired what I called "Operation Sundown." I thought if we could stay close in the voting throughout the day, we could make up the votes after sundown when the Rabbi and his followers would be observing Sabbath. Voting didn't end until midnight. Rabbi Chaim had been playing by the rules all week and beating us. Maybe we could use his rules to win.

But Rabbi Chaim beat me here, too. In press releases published that day on Jewish blogs, he encouraged supporters to vote before sundown, and they responded, even though on previous days, supporters voted in the evening. By 5 p.m. when voting for the Friendship Circle slowed to a trickle, they were up by 900 votes. There was no way we could get that many votes in the time remaining.

While it's said in the Old Testament that God made the sun stand still so that Joshua could finish destroying his people's enemies, Rabbi Chaim didn't need any extra time to defeat us (we finished second in the contest and out of the money) or the 398 Boston charities behind us. The sun set on time that Friday.

Succeeding with online contests

Here are some tips for succeeding with online contests:

- ✔ **Go back to prospecting circles.** Start with your supporters first, the people that know you, and work outward. (See Chapter 3 for more on the circle strategy.) Your supporters are critical in getting your message out.

- ✔ **Reach out to supporters in every way possible.** Direct mail is a possibility, and e-mail is a great place to start. But focus on Facebook, Twitter, LinkedIn, blogs, and other social networks your supporters favor.

- ✔ **Don't give supporters an excuse to say no.** Give them everything they need to make voting and sharing the vote easy. Some nonprofits create custom landing pages and give them a unique URL so that supporters don't have to go searching for the right page. Give your online audience prepackaged tweets and Facebook postings that they can share immediately with their contacts. Forcing them to create their own material — even a 140-character tweet — just gives them a reason to say, "I don't have time."

- ✔ **Make it fun!** Share fun postings with all your supporters. Create contests within the contest for voters. Offer incentives (for example, T-shirts, key rings, and so on) for votes. Continue to educate supporters about your mission. And, of course, thank them for their efforts!

Understanding the good and the bad of online contests

Our firsthand experience with online contests (see the sidebar "How a computer-savvy rabbi kicked the butts of Boston's biggest charities") illustrates the rewards and challenges of online contests.

Here's what you should remember before that first vote is cast:

- ✔ **Online contests can be a lot of work.** For the two-week period we participated in the Virgin America contest, it seemed like all we did was call and e-mail people begging for votes. We put a lot of other work on hold. And we still came up empty handed. Keep in mind, too, that a lot of online contests last a lot longer than two weeks.

- ✔ **Online contests can be incredibly invigorating!** For two weeks, our office of 20 people was a real team. Major gifts' staff, cause marketing, foundations, and operations all worked together on one goal. It was exciting, and the people we reached out to caught our enthusiasm. We lost, but it really felt as if we had fought a good fight together.

✔ **Losing makes you feel like a real, well, loser.** We know firsthand just how depressing losing can feel. You really need to consider this potential outcome before you jump into online contests. A lot of small nonprofits gravitate to contests because they look like easy money, and bigger nonprofits are focused on other opportunities. But losing can be devastating to a small staff. You have to weigh whether your nonprofit has the resources and emotional fortitude to participate in something so draining and be a winner even if it loses.

✔ **Use contests to shine a spotlight on a program you really care about.** Our goal in participating in the contest was to raise money for the hospital's pediatric AIDS program, which had recently had its funding cut. Not only did we get to talk to many people about it and to galvanize support, but the hospital staff and our supporters learned so much more about the program. The contest was an inspirational and educational experience for everyone.

Chapter 10

The Next Frontier: Location-Based Cause Marketing

In This Chapter

▶ Explaining location-based marketing and the standout services

▶ Taking the first steps to creating a location-based program

▶ Adding QR codes to your campaign

S ome cause marketing tactics have been around since it first appeared in the mid-1970s. But with the rise of smartphones, the mobile web, and location-based services, cause marketing is set to change like never before.

In this chapter, we identify the major location-based services (LBS) and explain location-based marketing (LBM). We also look at how you can apply location-based marketing to cause marketing with badges, offers, and awareness.

But not so fast, you say. Location-based services are just a couple years old and are still a niche marketing tool. Nevertheless, we make the case for jumping in now and sticking with these cutting-edge players.

Finally, we give you suggestions on how to get started and leave you with one more reason to get out your smartphone: QR codes.

Understanding Location-Based Marketing and Services

When you market a product, service, or cause to a customer or potential customer based on their current location, that's called *location-based marketing,* or LBM. While the term LBM is linked with its technological counterpart smartphones, location-based marketing isn't new. Stores that hang signs or ads in their window wooing passer-bys into their stores are using location-based marketing.

However, the new location-based marketing is being driven by GPS-enabled smartphones and a slew of location-based applications. The following sections share our top three location-based services.

Foursquare

Foursquare is a location-based social networking service that's primarily used on smartphones with GPS (Global Positioning System) — that thing on your smartphone that tells the world exactly where you are.

Foursquare is similar to other location-based services in that users check in at venues with their smartphones. For example, if you were stopping by a bakery shop, the GPS in your phone would identify your location and you could check in to the shop, thereby sharing your whereabouts with your friends on Foursquare.

Foursquare rewards check-ins with points and badges and even offers for special discounts and incentives.

There's good reason why Foursquare tops our list: With 7 million users, Foursquare (see Figure 10-1) is by far the largest service dedicated to location-based activities. It also has many of the features that are common to nearly all of the largest services:

Figure 10-1: Foursquare features include check-in, mayorships, specials, who's there or nearby, and social sharing.

- ✔ **Signup:** Creating an account is free, and you'll be asked to create a basic profile, which will include your e-mail address and even your phone number.

- ✔ **Check-in:** Users can check in to a location with a few touches of a smartphone app.

- ✔ **Access to specials, awards, or rewards:** In exchange for checking in, users receive incentives, badges, titles, and coupons to make using the app fun and to get and keep them shopping.

- ✔ **Stalking:** Just kidding. But Foursquare can tell you who's where or nearby. If you check in to a wine store that another Foursquare user has checked into, his name will be visible to you, unless he chooses not to share it with the world. Foursquare allows you to check in to a location without identifying yourself — a great feature if you and your spouse are avid Foursquare users, but you want to keep your Dairy Queen habit to yourself!

- ✔ **Social updates:** You can share your check-in, location (with a picture, if you choose!), on social media sites, such as Twitter and Facebook, or by e-mail or short message service (SMS).

Facebook Places

Not to be outdone by Foursquare (see preceding section), Facebook created its own location-based service, Places, so that Facebook users could check into venues with their smartphones and let friends know where they are and what they're doing.

Why Facebook Places is on our list: 600 million people, to be exact. Facebook is the behemoth of the social media world. To bypass Facebook Places (see Figure 10-2) is to ignore the elephant in the room, which is impossible and potentially dangerous.

Facebook Places was launched in August 2010 as a simple check-in service linked to a Facebook profile that allowed you to include (or tag) other Facebook users in your personal check-ins.

Similar to a Foursquare check-in, Facebook Deals (see Figure 10-3) arrived later that year and allowed business owners to add incentives to users for checking in. They include discounts, free merchandise, or other rewards. Of course, Facebook Deals include charity deals where businesses pledge to support a cause when you check-in.

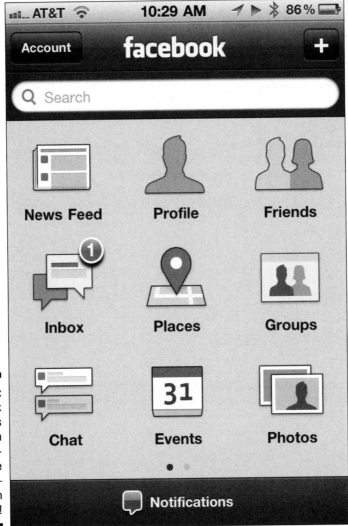

Figure 10-2:
Facebook
Places is
location
market-
ing for the
masses —
600 million
to be exact!

SCVNGR

Why SCVNGR (pronounced "Scavenger") is on our list: While this Cambridge, Massachusetts, start-up has far fewer users than either Foursquare or Places — somewhere north of a million — it has a strong gaming component that makes it unique and represents a different opportunity for causes and companies interested in location-based services.

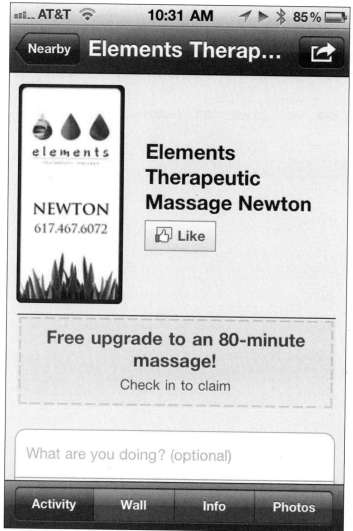

Figure 10-3:
Facebook
Deals for
Places are
visible to
users when
they check
in to a
business.

On SCVNGR (see Figure 10-4), it's not about the destination, although you can check in to one like on Foursquare and Places. It's about the journey. You earn points by answering a question, snapping a picture, or scanning a QR code. You can follow one of the preloaded treks in SCVNGR or create your own.

While most location-based services have a natural appeal to younger users, the gaming component of SCVNGR puts it squarely in the hands of Millennials.

Figure 10-4: SCVNGR is less about check-ins and more about challenges.

Runners-up

While our favorites are Foursquare, Places, and SCVNGR, many other note-worthy location-based services exist. Two of them are

- ✔ **Gowalla:** The horse race between Gowalla and Foursquare for the top location-based service was a lot more interesting in early 2010, but Gowalla still boasts over a million users. Also, with New York-based Foursquare dominating in the East, Austin-based Gowalla is the Foursquare of the West.

- ✔ **Yelp:** Best known as a crowdsourced online yellow pages with ratings of everything from restaurants to hairstylists to dentists, Yelp added check-ins late last year. The power of Yelp lies in the fact it has an existing community like Facebook but a business focus like Foursquare.

Applying Location-Based Marketing to Cause Marketing

Foursquare, Places, and SCVNGR all give businesses the option to offer rewards and incentives to people who check in. The cause marketing version of an offer is for a business to reward a check-in with a donation to a cause. It's action-triggered donation on your smartphone!

Here are a few ways location-based marketing can become location-based cause marketing.

All of our location-based services of choice give businesses the option to offer rewards and incentives to their customers for checking in. The cause marketing version of an offer is for a business to make a donation to a cause specified by the business. The following section describes how this works.

Badges

The American Red Cross was the first major cause to launch a Foursquare badge. Users can earn the badge, shown in Figure 10-5, by donating blood.

Badges are generally not easy for smaller nonprofits and companies to get. Services like Foursquare appear to be focusing on well-known brands that will resonate with their user base. Badges also aren't free. They can cost thousands of dollars.

While a badge is probably not in your immediate future, it is something to aspire to. A badge says something about your organization and digital prowess that others will note. Being a leading brand that can earn a badge and knows its value as a symbol of LBM prowess is a cause or company you want to be.

The good news is that even if your aspirations are much more modest, getting a badge should become easier and more affordable as location-based services mature. But by then the bloom will be off. Wouldn't you rather be one of those cool early-adopters that everyone remembers?

Figure 10-5:
American
Red Cross
Foursquare
badge.

Offers

When LBS users check in to a business, they're informed that a donation has been made to a cause.

When Facebook users in and around Austin, Texas, checked in to outdoor gear retailer REI via Facebook Places, between $1 and $50 dollars was donated to the Hill County Conservancy, a nonprofit land trust that works with land owners, attorneys, and government to set up conservation easements (see Figure 10-6).

REI reported over 1,400 check-ins that raised $8,191 for the conservancy.

Figure 10-6: This Facebook Deal helped REI raise $100,000 for charity.

One of the more creative cause marketing partnerships was a New Year's promotion in Times Square between teen clothing retailer American Eagle and SCVNGR that benefited Big Brother Big Sister.

To raise money for the nonprofit, users were asked to complete a series of challenges, including sharing their 2011 resolutions (see Figure 10-7). For each challenge completed, American Eagle donated $5 to Big Brother Big Sister, which SCVNGR matched for a total donation of $10 to Big Brother Big Sister.

oldies but **Goodies**

Figure 10-7:
One of the
challenges
users had
to complete
was to snap
a picture
of them-
selves with
this Times
Square
billboard.

Here's how to create your own location-based cause marketing promotion:

1. **Choose your partner.**

   As with all cause marketing promotions, you have to start with a partner. No partner, no cause marketing. If you're a company, you need to
   choose a cause to support. If you're a cause, you need to find a company
   that wants to exchange a check-in for a donation.

2. **Choose a location-based service for the promotion.**

   If you think your audience may be a savvy location-based community,
   choose Foursquare. If Facebook is your strongest social media platform,
   try Places. If your supporters are younger and up for a challenge, check
   out SCVNGR. And if your first program with a location-based service
   doesn't work, try another! (For more on location-based services, see the
   section "Understanding Location-Based Marketing and Services," earlier
   in this chapter.)

3. **Decide how you're going to track donations.**

   Perhaps the best way to track donations is to use the back-end analytics that Foursquare, Places, and SCVNGR offer users. Another way
   to track check-ins is to ask users to take the extra step of tweeting or
   posting their check-in on Facebook. This is what McDonald's did in
   a cause marketing Foursquare effort for the Ronald McDonald House
   Charities. McDonald's made a $1 donation to Ronald McDonald House

Charities whenever a Foursquare check-in was sent to Twitter with the McDonald's Philadelphia handle @McDPhilly. This strategy made for easy counting either daily or weekly on one of the many services that allow you to search keywords or handles on Twitter.

Awareness

A powerful component of location-based cause marketing is how it can alert consumers to cause promotions either at the register or in the aisles. When users check-in to a store — and they do this for a variety of reasons ranging from collecting points, earning badges, or getting special deals — they can be notified that October is National Breast Cancer Awareness Month and the way they can help.

In the Foursquare promotion executed by Big Hearts Little Hands profiled in the sidebar, the cause used the Tip section — that part of Foursquare where you can alert users to a suggestion, comment, or recommendation — at 600 locations to alert consumers to their cause.

Location-based services likes CheckPoints helps you locate multiple deals and specials within a venue. For example, during Breast Cancer Awareness month in October, CheckPoints could highlight all the pink products in the store that benefit cancer causes.

You could do this location-based cause marketing, too. It all starts with a partner.

Dealing with the Reality of Location-Based Marketing

Experts tend to agree that, over time, location-based marketing will be a big part of consumer marketing (and with it cause marketing). But you wouldn't know that based on the current number of users. Consider this reality: Facebook is 85 times bigger than the largest location-based service, Foursquare. Heck, the Earth is only 49 times bigger than the moon! Imagine if the Earth was a big as Facebook. We'd have lots of open spaces, to say the least.

Moreover, most LBS users are well-educated young men, and not the shopping moms that marketers love. But with the convenience and couponing that comes with location-based marketing, moms may very well be the next big adopters. Moms are already eager smartphone users.

A recent study by BabyCenter found that having kids is a trigger for women to adopt smartphones, and with good reason. Smartphones are super-portable, and you can use them one-handed when you have baby in the other. Key features of the smartphone for moms are the camera and apps for staying organized and keeping the kids entertained. Sixty-eight percent of moms said that they use their phones for shopping, with nearly half saying that they took an action (unspecified) after they saw an ad on their phone.

Location-based marketing won't take hold overnight, but hesitation has always preceded major cultural and technological shifts.

Take some of these shifts we surmised from history:

> *Steel swords will never work. Besides, iron is nonstick.*
>
> — King of the Gauls, 1 B.C.

> *Printing press? But what will we do with all the monks?*
>
> — Pope Sixtus IV, 1501

> *I bet I can shoot this arrow faster than you can shoot that gun.*
>
> — Dead Wompanoag Chief, 1676

And don't forget the automobile. In 1900, there were just over 4,000 built in the United States. At the time, the United States had a population of 76 million. That's well less than 1 percent with cars.

Few drivers. Mostly male. Educated mavens. Are we talking about the users of cars in 1900 or the early adopters of location-based services in 2011?

The turn of the century probably didn't seem like a great time to jump into the car business. But smart people like Henry Ford recognized the opportunity of the Tin Lizzie, the nickname for his signature Model T and the important societal shift that was about to occur.

While not as dramatic as the emergence of the automobile, plane, or electricity, location-based marketing will nonetheless change marketing, advertising, and cause marketing — forever. Now isn't the time to let the future drive by you, especially when change in 2012 is moving a lot faster than the Model T, which had a top speed of just 45 miles per hour!

Jumping in to location-based marketing

Here are five reasons to start and stick with location-based marketing for your cause:

✔ **Men, men, men.** Because twice as many men use location-based services as women, location-based marketing may be a great fit for male-oriented brands in the gaming, consumer electronics, and sportswear industry. And what about male-focused causes like City Year, testicular cancer groups, and charities that raise money for lumberjacks (yes, they exist!), police officers and firefighters?

✔ **The web is dead. Long live the mobile web.** It's expected within a few short years that global Internet consumption on mobile devices will surpass the same activity on PCs. This transition will dramatically impact how products and services are marketed to us when we are in or near our favorite stores.

✔ **Pinups won't last forever.** No one is sadder than we are because we've raised a ton of money and awareness with them, but the bloom is already off pinups, which have been around since at least the 1970s, and their bar codes, well, are numbered. Location-based marketing is a new opportunity for cause marketers to engage consumers where they shop and when they care. Shoppers that check in to a retailer will be asked to support a cause, possibly in exchange for savings on purchases. Soon they'll be able to make the donation right from their phone via a mobile app.

✔ **Don't wait for users. Enlist them.** Don't wait around for Foursquare to become Facebook. Create your own success now. Find ways to integrate location-based marketing into your existing programs and events. If you're doing a walk in conjunction with a cause marketing program with a retailer, you could extend special privileges to existing customers that check in the most (these people are called *Mayors* on Foursquare and *Dukes* on Yelp) and then walk at your event. Maybe being mayor gets them a free t-shirt, a ride in the pace car for the last mile, and so on (see Figure 10-8). The point is that you want to incentivize people to become users, instead of just waiting around for them to sign up on their own.

Figure 10-8: Most location-based services have a designation for the user that's checked in the most to a business.

✔ **We're not talking about a huge investment of time.** Location-based marketing needn't be time-consuming after you get up to speed. Foursquare may be tiny compared to Facebook, but it's also a lot less sophisticated.

Reaping the rewards of location-based marketing

We know — you're busy. You have a lot of other things on your plate besides Foursquare. We get it. Fortunately, staying current on the developments of location-based marketing is neither complicated nor time consuming. Just do these three things:

✔ **Use location-based services.** Not for your organization, but for *you!* Get comfortable with how it works and its different functions.

✔ **Find ways to get others to use location-based marketing.** Find a way to add location-based marketing to every program and event you do.

✔ **Stay abreast of the latest developments of location-based marketing.** That way, you can keep progressing and using the service effectively. A good blog to follow is www.aboutfoursquare.com.

We're speaking from experience on location-based marketing. Of all the social media tools our organization uses, location-based marketing requires the least amount of work. But it's a load of fun.

It also currently delivers the smallest return. But like the seeds you plant in the spring, we know that will change. And one day we expect to harvest a bumper crop.

Getting Started with Location-Based Marketing

If you haven't tried your hand at location-based marketing before, don't be intimidated. Location-based marketing was made for you! Foursquare alone boasts tens of thousands of businesses experimenting with offers and specials. Most of these are small businesses that are using location-based marketing to connect with consumers and level the playing field with larger competitors. Join the crowd.

As you get started with location-based marketing, keep the following pointers in mind:

✔ **Consider your location.** Obviously, on the for-profit side, Foursquare is perfect for stores and restaurants and coffee houses and any other business with foot traffic. On the nonprofit side, museums, cultural centers, historical sites, and schools are just a few of the organizations that should "claim their venue" on location-based services like Foursquare and Facebook Places (see Figure 10-9). You might just connect with a cause or company because they checked in to your location on Foursquare.

Figure 10-9:
Adding your company or nonprofit on Foursquare is easy and necessary if you want to create an offer on Foursquare.

Add Venue

Make sure you've read our style guide and house rules before saving your changes.

Name:

add a venue

Address: Cross Street:

Not sure? Check **Google Maps**.   Like: "at 5th Ave." or "btwn Essex & Ludlow"

City: State/Country:

Postal Code:

Twitter: Phone:

@

Add Venue

✔ **Find a partner that wants to experiment with you.** It's important to identify a partner that's as interested and curious as you are about location-based marketing. We found our lab partner with Finagle-a-Bagel, a nine-store Boston bagel chain. We wanted to work with a retailer on Foursquare, and Finagle-A-Bagel wanted someone to help them replace their traditional loyalty program with a location-based program that was less expensive and social. Working together was fun and rewarding for both of us (see Figure 10-10).

✔ **Take one step back to take two steps forward.** Sometimes the key to success with location-based marketing is sowing and then reaping. This was the case with our friends at Finagle-A-Bagle. The company wanted to support our cause, but it needed help getting its location-based marketing program started. Most causes wouldn't think to help a partner with something that didn't directly benefit them. But if partners help each other, they can grow a larger opportunity and share the bounty.

Figure 10-10:
Our location-based cause marketing program with Boston's Finagle-a-Bagel began by us helping them to update their traditional loyalty program to one that was social.

FINAGLE SOME SAVINGS!

FOR DEALS & PROMOTIONS ON YOUR FAVORITE FOOD

OUR **FREQUENT FINAGLER** PROGRAM HAS GONE SOCIAL!

CHECK-IN ON FOURSQUARE
FOLLOW US ON TWITTER
LIKE US ON FACEBOOK

ALSO, SIGN UP FOR DEALS & PROMOTIONAL EMAILS ON OUR WEBSITE

WWW.FINAGLEONLINE.COM
WWW.FINAGLEABAGEL.COM

✔ **Test a variety of services.** Do you know who's going to be the survivor in the location-based services wars? Will it be Foursquare because it has the most users? SCVNGR because it's the most interactive? Or will Gowalla resurrect itself and roll east? I don't know. Neither do you. That's why you have to try different services. Decide what you like about each of them, and which appeals to different audiences. (For more on your choices, see the section "Understanding Location-Based Marketing and Services," earlier in this chapter.)

✔ **Use the services as-is.** It would be nice if you could just pick up the phone and call Facebook or Foursquare or Yelp and have it tailor its service to your needs like you can tailor clothing to your tiny waist or long legs. But that isn't going to happen. All these companies are growing very quickly and have not staffed up to meet all the calls and requests from customers. Our advice is to focus first on using the services as is. On Foursquare, this means sticking to basic functions, like building your program around Mayors, check-ins, tips, and specials.

✔ **Be realistic in your expectations.** You're not going to raise a lot of money from location-based cause marketing to start. Estrella's success was a wonderful exception, but hardly the rule. (See the sidebar "Foursquare tip leads to big win for Chicago charity" for more on Estrella.) But with perseverance, you'll raise some money and tap into a vein of opportunity that will deliver deep rewards in the years ahead. But the mining must begin now.

Foursquare tip leads to big win for Chicago charity

Estrella Rosenberg's goal was to raise awareness, not dollars, when she registered her two charities, Big Hearts Little Hands and One Hundred Squared, which focus on congenital heart defects, for Foursquare in April 2010.

Estrella and her team started by creating a hashtag, #100X100, which stood for 1 in 100 (the number of children born with a heart defect) on the 100th day of the year, April 10. Then they recruited volunteers to commit to a grass-roots effort to use Foursquare to spread the cause's message.

The hashtag on Foursquare wasn't necessarily for Foursquare users. Its main value was that when checking in, many users would share their check-in with their followers on Twitter. The hashtag on Twitter was an easy way for supporters to highlight their support of the program. It also gave Twitter followers an easy link to get more information about it and gave Estrella and her team a powerful metric to measure the impact of the campaign. (You can read more on Twitter hashtags in Chapter 9.)

The night before the target date, volunteers added this tip to 600 Foursquare locations: "1 in 100 children are born w/ a heart defect. Pulse-Ox screening saves lives — you can, too! Check in with the hashtag #100X100".

On the awareness front, Estrella was very pleased with the results. One of the benefits of using Foursquare is that it connects with Twitter and Facebook. This means that one check-in on Foursquare could end up on two more platforms.

But something else happened.

A woman saw the #100X100 hashtag and offered to give the cause $1 for each time the hashtag was used on April 10th. By 11:45 p.m.

that evening, the hashtag had been used 11,703 times on Foursquare, Twitter, and Facebook. The donor was so impressed she gave the charity $25,000, which was enough to pay for 12 surgeries in developing countries.

Estrella's Foursquare program for the charities she founded raised awareness and money and saved 12 lives. It also didn't cost her a dime, and she executed the entire program in just a few days.

The program is an excellent example of a cause using a location-based service as is and leveraging its connection with other social networks. To give this program a cause marketing twist, enter tips — suggestions, comments, and recommendations that you leave behind for other users — for your business partner's stores so that when consumers check in, they see the company-cause connection and how they can help.

Looking for a visual link with consumers? Take advantage of a Foursquare feature Estrella didn't have: Add a picture of your cause to the venue (see figure).

Target - S Clark St
1154 S Clark St
at W Roosevelt Rd
Chicago, IL 60605
(312) 212-6300

CHECKINS HERE
847

Are you the manager of this business?

FROM THE TOP 12 LISTS

100x100 tip on Foursquare

Estrella did this...
1 in 100 children are born w/ a heart defect. Pulse-Ox Screening saves lives! You can too - check in w/ the hashtag #100X100 (April 10, 2010) [Link]

Linking Consumers to Your Cause with QR Codes

Imagine you visit your local supermarket and at the register you donate to a local food pantry. You buy a pinup for a buck. On your receipt is a barcode with a message saying that you can learn about the cause you just donated to by scanning the barcode with QR reader on your smartphone.

In your car before you leave the parking lot, you quickly download the app to your phone and scan the barcode. It links you to a one-minute video on a food pantry like no other. It's run out of a local hospital. The pantry started by feeding a few thousand patients every year. In 2009, it fed 75,000 men, women, and children. The video closes with an image of a food line that snakes down the hallway and around the corner. It is after all the busiest day of the year, the day before Thanksgiving.

Wow.

How QR codes work

Causes are using RFID tags or QR (Quick Response) codes, as they're the most commonly called, to add context to gifts and personal history to donated items. *QR codes* are offline hyperlinks that direct cellphone users to online content. This 2D barcode can be read by a free QR reader app that you can download in the iTunes or Droid app store.

Once you've scanned the QR code, it can redirect you to just about anything: a web page, call a phone number, calendar event, contact info (such as a vCard), e-mail address, SMS text message, and even geolocation information.

For example, City Harvest, a New York food bank, is using QR codes on advertisements in print, phone kiosks, transit shelters, and on Facebook (see Figure 10-11). With QR codes, cellphone users can go directly to the City Harvest website, read facts about City Harvest, view a video illustrating City Harvest's work, and make a donation online.

Figure 10-11: These creative and eye-catching codes were used in a campaign for New York's City Harvest.

We used a QR code last year on a pinup to direct supporters to our Halloween Town website (see Figure 10-12). Think of QR codes as offline hyperlinks taking people where you want them to go online without the hassle of entering a URL.

Think of the potential for cause marketers to make transactional programs less, well, transactional and more meaningful. When you pick up a coffee mug at Starbucks that supports Product (RED), you can scan the QR code to hear the story of an African man who benefited directly from the life-saving HIV drugs Product (RED) provides and Starbucks funds.

Figure 10-12: The QR code on this pinup was the first of its kind. It directed users to an event website.

Donors scanning QR codes for cause content won't happen overnight. But adopting QR codes will build a stronger charitable and emotional connection among causes, businesses, and consumers.

And like location-based marketing, it's best to get busy with QR codes now.

A quick guide to QR codes

QR codes are easy to make. You can create your own www.QRstuff.com or www.Kaywa.com or use Google's QR creator http://createqrcode. appspot.com. If you're uncomfortable making your own, your local printer can create and affix one to any item.

You can use a QR code anywhere, even online instead of a traditional hyperlink! But remember, QR codes are best thought of as offline hyperlinks.

You can even tell how many people have clicked on your QR code. The same site where you created the QR code generally allows you to track and measure clicks on the code. Check this out before generating a code. Some tracking services can be accessed only for a fee.

We have used QR codes on many of our pinups to promote events and cause marketing partnerships. Simply direct the QR code to a dedicated event page, your organization's home page, a partner page, or Quora page that you've created for a specific program you want to promote.

In Chapter 9, we share our experience using a QR code on a pinup that links to a Quora page that answers questions about a specific cause marketing partnership.

Part V
Expanding Your Cause Marketing Plan

The 5th Wave   By Rich Tennant

©RICHTENNANT

ADVERTISIN' DEPT.

"Snappy ad copy. And it really got my attention."

In this part . . .

*P*art V is all about measuring the success of your
cause marketing campaign to ensure that it is indeed
win-win-win for company, cause, and consumer. We also
introduce resources to further your education on cause
marketing.

In this part, we look at the metrics behind determining
cause marketing success and how to use them to land
new partners and repeat your success. We also cover new
tactics like working with celebrities, text-giving, and affiliate cause marketing to add to your momentum. In addition, we share our best tips for staying on the cutting edge
of cause marketing. We give you groups to join, important
blogs and publications to read, and key folks to follow on
Twitter.

Chapter 11

Measuring and Building on Your Success

In This Chapter

▶ Gauging the success of your first program

▶ Using the momentum to launch another program

▶ Adding new tactics to keep the ball the rolling

Completing your first cause marketing program is a major achievement. And you'll no doubt learn much from the experience. But with completion comes the void: What now? How do I capitalize on my success?

In this chapter, we explain the ways to measure the results of your program, especially if you're a small cause or company without the resources to invest in traditional analytical tools, such as focus groups and expensive marketing consultants. We also share proven ways to grow your next cause marketing program with celebrities, affiliate cause marketing, and text-to-give.

Measuring the ROI of Your Program

Everyone talks about how great cause marketing is for causes and companies, but how do you measure greatness when the program is over? If your cause or company is like ours, you don't have money to invest in focus groups or market research to determine whether a program has really enhanced a cause's visibility or improved a company's favorability with customers.

You can use inexpensive but effective ways to measure the impact of your program beyond the obvious result of how much it raised. Start with these questions:

✔ **Did your program have a tangible goal that you can measure?** This is the easiest measurement and where you should begin. It's also one that will make you feel really good! Many cause marketing programs have a tangible outcome from supporting the program. For example, when Facebook users Liked Woodchuck Cider's page, they pledged to plant two trees with American Forest. By the end of the program, Woodchuck had pledged to plant 13,618 trees. That's a number supporters can get their arms and hearts around.

✔ **Overall, how was the program received?** Did customers and employees respond favorably to the program? If it was point-of-sale, did you get many complaints from shoppers about being asked to give at the register? Did employees complain that the program was hard to sell, complicated, even painful for them to execute? Also, don't hesitate to speak with several regular customers for their perspective.

✔ **What about employee engagement?** Getting hard numbers on customer engagement with cause marketing promotions can be complicated and expensive. But understanding the impact of cause marketing on employees is easier as the audience is smaller and accessible. Talk to your managers and rank and file employees about the program. Customers aren't the only ones that benefit from cause marketing. It can also boost employee satisfaction and loyalty, which has its own bottom-line benefit.

✔ **How many coupons were redeemed?** As we introduce in Chapter 7 and also discuss later in this chapter, coupons are a regular part of our cause marketing programs (see Figure 11-1). They offer great value to the consumer and are a good gauge of consumer interest in the program. Most of the coupons on our pinups can't be used immediately. Shoppers can use them on their next visit or during the following month.

Figure 11-1: Coupons on pinups are a great value to consumers and a useful tool for you to track engagement with the program.

Not only can retailers track their redemptions, but they can also track — with a small numerical code we put on the back of each coupon — coupons distributed by other retailers in the program. Redemptions demonstrate consumer interest in the program and the power of combining cause marketing with cross-promotion.

✔ **Did you take the promotion out of the store?** Our cause marketing programs are rarely one-dimensional. We combine in-store promotions, such as pinups or purchase-triggered donations, with special events, social media, and traditional TV, radio, and print. In short, we have a lot to measure and share with partners. If you can, don't limit your program to just one element, such as point of sale. It's easy for one thing to go wrong. You want to have a lot of areas to evaluate and many successes to brag about.

✔ **Did you get your money's worth?** We always throw this question out to a partner because the most lucrative cause marketing program is the one for which you don't have any expenses to account. We usually save this for our final point to our partner after we've shared the many rewards of the program. To it, we add, "Oh, yeah, and it was free. Great ROI, right?"

Building on Your First Program

A lot of people think that building on that first program is all about getting partners to do more for you. Doing more is a great destination, but it's an end not a means.

How do you plan to reach your goal? Education, mutual value, and new areas of opportunity are the building blocks that will take your cause marketing program to the next level.

Educating partners

After you finish your first cause marketing program, your goals are twofold: Educate your partner on the highs of the program and build a stronger connection to your cause's mission.

Here are some key actions to take following the program:

✔ **Emphasize the turnkey nature of the program.** If you take the advice we give you in the book, then the cause should create, operate, and execute the cause marketing program. The only thing the cause shouldn't do is what has to be done by the company (for example, solicit shoppers at the register) or what the company wants or insists on doing.

✔ **Meet your contact's boss.** If your response is that you dealt with the owner, president, or chief executive officer and don't have a boss to meet, you've already achieved this goal. But a lot of cause marketing programs don't begin with the top dog at a business. Many of our programs began with a mid-level marketing person. But you don't want it to stay with them. Making a personal connection with the head of the company potentially makes your program more personal, visible, and long lasting. A common ingredient to our longest and most successful programs is CEO commitment to the program.

✔ **Teaching about cause marketing never stops.** Because cause marketing may not have an immediate bottom-line benefit to their business, business owners need to know that the favorability cause marketing delivers is like soaking rain after a dry spell — it takes time to seep in. But when it does, it makes everything a lot greener!

✔ **Show the impact and say thank you.** Invite the business owner, managers, and employees of your organization to show them how you're using the donation! No time for them to come to your nonprofit? Visit them with some of the dogs and cats that benefited from their support of your animal shelter. Show them all the people they fed or made smile or gave a place to sleep. Bring some kids in to their business to sing to them! Our hospital has an annual fall event that raises over a million dollars for our Grow Clinic, a program that helps undernourished inner city children. After the event, the children will sometimes draw and color thank you notes to the donors. This means a lot to our donors and keeps them engaged.

✔ **Stay top of mind.** Joe has a saying with our partners: "You are never far from my mind." And they really aren't because he's always talking to them and blogging, tweeting, and Facebooking about them, too. Digital tools are a great way to stay connected with partners. While they don't replace human contact, they're a great substitute for the times in between face-to-face meetings.

Establishing new points of value

Right after your first program is an excellent time to start talking about what your next program with the business will look like. It shows that you're thinking progressively about your partnership and not resting on your laurels.

But talking and *bringing* fresh ideas to the table are two different things. Like companies that are also introducing new products and services to spark consumer interest, you have to constantly strive to engage your partner in a new, interesting promotion.

Our first promotion with iParty, a 50-store party supply retailer in New England and Florida, was a simple pinup (see Figure 11-2) that it sold at its stores for a buck.

Our next promotion with iParty was a pinup with coupons (see Figure 11-3) and reflected the addition of other retail partners that had agreed to sell the pinup for $1 in their stores. Pinups with coupons represented an important new twist in our cause marketing as iParty coupons were now being distributed to potentially new customers by other retailers. This new twist to the program was a fresh idea that kept iParty engaged with our cause.

Later that same year, we launched a Halloween event in partnership with iParty called Halloween Town (see Figure 11-4). To the pinup and cross-promotion, we added a special event that gave iParty additional exposure with 15,000 moms and kids the weekend before Halloween. One in five people that attended the event said that they learned of it from the pinup.

iParty stepped up its support for our organization by increasing the number of point-of-sale programs they did for us from one to three, which raised $160,000 for us.

Building on your first cause marketing program is not just about getting the green light to repeat the program. The standards for marketing and promotion in business, especially with retailers, are too high for that. You have to be progressive, creative, and client-focused to be successful. Or you'll quickly find yourself starting anew with another company.

Figure 11-2: Our first promotion with iParty was a simple pinup that sold for $1 at the register.

Proceeds of this Ice Cream Cone will benefit food pantries in New England and Florida serving underprivileged children.

iparty

Helped feed a child

Working a businesses' circle of influence

In Chapter 3, we talk about prospecting circles and how you're better off starting your outreach by targeting businesses that already support your cause, then moving on to businesses that know you, and finally going to businesses with which you have no connection whatsoever.

The powerful opportunity you have after a program is successfully completed is to tap the circle of power of your new friend and partner. Here's how:

- ✔ **Ask them who they know.** Businesses don't operate in a bubble. They know and work with many other businesses. Who can they introduce you to? Our relationship with iParty led to another partnership with a large restaurant chain. The connection? The two owners knew each other.

- ✔ **Don't forget their vendors.** Businesses buy their supplies and goods from other businesses. Because many of these companies are business-to-business (B-to-B), they're not appropriate for the point-of-sale and purchase-triggered programs that work well for business-to-consumer companies (B-to-C). However, your vendors may have connections with businesses that may be appropriate for this type of a program. Ask your partner whether he can introduce you to some of his vendors. It's an easy ask, vendors will be motivated to help you because of who asked them, and it could open some very important doors for you.

- ✔ **Identify companies that respect and admire your company partners.** A few years ago, we had a cause marketing partnership with Staples. (We recruited Staples in part because they were the office supplier for the hospital where we work. Approaching vendors works!). Recruiting Staples was a big win in two ways. First, they planned to do a program in 150 stores, and with good foot traffic, we would raise lots of money. Second, having Staples aboard gave us an edge in recruiting new partners. The reason was simple: Companies either wanted to be involved in a program that Staples was part of (and why not with all those stores and customers at their back?) or join us for another program because working with Staples was all the proof they needed that we were a great cause to partner with. (These companies are the Deferrer decision-makers we discuss in Chapter 6.) Every company that you work with has other companies that respect and admire what they do and would love to work with them. Your goal is to find them!

Thinking outside of point-of-sale

We are admittedly point-of-sale junkies, but with good reason, as we explain in Chapter 7. Point-of-sale is easy, lucrative, and cost-effective, and it works well with events and social media, among other things.

How to succeed with coin canisters

Our coin canister success with Finagle-A-Bagel was impressive but not unique. Coin canisters can work for you as well.

Thanks to our work with Finagle, we've learned why coin canisters worked so well in their stores and what things are needed for them to work in any store:

✔ **You need busy stores with lots of foot traffic.** The reason why canisters worked so well in Finagle was that it operates very busy stores. Busy stores mean lots of customers, which means more donors to fill the canisters.

✔ **Cash has to be king.** At a bagel store, where people are generally just spending a few bucks on a bagel and coffee, cash is the currency of choice. No cash transactions, no extra change for the canister.

✔ **No tips allowed.** If your coin canister is competing against a tip jar for employees, you'll lose every time. At the Starbucks Joe goes to outside Boston, he once asked a cashier how much employees collected from the tip jar each week — $50 per employee! Do you really think a cashier making just above minimum wage is going to set aside the tip jar for your coin canister? Yeah, right!

✔ **It needs to be front and center.** A coin canister has to be directly in front of or next to the register where change is made, or people won't give. This seems like common sense, but we're always amazed how canisters are pushed aside or compete with a common retail problem: counter clutter. Counter clutter includes all sorts of advertisements for specials, gum, Slim Jims, cigarette lighters, you name it. You want to work with a retailer who can help you reach their customers for a change donation with a clean, laser-like focus, not give them Attention Deficit Disorder!

✔ **Security is key.** One of the biggest challenges with coin canisters is security. Sadly, they're stolen all the time! At Finagle, the canisters are bolted to the counter and protected by a cobra (half-truth!). You can secure a canister in other ways, such as a chain or wire that runs from the canister to the register or another secure object. Whatever you choose, make sure that it's something that when a customer walks away, he can't walk away with your canister (see figure).

POS is an ideal first, middle, and last cause marketing program for local causes and companies. But it doesn't have to be a standalone or permanent program. Simple pinups can evolve to include coupons, co-marketing partners, and event promotions. Nevertheless, sometimes point-of-sale isn't the right fit, and you need to use a different cause marketing tactic.

When we recruited Boston-based Finagle-A-Bagel (a nine-store bagel bakery and cafe) as a cause marketing partner, we truly thought we had hit the point-of-sale mother lode! With thousands of hungry people piling into its busy stores stores each day for freshly made bagels, we started to count are egg bagels before they were made.

The dough just wasn't there.

While our point-of-sale program with Finagle raised thousands of dollars for our cause, it didn't raise the tens of thousands we had hoped for. Our pinups didn't sell well, and everyone involved was disappointed.

A post-mortem showed we didn't do a great job analyzing our target Finagle customer. This customer visited the story daily, usually in the morning, and frequently bought a bagel with cream cheese and a small coffee.

For this customer, pinups were a nuisance. They happily gave the first time, but they didn't like being asked every day. Also, because their average order was just a few dollars, adding an extra dollar to their tab — even to support a cause — seemed like a lot to ask. Adding a dollar or two is less of a problem when you a run a pinup program at a supermarket or department store chain. Shoppers spend a lot more, and donating a dollar isn't a big deal.

After our first program with Finagle, we sat down with its senior management team and hammered out a new direction:

- ✔ Finagle agreed to sell travel coffee mugs — branded with both our logos — at its locations, a portion of which would benefit our cause.
- ✔ Finagle also agreed to install coin canisters in all its stores to collect loose change from customers. (Coin canisters, shown in Figure 11-5, are a form of point-of-sale, but there's no ask, which makes them a type of passive cause marketing.)

These two adjustments raised $25,000 in 18 months. It also meant happier Finagle customers and employees.

Building on a cause marketing program doesn't always mean big successes with every program. Sometimes you'll only see small growth, or none at all. The key is to keep pushing forward. You may retreat, but don't ever, ever, surrender.

Figure 11-5:
Instead of pinups, Boston-based Finagle-A-Bagel switched to coin canisters, which were a big hit with customers and raised $25,000 in 18 months.

Dealing with Unhappy Partners

This entire book is about the building blocks of cause marketing and what you need to do to succeed and keep all parties happy. But having the occasional unhappy sponsor at the end of a program is part of the learning curve and can happen to the best of us.

Here are a few tips on what to do when sponsors lose their happy face:

- ✔ **Don't take it personally.** If you've been a good, dedicated partner, you should feel good that you gave it your best. Your commitment will shine through to everyone involved. You just came up short in delivering the goods. It's about what was agreed upon and what was delivered. It's not a reflection on whether you're a good or bad person. Lighten up.

- ✔ **Let them vent.** This is always a tough one for us because we both want to argue our case. But you have to bite your tongue. Deep down, you may want to show the sponsor that you're right, and they're wrong. But we've tried that. It doesn't make the situation any better. What will make it better is letting the sponsor vent. And just don't tune them out. Remember, they're sowing the seeds for what can become a productive conversation.

- ✔ **Acknowledge. Explain. Repeat.** The next step after venting is acknowledging *their* disappointment: "I'm sorry you were disappointed with the pinup design." Then, very briefly, explain yourself: "We discussed that this was the best design we could do on such short notice." If it wasn't discussed, then say you should have communicated it better and you will next time. Focus on how you will make things better *next time*.

✔ **Focus on the positive.** If you apply what we talk about in this book, all your programs will have lots of value for partners, which means even in a sea of negativity, you'll have a few positive beacons to point to. We remind sponsors of their windfall so that we can frame their complaints. We don't dismiss their concerns, but we do want to put in to perspective what was delivered and achieved.

✔ **Focus on the fix and the future.** When partners complain about an issue we always talk about how we plan to do things differently with them the next time. We get them psychologically focused on doing the program again, but better.

✔ **Take the fight to them.** When talking about next year, we always take time to discuss what the sponsor needs to do to improve the program. The "fix" is always a joint effort.

Addressing Common Partner Complaints about Cause Marketing

We've heard every complaint and comment under the sun about cause marketing! We've thought through all the responses and have them here for you so that the next time someone claims you dropped the ball, you can catch it before it falls.

Keep in mind that we wrote these answers as if we were sitting across from a partner. It's not exactly the right time to rattle off lots of stats or whip out a PowerPoint. Feel free to use these answers verbatim as we would — minus the Boston accent, of course.

✔ **I feel like cause marketing only reached my existing customers. How does this help me?** In-store cause marketing programs do target existing customers, but they target them in a different way. Other forms of in-store promotion are meant to build attention to drive sales. Cause marketing enhances your favorability with customers by drawing attention to your corporate values. There's nothing else in your marketing program that's serves that purpose.

✔ **Maybe I should have just donated money to you and focused my efforts on advertising?** Advertising is great, but it doesn't do what cause marketing does. Advertising is about visibility and promotion. Because cause marketing increases your favorability with existing and potential customers, it gives you a competitive edge that goes beyond product and price. Advertising should be part of your marketing mix, but so should cause marketing.

✔ **I'm not sure I want to bug my customers again by asking them to give to your cause at the register.** Customers don't have a problem with cause marketing. As a matter of fact, the support of moms for cause marketing — a key customer for you — is over 90 percent. What consumers don't like are programs that are ill-conceived, inauthentic, poorly executed, or overdone. We can iron out the problems we had with this program through training, communication, and better timing. Don't throw the baby out with the bath water.

✔ **The program we chose didn't work for my cashiers who already have many responsibilities at checkout.** You're not the first business to say that a particular cause marketing program didn't work for them. It happens. The good news is that there are other types of cause marketing programs. We can also take a better look at the actions of your cashiers to see whether we can streamline the program and make it work with their other responsibilities. For example, with another partner we work with, we found that cashiers were getting bogged down because they had to upsell the shopper and ask for a gift during the same transaction. So the next time we did the program, we added the retailer's special offer right on the pinup so that cashiers could use it to explain their special offer while also using it to ask for a donation.

✔ **How do I know the cause marketing program worked?** The program raised a lot of money so that says something about the response from consumers and employee support for the program. Another thing to do is to dig a little deeper to find out what customers thought about the program. This is a good question to ask your employees as they're the ones who talked to the customers. Finally, it's important to remember that the benefits of cause marketing don't occur overnight. Building loyalty, trust, and admiration with your customers takes time. What cause marketing does for a business is nothing short of incredible. The dividends cause marketing pay are worth waiting for.

✔ **Now that I've done a cause marketing program for you, every nonprofit in my area is calling me! What should I do?** There's nothing wrong with focusing your efforts on one or two key charities and saying no to the rest. Of course, saying no is easier when you don't have to keep saying it to people by phone or in person, which can be uncomfortable, if not annoying. Some of our partners have created areas on their websites that explain their charitable giving program. Then when they get questions about giving, they can just refer people to their site. What seems to work best for most businesses is to make a real commitment to one or two charities and then offer smaller giving opportunities to the rest. Perhaps all nonprofits can apply for a small grant from your company's foundation. One of our retailers has shopping days for charities so that they can buy things they need at a generous discount. Another chooses a different charity every month to give the canned goods collected from a company-wide food drive.

✔ **My customers had lots of questions about the program and the nonprofit it supported. It was time consuming and confusing for employees. Is there a better way to communicate this information to customers?** Three things: First, we can ensure that your next cause marketing promotion has a takeaway that will give consumers the information they need. Second, we can put a QR code on the promotion so that shoppers with smartphones can just scan the code and bring up all sorts of additional information about the program. Third, we can devote some more time to training your employees so that they can answer questions quickly and accurately. Questions from shoppers are a good thing. It shows interest and gives employees a chance to reinforce the company's commitment to the nonprofit's mission so the company can earn its halo with consumers.

✔ **Most of the other cause marketing programs I see my competitors doing are for large, national nonprofits like Komen, St. Jude, and UNICEF. Why should I continue working with a local partner like you?** Showing your commitment to a local nonprofit like ours really demonstrates your commitment to the community. A study (2010 Cone Cause Evolution Study) last year showed that over 90 percent of consumers think companies should support an issue in the community where they do business. Supporting a local nonprofit is good for the community and good for you.

✔ **This program was great! I'd like to replicate it for other charities we support. Will you help me?** We create these cause marketing programs to support our organization, but it's great that you want to help another cause. We can be helpful to you and the organization you want to support. But we can't do it for free. We can work with the other organization, and you can split the proceeds raised between the two charities. This is about creating a bigger pie for all us. You bring the venue that will help raise the money, and your favorite cause brings the motivation to do a second cause marketing program. We bring the expertise in running a successful cause marketing program. As long as it's win-win-win, you can count us in.

Incorporating New Strategies

All the different cause marketing programs we discuss in this book are the building blocks for your success. Point-of-sale, purchase and action-triggered donations, digital cause marketing, and the other types are programs you can use and succeed with for years.

However, you can add new strategies to your program or use them alongside these existing tactics.

In this section, we look at three new strategies: adding star power, tapping the relationships of others, and harnessing the power of mobile technology for a text-to-give program.

Working with celebrities

The point that celebrities can play a huge role in cause marketing promotions may be a bit of an understatement when you look at the success of big cause brands like Product (RED), Livestrong, and St. Jude Children's Research Hospital. Where would these causes be without Bono, Lance Armstrong, and Marlo Thomas?

While individual results vary, celebrity involvement can generate tremendous awareness and interest in your cause marketing campaign. According to the 2010 Cone Cause Evolution Study, Americans are 54 percent more likely to take notice of a cause-related campaign by a company or nonprofit if a celebrity they know supports it. Americans also said that when a celebrity's support for a cause is sincere, which nearly three-quarters of respondents said they could detect, a whopping 81 percent said that the celebrity could play a significant role in raising awareness for the issue. Having a music icon like U2's Bono (see Figure 11-6) makes Product (RED) appealing to donors, but what makes it one of the most successful cause marketing campaigns ever is that the companies that run (RED) campaigns are "cool" by association. This is not just any halo; this is a hip halo, and it's the ultimate image boost.

So, celebrities are called stars for good reason. But like finding a constellation in the night sky, you need to find the right combination of stars to make your program work.

Figure 11-6:
Irish rocker Bono makes raising money to end AIDS in Africa the right thing, but also the cool thing, to do.

Finding the right celebrity for your cause

We've used several approaches to identify and track celebrities for our cause:

1. **Brainstorm with your staff, board, and supporters on celebrities with a local connection.**

   Include local news TV and radio personalities, sports stars, and Hollywood celebrities that once or now call your area home. The list should even include actors that may be temporarily calling your town or city home because of a movie shoot. Your city or state's film office can tell you which movies are filming in your area. (Working with our local film office is how we got Dwayne "The Rock" Johnson to join us at one of our fundraising events.)

2. **Plug all this intelligence into your database and categorize or tag it as Celebrities so that you can sort and find the information easily.**

   For more on how to use CRM solutions, see Chapter 3.

3. **Research your list of celebrities that you compiled in Step 1 to see who might be a good fit for your cause.**

   Many celebrities have websites and foundations where you can find out about their interests, challenges, backgrounds, and passions. Use these tools to narrow down your list of suitable celebrities.

4. **Start forming your approach around celebrities with whom you have the strongest connection either through mission or relationship.**

   See the next section for ways to increase the likelihood that a celebrity will work with your cause.

Increasing your chances of working with a celebrity

Celebrities are busy people, and they have lots of choices on causes they can support. Here are some ways to ensure that your pitch doesn't end up on the walk of shame:

- ✔ **Have a plan.** This meeting isn't the time to be starstruck. You need to develop a plan that outlines exactly what you want the celebrity to do for you, when, and with whom. Times, dates, location, and other relevant details are all critical to the celebrity and his representative (the person you'll ultimately be working with).

- ✔ **Be specific.** Saying "We'd really like to work with you somehow" isn't going to cut it. You need to be specific and concrete. "We'd love you to be the spokesperson for our next cause marketing program in September when we work with these three companies. . . ."

- ✔ **Be sensitive to their time.** Be clear on how much you expect of them. If their image is going to appear on your pinups, will you need them for a photo session? If they're doing a signing at a store, how long will they have to be there?

- ✔ **Coincide your promotion with their schedule.** For example, after October, a lot of professional baseball players aren't around unless they happen to live locally (in which case, they may prefer to do something in the off-season). So plan your campaign during the months when they're playing. The same with actors. It's hard to get them to support your program when they're filming a new movie in London or Tibet. But they may be more likely to help you when they do the premiere for that movie in New York City where your nonprofit is located.

- ✔ **Do it all.** Make it clear to the celebrity and his representatives that you will make this a turnkey, engaging, and powerful experience for them. They need to be assured that you are hard-working, committed to them and the cause, organized, and flexible.

We love working with celebrities, but we don't make our cause marketing program dependent on them. Actors get divorced or finish movies early, or sometimes not at all. Sports stars get injured or traded or both. Rock stars leave town on a whim or go into rehab. (We're generalizing, of course, but you get the point!) Make sure that your program can continue when your glitzy, twinkling celebrity becomes a fallen star.

Using affiliate cause marketing

In business, *affiliate marketing* is when one company rewards an individual or another company for selling its products or services. A lot of times you see affiliate programs advertised on websites. If you buy a book or sign up for a program through the site, the owner of the site gets a percentage of the sale.

Affiliate cause marketing is when a cause rewards a business or another cause for securing a cause marketing partnership.

The following sections outline how affiliate cause marketing works.

A cause rewards another cause

A cause rewards another cause when one of them either brings a corporate partner or assets to the table that the other cause can leverage to create a cause marketing program that benefits both of them.

One example is our relationship with the Boston Bruins Foundation, the charitable arm of Boston's professional NHL team (see Figure 11-7). The Bruins Foundation was interested in growing its brand in Boston but lacked the expertise we had in executing promotional cause marketing programs. But what the Bruins did have were great assets. The team could offer player appearances at their potential partners' stores, a check presentation on the ice at a home Bruins game, promotion on its gigantic jumbotron, and so on.

We took the Bruins Foundation's assets and combined them with our cause marketing skills to create a program that recruited new corporate sponsors and raised over $50,000 its first year.

The Bruins Foundation had the assets, and we had the expertise in cause marketing, which we leveraged to recruit partners and execute a cause marketing program that benefited both our organizations.

The Bruins Foundation liked the promotion they got from the partnership and we made some new friends and raised some great money.

The other potential scenario with affiliate cause marketing is that you connect with a cause that already has a corporate partner but has no idea what to do with them. In these instances, we offer to execute the cause marketing program on their behalf and share the funds raised.

It's win-win for both causes. While you may be thinking it might be smarter for the cause with the partner to soldier on by itself, partnering with another cause that has the cause marketing expertise and this book under its arm will save time, reduce stress, and raise more money.

Figure 11-7:
Our partnership with the Boston Bruins Foundation combined its star power and promotional muscle with our cause marketing expertise and business contacts.

The cause rewards another business

Several years ago, we were feeling burnt out. We were putting on great events and combining them with our cause marketing to raise money and awareness for our nonprofit. Cause marketing and special events are a great combination, but the two together can be a lot of work!

We concluded that while we wanted to be in the cause marketing business, we wanted to limit our planning and production of special events. But how?

Joanna found the answer amid the informative and hilarious food reviews of the Phantom Gourmet television show. This popular show airs throughout New England and is well known for its spot on reviews by an unknown phantom food critic and gastronomic outings throughout the year.

It was these popular and well-advertised events that interested us the most. For example, Phantom's *BBQ Beach Party* drew a large crowd and plenty of promotional heft thanks to the TV and radio show and website. These were assets we could turn into cause marketing gold with business partners that were hungry for new, creative concepts.

Look for partners that have assets you can use. Don't make our mistake and think you have to create everything yourself. You're a cause marketer, not an event organizer. Always be looking for things you could use that would help you build a better program or attract a holdout partner.

Dave Andelman, the founder of Phantom Gourmet, was receptive to working with us. He liked the idea of supporting a good cause while our retail partners promoted his BBQ Beach Party at the register. This is where he leveraged our assets:

- ✔ As a nonprofit, we had the partners and the leads to create a cause marketing program that would promote his brand and his event.

- ✔ We could also act as a sales and marketing arm for his company because we had sales professionals on staff with the experience and expertise to market large events, such as the BBQ Beach Party. But this time it wasn't our event; it was theirs we were selling.

We leveraged the exposure Phantom could offer partners on its radio and TV shows and recruited four partners with a combined 342 locations. In less than four weeks, they raised close to $120,000.

Since Phantom Gourmet, we've partnered with other *properties* (any business with assets we could leverage ranging from cultural attractions to radio stations) to market through their events. The opportunity is to link cause marketing with a successful event from which you can use its promotional assets and leave the hard work of planning and organizing the event to someone else. The result is better cause marketing with more partners that raise more money.

Adding text-to-give

Giving via texting on mobile phone — *text-to-give* — really took off in 2010 when a devastating earthquake struck Haiti. The American Red Cross alone raised $32 million dollars when generous donors used their mobile devices to type "Haiti" to 90999 to donate $10 (see Figure 11-8).

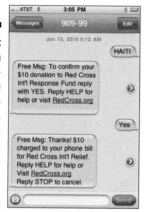

Figure 11-8: In just ten days following the earthquake in Haiti, donors gave $32 million in aid via mobile giving.

Considering the outpouring of support for Haiti, you might conclude you should include a keyword and number (called a *short code*) on all your cause marketing materials so that you can reap millions from text-to-give. Unfortunately, text-to-give doesn't work that way.

The urgency of the situation in Haiti and the terrible images of the disaster being transmitted around the globe motivated people to give and their mobile phones were an easy, fast way to help.

A pinup, cause product, or Facebook page with an appeal to text-to-give wouldn't get the same attention. But here are two ideas that just might work, if you have the right partner:

- ✔ Team up with a media partner, particularly from TV, radio, or outdoor advertising. Your goal is to convince them to donate air-time or space to share a compelling story, image, or message from your cause and to encourage supporters to text their donations. A great example of this concept at work is the "I am here" campaign by Mobile Loaves & Fishes in Austin, Texas, which sought to raise awareness of the homelessness and of one man: Danny Silver (see Figure 11-9). By simply text messaging "Danny" to 20222, donors could give $10. The campaign raised enough money to get Danny and his disabled wife off the street and into a home.

To find out more about Danny Silver and the "I am here" campaign, scan the QR code on the left with your smartphone or visit `http://bit.ly/iIuPvb`.

✔ **Ask for a plug at a sporting event or concert.** You may have already experienced this one yourself. You're at a concert enjoying yourself, and the lead singer gives a plug for her cause and asks you to text a donation from your phone. Singer Adam Lambert of *American Idol* fame has raised hundreds of thousands of dollars for Donorschoose.org by asking fans at concerts to donate. Or maybe you're at a sporting event and the announcer asks you to watch the jumbotron where a bald child stricken by cancer is shown, and a number flashes on the screen for you to text a donation to a cancer hospital. That's just what the Washington Nationals major league baseball team did in 2008 (see Figure 11-10) when it asked fans to donate $5 to a pediatric diabetes care complex at Children's National Medical Center in D.C.

But just as a point-of-sale program can happen at one store, text-to-give could be added to a high school football game, a pancake breakfast, a city festival, or local concerts. Just be realistic about how much you'll raise if Lady Gaga isn't scheduled to appear and give your organization a plug.

Figure 11-9:
The billboard to launch the "I am here" campaign and help Danny Silver and his wife was donated by a local outdoor advertising company.

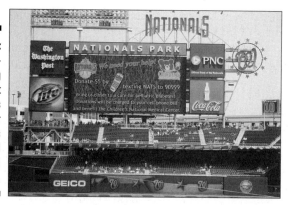

Figure 11-10: The text-giving program at Nationals Park for Children's National Medical Center.

Keep these key points in mind about text-to-give:

- ✔ **Consider the audience you want to reach.** The type of people who rely on text messaging is growing every day, but it's particularly strong among *Millennials* (men and women born during the 1980s and '90s). If your group primarily works with and raises money from seniors, you may want to consider another strategy.

- ✔ **You'll have to choose a third-party vendor to execute your campaign.** Text-to-give isn't something you'll do in-house. A list of approved application service providers evaluated on functionality of their mobile platform, mobile marketing service capabilities, financial viability, commitment to pioneering the mobile channel, geographical coverage, transparency of ownership and governance, and so on is available on the Mobile Giving Foundation's website (www.mobilegiving.org).

- ✔ **Giving options are limited.** The most popular amounts are $5 and $10, but the Mobile Giving Foundation is testing $20 and $25 gifts. Currently, there are no recurring text donations.

- ✔ **Make sure that you understand the fees.** Providers typically charge for setup, monthly usage, and per-message usage.

To find out more about text-to-give, visit the Mobile Giving Foundation's website (www.mobilegiving.org).

Chapter 12

Exploring Other Cause Marketing Resources

In This Chapter

▶ Exploring offline and online resources for networking and education

▶ Gaining knowledge about cause marketing from key people, companies, and causes

*T*his book is a beginning for your education on cause marketing. No one resource can be your Bible on cause marketing because the field is too big and changing too quickly. In conjunction with reading and using this book to understand and execute your cause marketing plans, you should plan to check out a number of other good resources.

In this chapter, we begin with perhaps the most timely, important, and comprehensive resource for cause marketing: the Cause Marketing Forum. From there, we explore five key cause marketing blogs that will enrich your understanding of cause marketing and update you on the latest tools and practices. To get you connected with cause marketers online, we have a great list of people for you to follow on Twitter.

As in most fields, there are a few exceptional cause and corporate leaders that practitioners should regularly follow. These organizations set the pace for the cause marketing field. Our watch list includes two causes and two companies.

Finally, we highlight three online publications that are an ongoing source of news and information on cause marketing. You should sign up for their newsletters or add them to your online reader today.

Joining Cause Marketing Forum

Whether you're a cause or a company that's based in the United States or another country, you should visit the Cause Marketing Forum (CMF) website (www.causemarketingforum.com) and become a member.

Cause Marketing Forum, Inc. was founded in 2002 with the goal of increasing the number of cause marketing partnerships by giving nonprofits and businesses the practical information and connections they need to succeed.

David Hessekiel founded the organization after years of volunteering for good causes and a career in journalism, publishing, and consumer marketing.

There's just one word to describe what David has accomplished and the tremendous resource CMF is to companies and causes: remarkable.

Just by visiting the Cause Marketing Forum site, you have free access to its Knowledge Center, which contains Cause Marketing 101, Research & Reports, and Newsletter Archives (see Figure 12-1). These three areas alone are invaluable to budding and seasoned cause marketers!

Figure 12-1:
Cause
Marketing
Forum's
Knowledge
Center is
open to all.

If you become a member of Cause Marketing Forum, you get a bunch of additional benefits:

✔ You get free access to its live teleconference series by cause marketing masters. These sessions are taught by some of the best people in cause marketing — including us — and are only a phone call away from your home or office.

✔ Missed a teleconference? No problem. They're archived for members on the Cause Marketing Forum website. You can listen to the one you missed and even to the ones that were recorded before you joined whenever you want.

✔ You get the Cause Marketing Forum newsletter every month with the latest news and insights. Sure, you could wait a month or more and read it in the CMF archives, but if you're like us and serious about cause marketing and want the latest news, information, and insights, you'll want this fresh from the Cause Marketing Forum team.

(The rates of membership vary depending on whether you're joining as an individual, a group, or a company. There's something for every price point. See the Cause Marketing Forum site for details.)

With membership, you'll also receive a discount on Cause Marketing Forum's annual conference, which usually occurs the first week of June in Chicago. If you're a cause marketer, this conference is on your calendar and circled in red!

We've found the conference helpful in three important ways.

✔ A main part of the conference is the Halo Awards, which recognize some of the best cause marketing campaigns of the past year (see Figure 12-2). The awards are given for just about every category you can imagine: best transactional campaign, best digital marketing campaign, best video creative, and so on. It's inspiring and educational to hear about all these great campaigns and to meet the people behind them.

✔ There's simply no other place besides the Cause Marketing Forum conference where you'll meet so many people from cause marketing! In many ways, cause marketing is still very much a niche industry. And while it's growing, there are few dedicated forums where cause marketers can meet, talk, and learn from each other. Thankfully, the Cause Marketing Forum conference is one of them.

✔ After awards and networking, the Cause Marketing Forum conference is very much about education. It offers breakout sessions on everything from cause marketing legal issues to working with celebrities to using social media. This is hands-on training and learning delivered by experts to peers that will fuel your cause marketing efforts for a whole year.

Figure 12-2:
The Halo
Awards
at Cause
Marketing
Forum's
annual
conference
recognizes
the best
cause
marketing
campaigns
of the past
year.

Reading Five Must-Read Blogs

A blog is a versatile tool for people to share their insights, experience, opinions, and expertise, among other things. The five blogs we share in this section are regularly updated with content on cause marketing and related topics. Collectively, they offer a wealth of information that is interesting and useful to both causes and companies that want to learn more about cause marketing and how to execute successful programs.

CompaniesandCauses.com

CompaniesandCauses.com (see Figure 12-3) is the official blog of Cause Marketing Forum, which is produced by CMF's director of communications Megan Strand (who's also the technical editor for this book!). (For more on the Cause Marketing Forum, see the previous section.)

To give you a flavor for the CMF blog, here are five posts:

- ✔ "Help Mollye Help Tornado Victims"
- ✔ "Mom Bloggers: The New Cause Ambassadors"

✔ "Getting Cause Marketing Credit Where Credit is Due"

✔ "The Value of a Non-Branded Acts of Cause Partnership"

✔ "Thinking Like a Brand Manager: A Primer for Nonprofits"

SelfishGiving.com

Joe's blog, *Selfish Giving* (www.selfishgiving.com), is the web's No. 1 blog on cause marketing (see Figure 12-4).

Joe started his blog in 2004 as a way to track ideas and to share them with others. Today, Joe posts twice weekly on a variety of how-to cause marketing topics ranging from point-of-sale programs to cause marketing with social media to location-based cause marketing and the impact of mobile technology.

Selfish Giving is focused on serving small causes and companies and teaching them to raise money and build awareness with cause marketing.

You can follow Joe's blog in several ways. You can sign up for his e-mail newsletter, watch for his blog post links on Twitter, Like his Facebook page, or subscribe to his blog's RSS feed.

Figure 12-3:
Companies
and
Causes.
com.

Here are five posts from Selfish Giving that highlight what Joe blogs about:

- ✔ "Food Bank Bags $15k with Cause Marketing, Social Media"
- ✔ "What's The Best Cause Marketing Program for My Business?"
- ✔ "Starbucks Mobile Payments May Give Cause Marketing a Jolt"
- ✔ "Foursquare Cause Marketing Starts with Loyalty Programs"
- ✔ "5 Tips for Businesses Looking for a Cause Marketing Partner"

Figure 12-4:
Selfish
giving.com.

CauseMarketing.biz

While Joe inspects cause marketing programs to see what he can learn and share with small companies and causes (see preceding section), Paul Jones at CauseMarketing.biz (www.causemarketing.biz) dissects them to see what makes some promotions successful and others duds (see Figure 12-5).

The longest published cause marketing blog on the web, Causemarketing.biz offers a tremendous amount of advice and insight. So much value from one site isn't surprising considering Paul's training: He's a former director for the cause marketing powerhouse, the Children's Miracle Network.

Figure 12-5:
Cause
Marketing.
biz.

Five sample posts from CauseMarketing.biz include

- ✔ "Displaying Multiple Cause Marketing Allegiances"
- ✔ "Some Questions to Answer When Cause Marketing With Franchises"
- ✔ "A Cool New Platform for Cause Marketers to Launch Virtual Paper Icons From"
- ✔ "Cause Marketing Customer Satisfaction Surveys"
- ✔ "How to Pay Your Nonprofit Cause Marketers"

Paul is based in Utah. You should check out his blog but also follow him on Twitter for his most up-to-the-minute insights: @PaulRJones (www.twitter. com/paulrjones).

Coneinc.com/WhatDoYouStandFor

Cone LLC is a Boston-based cause branding firm well-known for its long history in cause marketing and cutting-edge programs. It's no surprise that Cone has a blog — *What Do You Stand For?* — or that it's a good one. Cone's blog offers something different from either Joe's or Paul's blogs. It takes a broader perspective on cause marketing and explores issues of cause branding and corporate responsibility, the more mature siblings of cause marketing (see Figure 12-6).

You can read the Cone blog online or sign up for its weekly e-newsletter, which is excellent and chock full of additional insights and research.

WHAT DO YOU STAND FOR?

Women's Empowerment: Not Just a Social Issue
March 11, 2011 at 10:47 AM by Knowledge Leadership

Tuesday marked the 100th anniversary of International Women's Day. Stories about women flooded the media, many featuring companies that have dedicated cause–related programs addressing everything from women's health, to education, to self esteem. Amazing, forward–thinking programs recognize that women play a critical link in many of our global issues, and when we lift them up, society follows. With a topic so widespread and complex, companies must do more than create external programs. They must also look within their own walls to sufficiently recognize and reward the contribution of women.

Home
Cone Homepage
About What Do You Stand For?
Research & Insights
Brand Channeler

What is your reaction to the FTC's revisions to the Green Guides?
○ The guidelines are too restrictive
○ The guidelines aren't restrictive enough
○ The guidelines are just right

View Results
Share ThisPolldaddy.com

vote

All the top stories

Figure 12-6:
Cone's
*What Do
You Stand
For?*

Here are five posts from *What Do You Stand For?*

- ✔ "Technology Supporting Product Transparency"
- ✔ "Insights from a Master Storyteller"
- ✔ "Nonprofit Social Media Faux Pas: A Lucky Mistake"
- ✔ "Why to Think Twice about Cause Voting Campaigns"
- ✔ "Corporate-Nonprofit Partnerships: What to Do In a Crisis"

ForMomentum.com

For Momentum is a cause marketing agency that has worked with many companies and nonprofits on cause marketing campaigns. Founded and led by Mollye Rhea, who is well-versed in advertising, nonprofit, and corporate marketing, the For Momentum blog (see Figure 12-7), which you can link to at the company's website, offers many helpful insights on cause marketing from Mollye and other members of her team.

Here are five posts from ForMomentum.com:

- ✔ "Chipotle Mexican Grill - Food [& Cause Marketing] with Integrity"
- ✔ "Deliver ROI with Employment Engagement"
- ✔ "Key Steps for Successful Sales Process - Finding the Right Partners & Making the Links"

✔ Recipe: Cause Marketing + Crowdsourcing + Social Media

✔ Create Benefits that Sponsors Want

Figure 12-7:
For
Momentum
blog.

Following Ten People on Twitter Today

Joe loves Twitter. He finds a certain magic in it. So interesting. So quick. So current. So informative. So short, just 140 characters.

Twitter is a social networking and microblogging service that allows *twitterers* — those who use the service — to send and read messages called *tweets*. Tweets are text-based posts of up to 140 characters displayed on the user's profile page. You can check out Joe's page at `http://twitter.com/joewaters`.

Joe has learned a lot about cause marketing on Twitter, and so can you. Joe used the following criteria to pick the ten people you should follow on Twitter:

✔ **Joe chose real people as much as possible.** For him, Twitter is all about talking to people. He doesn't like talking to logos, brands, and billboards, and he suspects you won't either.

✔ **These people tweet . . . a lot.** There's a big difference between being on twitter and being active on Twitter. The people Joe chose for his top ten list are on Twitter every day.

✔ **Cause marketing is a focus.** But it's not their only focus. Chris Noble talks about his other business dealings in China. Noland Hoshino chats away about his daily workout. And John Haydon is, well, just being John. In short, don't expect talk about cause marketing 24/7.

✔ **Follow them and multiply.** The good thing about all these people is that when you follow them, they will lead you to many, many more new followers and open new paths to learning.

The following list covers Joe's top ten *tweeps* (twitter peeps, for those of you not well-versed in twenglish):

✔ **Twitter.com/Causeaholic:** Steve Drake is an expert in cause marketing for associations. His signature program, *Trees for Troops,* has delivered thousands of trees to U.S. military bases around the country and the world. Steve shares his insights on his blog *Causeaholic* (www.causeaholic.com) and *501Connect* (www.501connect.com).

✔ **Twitter.com/NolandHoshino:** Noland Hoshino is a passionate cause marketer who is CEO and cofounder of [B]cause Social Media Communications in Portland. He's on the cutting edge of cause marketing and social media — when he isn't volunteering and dressing up like a cow for his favorite charity: Heifer International!

✔ **Twitter.com/CFNoble:** Chris Noble is what every cause marketer wants to be when he grows up. Chris is a talented cause marketer who's focused on the technology behind giving. He's worked with some of the biggest names in business and has raised millions for good causes. The four brands of his company — Kompolt, WhatGives!, StudioGood, and Patron — are cause leaders. And you can learn about them all by following Chris and his business partner Joey Leslie (Twitter.com/jleslie).

✔ **Twitter.com/JohnHaydon:** John Haydon is not a cause marketer, but he's an excellent cause marketing follow on Twitter (see Figure 12-8). Here's why. John is an expert in social media for nonprofits — especially Facebook — which is becoming increasingly important for cause marketers. When John does come across a topic that's relevant to cause marketers, he does a great job connecting the dots.

✔ **Twitter.com/MeganStrand:** Megan Strand is the blogger at *Incouraged,* a blog that explores issues pertaining to cause marketing and social responsibility, (www.incouraged.com). She's also Director of Communications for Cause Marketing Forum, the leading organization for cause marketers. She's the leading woman behind its website, blog, newsletter, and twitter handle. As if she weren't busy enough, Megan was also the technical editor of this book.

✔ **Twitter.com/RealizedWorth:** Chris Jarvis works on the employee engagement side of cause marketing helping companies connect with communities through volunteering and social media.

Figure 12-8:
Each Twitter page has a short bio of the user, a link to its website or blog (usually), and a number of followers and tweets since they signed up for the service.

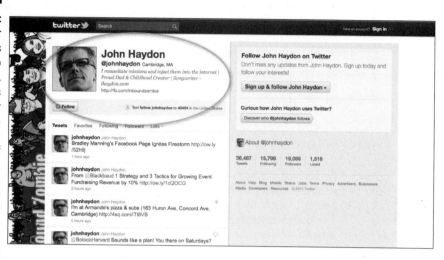

✔ **Twitter.com/GeoffLiving:** Geoff Livingston isn't a practicing cause marketer, but he has excellent insights on cause marketing, its contribution to society, and how it intersects with social media.

✔ **Twitter.com/ScottyHendo:** Scott Henderson blogs at *Rallythecause. com* and has led several high-profile campaigns, including *Pledge to End Hunger,* which helped Tyson Foods deliver 560,000 meals to four different cities for children in need and raised $28,000 for Share Our Strength. In 2010, he and his team at CauseShift launched *We Can End This*, a year-long initiative to spark innovation and create real, tangible solutions to end hunger in America.

✔ **Twitter.com/SchneiderMike:** Mike Schneider helps battle cancer each year by growing a mustache and raising money during "Movember". The rest of the year, Mike is one of the smartest guys I know on location-based services and marketing. That might be why Wiley Publishing chose him and location-based pro Aaron Strout (`http://twitter.com/aaronstrout`) to write *Location-Based Marketing For Dummies.* From reading Joe's blog and Chapter 10, you know that LBM will be a key area of focus for cause marketers in the years ahead.

✔ **Twitter.com/ConeLLC:** Recommending Cone is like suggesting a bunch of great people, not just one. Cone is a leading cause branding firm. Cone tweets insights and research on cause marketing and corporate responsibility. Combine Cone LLC's tweets with its weekly newsletter and blog, and you can brag to people that you are a cause marketing know-it-all. An active twitterer at Cone is Sarah Kerkian (`Twitter.com/sarahkerkian`) who leads their insights and research group.

Still want more Twitter handles?

Here are more cause marketing Twitter handles to follow to keep your Twitter stream teeming with learning:

- **Twitter.com/JocelyneDaw.** Jocelyne is the author of key books for cause marketers: *Cause Marketing for Nonprofits* and *Breakthrough Nonprofit Branding,* (Wiley), with Carol Cone.

- **Twitter.com/CarolCone.** What can we say? Carol is the Mother of Cause Marketing and an ongoing source of leadership and inspiration to everyone in the field.

- **Twitter.com/TweetCMF.** The cause marketing handle for Cause Marketing Forum, the leading organization for cause marketers.

- **Twitter.com/3BLmedia.** 3BL tweets the latest in Cause Marketing News, CSR, and Sustainability.

- **Twitter.com/PhilipsMcCarty.** Joe calls Phil the Godfather of Cause Marketing because he played such an instrumental early role in the development of St. Jude Children's Hospital *Thanks and Giving* cause marketing program, which raises tens of millions of dollars each year. Phil now shares his successful practices with some of the largest causes in the country.

- **Twitter.com/GoodConcepts.** Brian Powell is a Dallas-based cause marketer who is the managing director of cause marketing agency Patron.

- **Twitter.com/ MCCaliber.** Maureen Carlson is a very knowledgeable hospital cause marketer that started the cause marketing program at City of Hope. She works with hospitals around the country on cause marketing and corporate partnerships.

- **Twitter.com/Kanter.** Beth Kanter is a bona fide rock star in the nonprofit world. While her blog, Beth's Blog, focuses on how nonprofits are powering change with social media, cause marketing is an area of interest as well. We believe that cause marketing and social media will grow in tandem and that Beth has a lot to offer these fields. As a star in these areas of focus, she attracts many other great minds that you'll also learn from.

- **Twitter.com/BrighterCause.** Led by two talented strategists, Mindy and Megan, Brighter World Cause Marketing is a cause marketing and copywriting consultancy.

- **Twitter.com/KatyaAnderson.** Katya is author of *Robin Hood Marketing: Stealing Corporate Savvy to Sell Just Causes* (Jossey-Bass).

- **Twitter.com/MikeSwenson.** Mike is president of Kansas City-based Barkley, an advertising agency that specializes in cause marketing. Its campaigns include Lee National Denim Day for breast cancer.

- **Twitter/IEG.** IEG is a global authority on sponsorship, a close ally of cause marketing. IEG also discusses cause marketing and has some talented staff that write on the subject.

- **Twitter.com/JoinRed.** Product (RED) is pure-play cause marketing. It's pretty much all it does. If you're in to cause marketing, you gotta see red.

Keeping Tabs on the Frontrunners

Every year, we seem to revisit the same companies and causes to reinforce the best practices of cause marketing and gain new insights. These organizations have been executing successful cause marketing programs for years and consistently delivering new, innovative, and inspiring strategies.

Keeping tabs on these key causes and companies can refresh your cause marketing and keep your competitors at bay.

Share Our Strength

Joe has been a fan of Bill Shore's anti-hunger organization Share Our Strength (www.strength.org) since he read Bill's first book, *Revolution of the Heart* (Diane Publishing).

Share Our Strength has always been a leader in cause marketing. Its program with American Express, which replicated the first donation for purchase program for the Statue of Liberty in 1983, has raised $30 million since 1992.

In addition to working with large companies like American Express, Timberland, and Walmart, Share Our Strength has worked with restaurant chains like Capital Grille, which has 40 locations. In 2007 and 2008, this high-end steak house chain sold a signature martini adorned with a White Topaz and Diamond Caviar Rope Bracelet from acclaimed designer Steven Lagos (see Figure 12-9) for $1,000 each! The promotion raised more than $200,000.

But what really makes Share Our Strength special from a cause marketing perspective is all the standalone restaurants it engages with its programs. Many of the 4,000 restaurants that participate in their Dine Out No Kid Hungry program are independently operated. That's an impressive feat for a national nonprofit based in our nation's capital.

At every level, Share Our Strength is a winner — a winner to watch.

Figure 12-9:
This limited edition bracelet, created exclusively for The Capital Grille, sold with a special martini for $1,000 with 100 percent of the profits going to Share Our Strength.

Susan G. Komen for the Cure

Nothing excites Joe more than to arrive at the office and find the Komen for the Cure newsletter in his mailbox. He usually doesn't have time to read it until lunch, but it's the only thing he can think about that morning. When lunch hour arrives, it's everything he expected and more — always full of cause marketing programs of all types and sizes.

What's so great about Komen, you ask?

- ✔ **Komen is experienced.** A 13-year partnership with just one partner, BMW, has raised over $13.3 million through its signature program, *The Ultimate Drive*.

- ✔ **Komen has depth.** Komen calls nearly 200 companies corporate partners. `ww5.komen.org/CorporatePartners.aspx`.

- ✔ **Komen looks great in pink.** Komen's signature pink products, from handbags to shoes to candles, make it one of the most recognizable brands in philanthropy.

- ✔ **Komen has the pick of the litter.** Choose an industry category or leader, and Komen has a friend, including ones that serve pets (Purina PetCare)!

- ✔ **Komen isn't cheap.** Most of its cause marketing programs require a minimum six-figure commitment. You must pay for play.

> ✔ **Komen has a reputation.** Even men love Komen! Why else would the macho men of Major League Baseball swing pink bats or the burly men of the National Football League wear pink cleats?

Komen for the Cure's cause marketing program will inspire you . . . and probably make you a little jealous. That's normal. But you can discover a lot from Komen if you choose pink over green.

Starbucks

Starbucks is a leader in cause marketing, an adopter of new, interesting, and innovative strategies. Here are just a few of its programs we've admired through the years.

> ✔ **Ethos Water:** Five cents from the sale of each bottle goes to clean up the world's water supply.

> ✔ **Product (RED):** Starbucks donates five cents from the sale of each beverage on World Aids Day to Product (RED). Starbucks stores also sell cups, bottles, and traveller mugs that support (RED) with a donation when sold.

> ✔ **Conservation International:** Starbucks launched a Starbucks card to support CI. Each time customers used the card CI got five cents.

> ✔ **HandsOn Network:** Starbucks joined with HON to encourage customers to pledge five hours of volunteer time as part of Barack Obama's national call for service and encourage individuals to "create the change they wish to see." Starbucks rewarded customer pledges with a free cup of coffee (see Figure 12-10).

> ✔ **Starbucks Mobile Payments:** Earlier this year, Starbuck launched a new smartphone app that allowed customers to make purchases with their phones. While this app has yet to be combined with a cause marketing promotion, mobile payments will play a key role in the future of cause marketing. As it has in so many other ways, Starbucks may be setting a new standard for how cause marketing will be executed in the years to come.

It's easy to dismiss Starbucks as so unique and exceptional that there is no connection to you. You can only admire their achievements from afar. But wake up and smell the coffee. Most of Starbucks' programs are simple purchase-triggered donation programs expertly executed in its stores. Scaled appropriately, they could work for companies and causes of all sizes.

For more on purchase-triggered donation programs, see Chapter 8.

Figure 12-10:
Starbucks teamed up with the HandsOn Network for the Five Hour Pledge.

Toys "R" Us

It's easy for us to love the cause marketing Toys "R" Us does. With four young children between us, we spend a lot of time there!

As cause marketers, it's hard not to admire the shear breadth of Toys "R" Us promotions. In 2010, the toy store chain received a Halo Award by Cause Marketing Forum for Shaq Gives Back, a cause marketing promotion for the Marine Toys for Tots Foundation. Facebook users were encouraged to join Shaq by liking Toys "R" Us or Babies "R" Us to trigger a $1 donation to Toys for Tots.

The impact was impressive: The company's Facebook fans increased from 20,000 to almost 445,000. Nearly 30,000 users posted messages on its walls. The campaign raised $3.4 million and collected more than 335,000 toys.

In addition, Toys "R" Us contributed an additional $1 million worth of toys — nearly half of which resulted from the Join Shaq Facebook campaign.

Other cause marketing efforts include

✔ **Trick-or-Treat for Unicef:** As a national sponsor, Toys "R" Us embraced the program by distributing the iconic orange collection boxes, asking customers to support the program, and hosting parades in its stores where kids could design their own box. That's partner engagement!

✔ **Autism Speaks:** Toys "R" Us raised money for the nonprofit in its stores with point-of-sale and also sponsored the Walk Now for Autism Speaks at 80 locations around the country.

✔ **Make-a-Wish:** Toys "R" Us awards shopping sprees to young kids with life-threatening medical conditions. It has donated over $300,000 to help grant wishes to deserving children.

The lesson for companies and causes of all sizes is how Toys "R" Us leverages its assets — busy stores, in-kind donations, vibrant online presence, employee activation around the country — to help needy men, women, and children.

Toys "R" Us is a great place to buy toys. But when it comes to cause marketing, it doesn't play around. Neither should you.

Reading Publications That Follow Cause Marketing

There are so many different ways to find out about cause marketing. In addition to the other resources in this chapter, we follow these free, online publications every day.

It's worth noting that three of them, *Ad Age, The Huffington Post,* and *Mashable,* have sections dedicated to the cause world. *Ad Age* has Good Works, *The Huffington Post* has HuffPost Impact, and *Mashable* has Social Good. You should subscribe to these individual sections, but you can benefit from reading the general publications as well. We suspect you hear enough about the nonprofit world already. Read articles about seemingly unrelated topics in business, education, technology, and government and make the connections to cause marketing that others haven't. The words, "I wonder if we took this idea and applied it to . . . ." are how new ideas are born.

Ad Age

We subscribe to several daily *Ad Age* e-newsletters, including *Ad Age Daily* and *Ad Age MediaWorks.* While these newsletters closely follow the news and trends of the advertising world, cause marketing, social media, location-based services, and other emerging technologies are a key focus.

For example, consider this story on how the Girl Scouts are using Facebook and mobile payments to boost cookie sales (see Figure 12-11). This is a great story about how a Silicon Valley dad started a Facebook page so that friends and coworkers would know where his daughter was selling Girl Scout cookies. When people asked if they could buy the cookies with credit instead of cash, he signed up for Square, a credit card payment device that attaches to your smartphone and allows you to accept credit cards. In the first hour, the Girl Scouts sold 400 boxes.

We learned something in this article about giving, Facebook, mobile payments, and just how darn popular those Girl Scout cookies are!

Want to be a smart cookie? Have *Ad Age* delivered to your inbox for free and read it every day.

Figure 12-11:
Ad Age story on Girl Scouts using Facebook to sell cookies.

Philanthropy.com

Philanthropy.com is the online home of *The Chronicle of Philanthropy*, the No. 1 source of information and news for nonprofit leaders and fundraisers.

If you're a nonprofit, your office may already receive the print version of the *Chronicle*. It's a wonderful publication, but we suggest you follow the Chronicle's online activities via Twitter. @Philanthropy (http://Twitter.com/philanthropy).

From the Philanthropy Twitter handle, we link to great posts (see Figure 12-12) and are the first to hear of upcoming nonprofit webinars on everything from corporate giving to social media.

You can also follow Philanthropy by Liking its page on Facebook. (www. facebook.com/pages/Philanthropycom).

Figure 12-12: @Philanthropy on Twitter.

The Huffington Post

The Huffington Post is a popular online news site started by Arianna Huffington in 2005. You can learn a lot from The *Huffington Post,* but your daily reading assignment is in HuffPost Impact (see Figure 12-13), where *The Post's* cause writers and bloggers discuss issues surrounding causes, including cause marketing, which include Joe's posts on cause marketing.

Mashable

Mashable is a top source for news in social and digital media, technology, and web culture. It's also a great resource for the latest info and trends on digital cause marketing.

You can read Mashable online (www.mashable.com), or you can join the millions of followers and friends of Mashable's Twitter handle (www.twitter.com/mashable) and Facebook page (www.facebook.com/mashable) that choose to get their updates there (see Figure 12-14).

Figure 12-13:
HuffPost Impact focuses on causes.

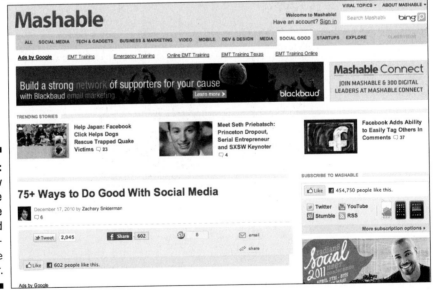

Figure 12-14:
We follow Mashable on the web and @mashable on Twitter.

Part VI
The Part of Tens

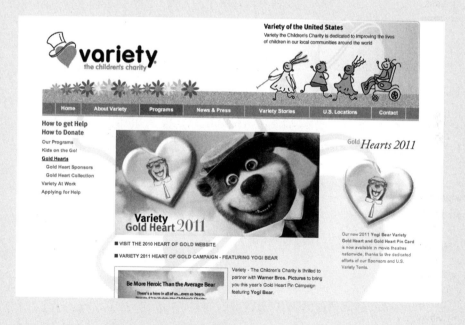

In this part . . .

In this part, we play Moses and give you our ten commandments for cause marketing. We also highlight ten mistakes to avoid in cause marketing and ten easy, low-budget cause marketing strategies for companies and causes on a budget. We also share ten cause marketing programs we wish we could take credit for and give you ten tips for delivering a presentation that would make Pericles, Abraham Lincoln, and Martin Luther King proud.

Chapter 13

The Ten Commandments of Cause Marketing

In This Chapter

▶ Adopting a code of conduct to follow for cause marketing campaigns

▶ Living by ten basic rules that will raise more money and protect your reputation

*T*he original Ten Commandments Moses brought down from Mount Sinai gave the People of Israel a basic set of moral and ethical rules to follow. While we don't consider ourselves the Moses of cause marketing bestowing commandments etched in stone to our readers, we do share his intention in bringing a simple code of conduct to the field. Fortunately for you, our medium is paper and not stone tablets!

Following these ten commandments of cause marketing will ensure that your program stays on track and far away from the dangers that destroy programs and reputations.

Thou Shall Know What Cause Marketing Is

There's no excuse for not knowing what cause marketing is (see Chapter 1). If you're a nonprofit, you run the risk of damaging your credibility with prospects and not converting them to partners. If you're a company, you may fail to understand the differences between cause marketing and traditional marketing and launch a program that will leave customers puzzled, if not angry.

Thou Shall Not Confuse Cause Marketing with Philanthropy, Sponsorship, or Social Responsibility

Cause marketing's first goal is marketing for both the company and the cause. While philanthropy is an aim of cause marketing, philanthropy is not its primary objective.

Cause marketing and sponsorship share a common thread: they're both win-win. Where they diverge is in the level of commitment between the partners and the tactics that make cause marketing unique. While sponsorship is generally a simple exchange of money for a promotional opportunity, cause marketing is a deep partnership (see Chapter 1).

In addition, social responsibility and corporate social responsibility (CSR) seem to be on everyone's tongues these days. The problem is that they use these words interchangeably with cause marketing, which isn't accurate.

CSR is an organization's commitment to operating in a way that is socially responsible. Cause marketing may be a reflection of the larger CSR strategy, but this is not always the case. For most organizations, cause marketing is a single tile in the mosaic that is their overall CSR strategy.

Starbucks' Shared Planet is its corporate commitment to do business in ways that are good for people and the planet (its CSR statement). Starbucks' cause marketing campaigns in support of Product (RED) reflect this overall corporate commitment but are just a small piece of a much larger CSR program.

Consider the Starbucks coffee cup in Figure 13-1 that's supporting (RED). Starbucks' support (RED) for red reflects its corporate social responsibility, its ethics, and its values. The portion of sales promotion it created to raise the money to put deeds to words is cause marketing. If CSR is the blueprint for change, cause branding is the wood that will be used to build it, and cause marketing is the hammer.

Social responsibility, CSR, and cause marketing share a bond, but they're not the same thing.

Figure 13-1:
This
Starbucks
ceramic
to-go cup
supports
Product
(RED).

Thou Shall Choose Cause Marketing Partners Carefully

In 2010, Susan G. Komen for the Cure taught everyone that you can't partner with just anyone. When Komen chose to partner with Kentucky Fried Chicken in *Buckets for the Cure,* which featured pink buckets at KFC restaurants (see Figure 13-2), you have to wonder if they saw any benefit beyond the millions they would raise from the program.

It didn't take long, however, before Komen ignited a firestorm of controversy as critics complained that Komen had aligned itself with a fast-food fat house that it should be criticizing, not promoting.

While Komen raised over $4 million from the program with KFC, some argue the cost to their brand was much higher.

Figure 13-2:
The pink buckets in KFC's program didn't soften the public's response to the program.

When it comes to partnerships, proceed with caution, or you just may do more harm than good. Take a cause marketer's Hippocratic Oath: "Do no harm." Don't damage your cause or company, the people you serve, or your trusted partner.

Thou Shall Create Cause Marketing Programs That Are Win-Win

The essence of cause marketing is mutual benefit (see Chapter 1). Just as non-profits hope to increase their visibility and raise money, companies aspire to enhance their favorability with consumers and, ultimately, drive sales.

If it's not win-win, it doesn't work. And it's not cause marketing.

Thou Shall Act Like a Business Person, with a Conscience

Cause marketing exists at the intersection of philanthropy, business, and marketing. If you're a cause, you have to be innovative, results-driven, and customer-focused like a business person because you'll be working with businesses that are focused on getting and keeping customers.

Companies, you also have to be giving, human, and humane, like a philanthropist, because you are, after all, dealing with a partner whose business is helping others.

A cause marketer balances himself between value and values.

Thou Shall Not Limit the Benefits of Cause Marketing to Money

If you're limiting the benefits of cause marketing to money, you shouldn't do it. For causes, there are better ways to raise money. Major gifts, grants, and even special events are more lucrative than cause marketing. The real benefit of cause marketing for nonprofits is the visibility and awareness it creates for your mission, which helps your organization and fundraising grow.

For companies, cause marketing can certainly be a sales driver, but companies were profitable before cause marketing, and many still are today without cause in their marketing. But adding cause to your marketing mix will enhance your favorability while other forms of marketing will give you only visibility. And study after study shows that given the choice between two businesses that sell similar products at similar prices, consumers will choose the business they view more favorably.

Cause marketing has many benefits for causes and companies (see Chapter 1). But doing cause marketing for the money is neither smart nor rewarding.

Thou Shall Make Your Cause Marketing Transparent for All to See

Consumers aren't fools. When they support a cause through a business, they want to know the following:

- ✔ **The cause that's getting the money.** Be specific and tangible. Make the cause real for the consumer. Don't say, "Funds raised will be directed to cancer charities." Instead say, "Funds support cancer care patients at Boston Medical Center."

- ✔ **If the money is earmarked for a specific program within the cause.** This information won't confuse the consumers; it will make the ask more directed and meaningful. "Monies raised will support The Kids Fund at Boston Medical Center."

- ✔ **How the money will be used.** Consumers want to know how the money they're donating will be used — so tell them. For example, say, "The Kids Fund provides a variety of necessity items — from eyeglasses to home medical equipment — for the hospital's pediatric patients. More than 25,000 children receive care at BMC, and they are among the neediest population in the Boston area."

- ✔ **If your promotion involves a purchase-triggered donation, be clear on how much the cause will receive from the sale.** Don't hide your giving behind "A portion of the proceeds will be donated to organizations that fight HIV/AIDS." Really? What portion? Which organizations? Consider this example from World Aids Day 2010: "For every (RED) beverage purchased at Starbucks, five cents will be donated to buy lifesaving medicines for those living with HIV in Africa."

Figure 13-3 shows a pinup we used for a program. We did a good job telling donors where the money would go and what program would benefit, but we should have mentioned that 100 percent of the proceeds go to the food pantries. We'll try harder next time

Figure 13-3: This was on a pinup we used for a program.

Thou Shall Not Expect Results Overnight

Cause marketing is not a quick fix. It takes time, effort, and resources to build a successful program. After you've executed a few, you'll have the credibility you need to launch more programs with new partners.

Credibility isn't given; it's earned. And you don't earn your cause marketing chops over night.

Thou Shall Use Social Media Strategically with Cause Marketing

Us telling you that you should use social media with cause marketing is a little like Moses coming down from Mount Sinai and telling people he just got the Ten Commandments from The Almighty. You have to trust us a bit on this one.

Companies and causes are awakening to the value of social media, the connection you can make with customers and donors, and how that connection can deepen an experience and a relationship.

If your business or cause is active on social networks, congratulations! Keep up the good work and don't rest on your laurels. The field is changing quickly.

If you haven't begun using social networks, you need to get busy. Many offline and online resources can get you up to speed on how to use social networks. But remember, the best way to learn how to blog, tweet, use Facebook, or check-in on Foursquare is to use these services yourself! Don't talk and don't just read. Do!

Commit yourself to using social networks for a week and you'll learn more about how to use them than you would ever have learned in a book about *how to use* social networks.

One resource we use is the daily *Smartbrief on Social Media*, which you can sign up for at www.smartbrief.com/socialmedia. *Smartbrief* (see Figure 13-4) gives a great summary of the top articles on social media trends and best practices.

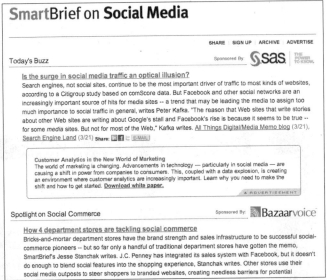

Figure 13-4:
Following the changes in social media can make you dizzy! Subscribing to *Smartbrief on Social Media* will help you get your bearings.

Thou Shall Not Overcomplicate Cause Marketing

The tactics behind cause marketing aren't brain surgery. The majority of programs are simple point-of-sale and purchase-triggered donations. As cause marketing pioneer Kurt Aschermann, president of Charity Partners, wrote in a post for Cause Marketing Forum's website (www.causemarketingforum.com):

> *Cause-related marketing really isn't that difficult. Just handle the relationship, deliver what you promise, and provide value to your partner. Best of all, cause-related marketing is fun and exciting. The sooner you master it, the sooner everyone will benefit from its incredible potential.*

Easy, right?

No one in Boston makes cause marketing look easier than the Jimmy Fund, the fundraising arm of the world renowned Dana Farber Cancer Institute. Not only is it an excellent, well-run fundraising machine, but the hope it gives to children with cancer resonates powerfully with donors.

One of the Jimmy Fund's most successful promotions is its partnership with supermarket chain Stop & Shop. This promotion, which has raised more than $50 million since 1991, is a simple register program that has cashiers asking shoppers for a dollar for kids with cancer.

The Jimmy Fund Triple Winner Game is powerful, effective, successful, and simple (see Figure 13-5).

Figure 13-5:
The Jimmy
Fund Triple
Winner
Game.

Chapter 14

Ten Common Cause Marketing Mistakes to Avoid

. . . .

In This Chapter

▶ Avoiding mistakes that can sabotage your program

▶ Knowing what cause marketing can and can't do

. . . .

Cause marketing has many rewards. They're highlighted through the book. We are, after all, big fans of the practice! But it also has hazards, and we want you to be clear on the mistakes that can damage your program or keep it from ever getting started.

Choosing the Wrong Cause or Company for Your Program

Companies that fail to choose the right nonprofit for their cause marketing campaign run the risk of building their program on a weak foundation. Employees and customers may respond indifferently, or worse. That's hardly the way for a company to earn its cause marketing halo.

Causes that choose the wrong companies can alienate donors and threaten their prospects for future partnerships. Causes must be careful not to put money before mission.

The guiding principles for causes and companies when choosing a partner are sincerity, authenticity, commitment, and transparency. We discuss in detail how to find the right cause marketing partner in Chapter 3.

Viewing Cause Marketing as Philanthropy, Not Marketing

While cause marketing certainly has a philanthropic objective, giving is not its primary focus. Companies engage in cause marketing to enhance their favorability with existing and potential customers. If their goals were strictly philanthropic, they could donate the money to causes and be done with it. Cause marketing allows companies to put their marketing muscle to work on behalf of the cause while promoting themselves and increasing the potential donation to the cause.

If nonprofits view cause marketing as philanthropy instead of marketing, they may not fully grasp the potential of a practice that is generally better at building awareness and generating visibility than raising large sums of money, especially on the local level.

When you think cause marketing is something else, repeat its name a few times to yourself. "Giving" and "charity" are nowhere to be found in the name. For more on what cause marketing is and isn't, see Chapter 1.

Being Unnerved by Competitors

The biggest obstacles keeping causes and companies from trying cause marketing are their demons. They psych themselves out before they ever get started.

For causes, it's the intimidation they feel from the high-profile causes that excel at cause marketing — the Product (RED)s, the St. Judes, and the Komens of the world. Yes, these causes have done well, but they can't stop you from trying and succeeding in cause marketing, even if one day you have to face them as competitors. Indeed, recent research from the 2010 Cone Cause Evolution Study shows that local causes may even have an edge with consumers. Forty-six percent of Americans believe that companies should focus on issues that impact local communities. And 91 percent said that companies should support an issue in the communities where they do business.

Companies, on the other hand, are unnerved by the level of commitment that may be asked of them and what they may be getting themselves into. Their larger competitors are an example they follow. In addition to in-store programs, these larger chains and businesses donate thousands of employee hours and millions of dollars to causes via corporate giving, foundations, and volunteer programs. That kind of commitment is just not possible for many small business owners. (According to the U.S. Small Business Administration, small businesses Represent 99.7 percent of all employer firms.)

The good news is that small businesses can give within their means and still make a difference. They can also choose cause marketing programs that tap their most valuable asset and gift, their customers, who generally can raise much, much more than any check written from the company checkbook.

The Goliaths of cause and business are big and mighty. But armed with the tools, training and right expectations, any cause or company can succeed in cause marketing.

Refusing to Be Transparent about Your Program

Look at enough cause marketing campaigns, and you're bound to see something like this:

"Proceeds from the sale of this item will benefit area shelters."

This kind of ambiguity begs the following questions from consumers:

- ✔ What proceed? A penny? A dollar? Two?
- ✔ What shelters? Shelters for people or animals?
- ✔ What area? My area? The area where the company is located? Or somewhere in Australia?

More than ever, consumers are demanding that causes and companies be more transparent about what charity the money will go to, to what program within the cause, and how much the charity will receive, either in total or from each purchase.

Regardless of what type of cause marketing program you execute, transparency should be the top concern. Cause marketing without transparency hurts your credibility, the very thing you're trying to build by doing cause marketing in the first place. Be clear, or your future will be cloudy and unsettled.

Making Your Program Overly Complicated

The writer Henry David Thoreau advised: "Simplify, simplify." As with most things in life, focus on what works in cause marketing and avoid what requires time and money but doesn't have a return-on-investment (ROI).

For example, in our experience, the two most lucrative and common forms of cause marketing are point-of-sale and purchase-triggered donations (see Chapters 7 and 8). Other types of cause marketing programs are out there (see Chapter 1), but these two work well for both company and cause and raise lots of money and awareness for nonprofits.

Another way that companies and nonprofits overcomplicate their program is by spending extra money and resources printing fliers, posters, and costly die-cut pinups to support their campaign. Fliers and posters don't work — or not enough to cover their cost — and pinups should be a simple design on an inexpensive paper stock.

The determining factor in a successful point-of-sale campaign are people — dedicated managers, motivated employees, generous customers. The key is knowing that regardless of the type of cause marketing program, people are the ingredient that make a program successful. And that's where you want to put your time and energy.

Streamline the material part of your cause marketing program to maximize its efficiency and success. The cause, company, and customer will all benefit.

Expecting Too Much of Your Partner

Our definition of cause marketing is a partnership between a for-profit and a nonprofit for mutual benefit (see Chapter 1). We like the dictionary definition of what a partnership is: the association of two or more persons who cooperate for profit. That's why we include partnership in our definition. It's also no coincidence that we included the words "mutual benefit."

But one of the quickest ways to ruin a cause marketing pact is for one partner to overburden the other or to not set clear expectations.

Sometimes the company makes too many demands for unnecessary material to promote the program or for incentives for employees. Causes overburden companies when they expect the business to do everything, except pick up the check when it's ready.

Cause marketing programs require equal effort from partners. A company supporting a cause, minus an engaged cause partner, isn't cause marketing; it's philanthropy. A cause promoting a company, minus an engaged company partner that isn't involving its company isn't cause marketing; it's sponsorship.

A work-work, win-win partnership between a nonprofit and a for-profit for mutual profit is cause marketing.

Being Too Focused on Cause Marketing

Yep, we said it. Sometimes when working with a company or cause, you can be too focused on finding the right cause marketing opportunity when the real opportunity for both is simply something else.

We certainly have faced this ourselves. A program doesn't go so well with a business — okay, it fails! — but we accept failure and move on to something else. Opportunity waits. Sometimes we switch to a traditional sponsorship or to an event. We'll even turn a company over to our major gift's team so that it can focus on an individual gift from its CEO.

Whatever the change in our approach is, the objective is to ultimately be open and flexible to cause marketing *and* opportunity, whatever form it might take.

Rewarding Supporters with Unnecessary Perks

We're big believers in incentivizing the people who make cause marketing programs such a big success. These incentives can range from a T-shirt to a $5 gift card to a pizza party for the store that sold the most pinups. Incentives work, especially when you're working with a team that's highly motivated.

What doesn't work is when causes and companies reward supporters lavishly at the expense of dollars or products that could have benefited the cause instead.

Take the high-profile case of New England Patriot Quarterback Tom Brady. After an auto accident in 2010, Boston media outlets reported that Brady got the $97,000 car he was driving as part of a sponsorship pact automaker Audi had with Best Buddies, a nonprofit with which Brady had played a major role for several years.

A spokesman for the car company said they gave Brady a car "in appreciation" of his work on behalf of Best Buddies. Sure beats a t-shirt, which is what other supporters got.

Brady has no official relationship with Audi, yet he accepts an expensive car from them in appreciation of his volunteer work with Best Buddies.

Bad call? Interference? Flag? You pick. Unfortunately, a penalty was never called on this play, and Audi replaced Brady's damaged car with a new one.

Steer clear of excessive perks and never lose sight of your ethics and the well-being of your brand. Brady was unhurt in the accident, but his Audi/Best Buddies and judgment were dead on arrival.

Thinking Cause Marketing Will Solve All Your Problems

We come across nonprofits every day that lurch from one trendy tactic to another, only to be disappointed when what was billed as the next great thing doesn't live up to expectations. Now, the cause and business world is abuzz about cause marketing.

For nonprofits, cause marketing is known for its media, celebrities, and million-dollar campaigns. Of course, this is true for only a very small percentage of charities, and in many cases, they've achieved this status only after many years, if not decades, of effort.

For businesses, cause marketing is the new shiny marketing tool that will have customers crowding the registers and talking glowingly of their company. But cause marketing is just one piece of the marketing mix, and expecting miracles from this one strategy is like expecting to drive a car with one wheel. You need a lot of other parts in place to make this car run.

Cause marketing isn't a cure-all. It's a strategy that needs to be approached opened-eye and realistic about the work and resources required to succeed and what can potentially be achieved.

Choosing the Wrong Type of Program

If a business is B-to-B and doesn't have a storefront with shoppers, a purchase-triggered donation program isn't the right fit. If a business sells a consumer product or service, but has no online presence, a digital cause marketing program that rewards Facebook Likes with donations won't work.

Choosing the right type of cause marketing is critical to the success of your program and your partnership. Start by first understanding your partner's single most important asset:

- ✔ Do they have lots of stores?
- ✔ Do they have a signature product or service?
- ✔ Do they have a large advertising budget?
- ✔ Do they have a large workforce?
- ✔ Do they have a vigorous and extensive online presence?
- ✔ Are their stores busy with lots of shoppers?
- ✔ Do they have a large or particularly dedicated workforce?

These questions will start you down the right road to picking the best cause marketing program for a partner, a journey we explore in detail in Chapter 3.

Chapter 15

Ten Low-Budget Cause Marketing Ideas

In This Chapter

▶ Exploring easy and inexpensive ways to jump-start your cause marketing program

▶ Bringing existing assets into play to accelerate your success

Working at a safety-net hospital in Boston, we're used to running cause marketing programs on a shoestring budget. We share much of our experience and advice throughout the book.

In this chapter, we summarize our top ten low-budget cause marketing ideas.

Looking Within

When you get started with cause marketing, you may think you need to put lots of time, energy, and resources into identifying and developing new partnerships. While work is always required to succeed at cause marketing, an easier, more effective route to success may be right in front of you.

For a cause, the better route may be focusing on existing relationships and partnerships. When we started at our nonprofit, we turned inward and focused on two existing relationships we had with CEOs that ran retail chains. These two retailers formed the foundation for our cause marketing program and helped us recruit new partners.

For a company, the clear course may be a partnership with a cause with whom you, your employees, or your customers already have a connection. Starting with a cause you know will save you time, energy, and money you'd spend meeting and vetting charities and finally selecting the right one.

The beginnings of a cause marketing program are not so much found as they are *detected*. If your time and energy are important to you, begin by looking in your closest circles.

Focusing on Pinups

You can raise money with cause marketing in many ways, but none of them are more cost effective than pinups. The cost for each pinup is minimal, usually less than a dime each (see Figure 15-1). While pinups generally sell for just a buck or two at the register, they have raised millions for causes.

It's no coincidence that some of the most successful point-of-sale cause marketing programs involve pinups.

Figure 15-1: In 2010, we raised $280,000 with this pinup program. Our expenses were just over 3 cents per pinup.

Setting Up a Simple Percentage-of-Sales Program

One of the easiest and most economical cause marketing programs you can execute is a percentage-of-sale program. Simply stated, a business, usually a retailer, chooses a service or product from which a certain percentage benefits your cause.

For example, say your nonprofit has a partnership with a local chain of three candle shops. You ask them first to do pinups to support your organization, but they balk saying they don't feel comfortable asking customers for money at the register. Plan B: How about a percentage-of-sales program?

Since Valentine's Day is just a couple weeks away, you choose a special lover's candle the business owner is sure will be a big seller. She agrees to give you 50 cents from the sale of each candle sold at her three stores.

The store owner sets up a special display for the promotion and signage at the register to let shoppers know they can celebrate their love while supporting a great cause by buying the candle. Keep in mind that cause products with a percentage-of-sale feature need more promotion — like signage — than a pinup that gets plenty of promotion from the cashier asking customers to donate.

Your cause helps spread the word by promoting the candle store and special cause marketing promotion to your internal supporters and stakeholders, helping to drive additional traffic to the stores.

At the end of the promotion, which could wrap up a couple days after Valentine's Day, the owner tells you how many candles she sold, multiplies that number by $.50, and cuts you a check!

Planning Shopping Days

If your cause or company is located or connected to a downtown shopping district, try a shopping event for a cause. Shopping for a cause can work several ways.

You can simply pick a day on which a group of businesses will donate a percentage of sales to a cause(s). Both the nonprofit and businesses promote the day to consumers and supporters in the weeks and days leading up to the event. This approach, which is turnkey and low budget, is classic cause marketing. The business helps a cause but also hopes its support will drive shoppers into their stores.

The next option is to ask area businesses to sell pinups along with donating a percentage of sales to a cause. Adding pinups to the shopping day will add expense, but it will also raise more money.

Finally, a good option to directly involve consumers is to combine shopping with walking. We called our event the *South End Shop Walk* because our nonprofit is located in Boston's historic South End, an up-and-coming shopping area with hip and trendy stores.

We recruited 50 stores, mainly small shops and restaurants, to offer discounts to "shop walkers" who had collected pledges for a special one-day shopping event. At the start of the day, walkers received a branded Shop Walk bag that entitled them to special discounts at participating stores along the route. Some of these stores also ran point-of-sale and/or percentage-of-sale programs to raise money for our cause. Some started a full month before the shop walk, which promoted the event and raised money.

Businesses loved the *South End Shop Walk* because it brought new customers into their stores. And since many of the walkers worked at the hospital or came from the neighborhood, there was a good chance they would return.

Shopping days should offer very targeted promotions. This is the key selling point for you, the nonprofit, when pitching a shopping day program to a retailer or group of retailers.

Shopping days are a good option if businesses are willing to give a discount, but hesitant to donate a percentage of sales to your cause or sell pinups to customers. Shopping days give you access to a new group of businesses that get to know and understand you and cause marketing. Maybe next time businesses will add the point-of-sale or percentage of sale to their support for your organization. Sometimes you have to take baby steps and build trust. Once businesses understand that you are giving something in return, they'll understand the win-win benefit of cause marketing!

Oftentimes, local business groups will develop promotions that drive traffic and raise money for good. We worked with the Downtown Crossing Association on *Retail Therapy,* a weekend event of shopping, specials, and live outdoor entertainment. The event drove traffic to retailers and raised money for programs for the homeless, a cause that was a key concern to this shopping district where the homeless regularly slept on benches and outside stores.

Businesses and business groups can benefit from a nonprofit's expertise in event planning and sales because *Retail Therapy* included two days of main stage entertainment and dozens of businesses that we, the nonprofit, "sold" into the event. All these businesses cross-promoted each other, and because the event benefited a cause, we leveraged our connections to newspapers and radio stations to get lots of great promotion for the event and our retail partners.

Businesses should understand that nonprofits have assets, too. It's important for you to know the ins and outs to finding the right nonprofit partner, which we discuss in detail in Chapter 3.

Using Social Media

Social media is powerful, ever-growing, and here to stay. It's also free. Social media and cause marketing belong together!

Social media teaches you cause marketing. Joe follows the key thought leaders and blogs in our industry via Twitter and Facebook. The best posts are *crowdsourced,* which means a large group of people he respects on the Internet help him decide which ones are worth reading.

Social media is a link in building strong partnerships. It's instant, informal, sometimes personal, and generally informational as a lot of sharing happens.

Think of social media as the letter that rarely gets lost, the phone call that more often gets answered, the e-mail that gets the reply, or the unannounced visit that is not turned away.

Soon, as social media evolves and location-based services gain momentum, social media will be used more and more for cause marketing promotions to raise awareness and money.

There are 600 billion people on Facebook. It's not going away. YouTube is the second biggest search engine after Google. It's not a fad. And with 59 percent of businesses on the INC 500 list using Twitter, do you really think everyone is only talking about what they last ate?

Whether you like social media or not, it's here to stay. It may not always be called WordPress, Facebook, Twitter, or YouTube, but the social genie is out of the bottle.

Making Your Program Easy to Find with SEO

More and more people are using search engines to find the things they're looking for. Looking for details on the side effects of the latest prescription from your doctor? Google it. Need an address? Try Google. Looking for a company's website? Don't bother asking for a URL. Google it!

People are searching for information on your cause marketing program. Your goal is to be as close to the top of the search results as possible so that people don't miss you and pick someone else.

If you have a blog and are using Facebook and Twitter, you're well-positioned for search engine optimization (SEO), the process of improving the volume or quality of traffic to a web site from search engines.

One of the most powerful ways to improve your ranking in search results are links *in to* your sites. When another blog or website references your post and provides a hyperlink back to your blog (which they can't do if you don't have a blog!!), you gain authority with search engines and boost your ranking in search results. For example, Joe has been writing his blog since 2004. The age of a blog is one factor that helps its search engine ranking. Despite cause marketing having more than 8 million search results, Selfishgiving.com is in the top ten (see Figure 15-2).

How do you get these links of gold for free? Local cause marketers can network with local bloggers and other nonprofit and marketing types who can blog about you and link to your posts.

Bottom line: Blog and link to blogs, which encourages other bloggers to link to your blog! Got it?

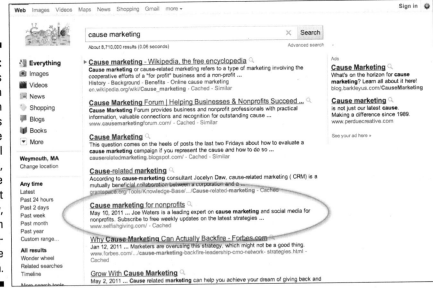

Figure 15-2:
Blogs rank high on search engines because you control keywords, update content regularly, and can offer text-rich niche information.

Building Your Program with Existing Events

Special events for fundraising can be very effective and lucrative for a non-profit. They can also be expensive and labor intensive and can come up short on return-on-investment considering all the time, effort, and money that you put into them. Perhaps this sounds like your events.

To maximize your events — and to tap an existing resource — we suggest a cause marketing twist. In addition to trying to secure sponsors— the backbone — of every event fundraiser, you also seek out cause marketing partners that would get sponsorship benefits in exchange for hosting a cause marketing program in its stores.

Here's how it works: Say that you have a fabulous walk every year for your cause. Thousands of people show up, you get great sponsors, and you raise good money. The event is a big success.

To kick off your cause marketing program, you leverage this successful event by approaching the local supermarket chain that has taken a pass on supporting the event every year because of the hefty price tag for walk sponsorships. You offer them a title sponsorship for free, with the requirement that they sell pinups in their stores the month before the walk and raise a minimum of $50,000.

You may be wondering what happens if your partner doesn't reach the $50,000. We generally stipulate that if the business doesn't reach the agreed upon amount, it has to do additional pinup programs to make up the shortfall. In all our years working with cause marketing partners, this situation has happened only once, and the business quickly and happily reached its goal with a second point-of-sale program.

It's important to find good partners and set realistic goals so that no one is surprised or disappointed (see Chapter 3).

The upside for the cause is you now have another promotional vehicle, the pinup, to promote the event and its sponsors, which makes partners even happier. The other benefit is that with the supermarket committed, you may be able to recruit more cause marketing partners for the program that are interested in the comarketing opportunity.

Events are existing assets you can put to work to build your cause marketing program. Events and cause marketing open the door to more partners and to more opportunities.

After you engage new retail partners in your cause marketing program, these companies can add value in several ways, such as TV, radio, in-store promotion, vendor relationships, or a much sought-after customer base that you can dangle in front of prospective retail partners. You can use their assets to build your own inventory of assets and recruit even more partners.

Teaming Up with Another Cause or Company

Here's the situation. You're a nonprofit with a good company that's eager to work on a cause marketing promotion, but neither of you have the expertise to execute it. A nonprofit across town has executed lots of cause marketing programs, but doesn't have a company partner for its next program. Oh, what to do!

The solution: Work together on the cause marketing program and split the dollars raised. The cause with the experience brings the expertise in running a program, and the cause with the company brings the opportunity for giving.

For example, our partnership with the Boston Bruins Foundation brought together our expertise executing cause marketing programs with a long list of marketing benefits that only a professional sports team could deliver to make this program a real winner with partners (see Figure 15-3).

We're surprised that more nonprofits don't work together on cause marketing programs. The reason probably is territory and money. Causes don't want to lose a supporter to the other guy, and they can't bear to split the money. Of course, they don't see two things.

First, without a successful cause marketing program a cause just might lose that company to another cause anyway. Second (and we say this all the time), 50 percent of something is better than 100 percent of nothing.

Figure 15-3:
Even though you're a nonprofit, consider working with other nonprofits when they bring something to the table.

Starting with Coin Canisters

Coin canisters (see Figure 15-4) are a great way to get started with cause marketing. They're inexpensive, and while generally a passive fundraising tool, they can raise good money and build a foundation for other cause marketing programs.

One of the best coin canister programs we know of has been held annually since after World War II in New England movie theaters by the Jimmy Fund (www.jimmyfund.org), the fundraising arm of Boston's Dana-Farber Cancer. In 2010, it raised $530,000. The money is raised with coin canister collections by ushers or volunteers after moviegoers see a short trailer on the charity's mission and services.

We've seen many very moving trailers over the years, including one with ironworkers from a nearby construction site talking of the bond they formed with kids with cancer as they welded iron outside their hospital windows. You can view this video through this link: http://bit.ly/1JsYM6.

Coin canisters, when done well, are a visible cause marketing program that demonstrate a company's commitment to the community and is a catalyst for discussing all the other things a business does for its favorite causes.

Figure 15-4:
Coin canisters work and are a great first step for any cause marketing program.

Joining Cause Marketing Forum

New York-based Cause Marketing Forum (CMF), which David Hessekiel, a former journalist and nonprofit volunteer, founded in 2002, is the leading source of information, training, and recognition for cause marketers. CMF has tons of free resources available right on its website, including a knowledge center with cause marketing basics, case studies, reports, and research.

For an annual fee, you get the membership newsletter, access to the CMF web teleconference archives, and a discount to CMF's annual meeting, which is a must-attend event. CMF is an excellent, affordable resource for cause marketers. We know this firsthand because we've benefited from CMF's resources for years.

Chapter 16

Ten Cause Marketing Campaigns We Wish We Could Take Credit For

- -

In This Chapter

▶ Highlighting programs that have inspired us and will inspire you

▶ Sharing ten top campaigns from which you can learn and grow

- -

*W*e've sighed for many cause marketing programs, but we love just ten. Here are our picks for the ten local cause marketing programs we wish we had thought of before these smart folks did.

Wehrenberg Theatres Gold Heart Pin

Wehrenberg Theatres with 15 locations throughout the Midwest supported Variety the Children's Charity of St. Louis through the purchase of Variety's 2011 Gold Heart pin. Movie-goers purchased the pins for $3 (see Figure 16-1). When they bought the gold heart with any concession combo, they received another select concession item for free.

The tie-in with concessions was a smart one, as many moviegoers want to buy a drink and popcorn for the show. The key, of course, is the ask at the counter. "Would you like to buy a Gold Heart pin for $3 to help Children's Charity? Buy it with a concession, and you get one free."

Figure 16-1:
Variety's
2011 Gold
Heart pin
featuring
Yogi Bear.

Whatever they're doing at Wehrenberg Theatres, they should keep it up. Over the past two years in 15 theaters, they sold 31,317 pins and raised $94,000. This year, their goal is $100,000.

Starbucks Leprechaun Lattes

Before Starbucks teamed up with Product (RED), it had a regional partnership with Jumpstart, a national early education organization based in Boston, involving a St. Patrick's Day drink fittingly topped with green foam, Leprechaun Lattes. Twenty-five cents from each drink went to Jumpstart, which raised tens of thousands of dollars for the nonprofit.

The program started at one Boston Starbucks in 2002 and then expanded throughout the Northeast. In 2005 alone, 53,000 lattes topped with green foam were sold (see Figure 16-2).

Although Starbucks is an international company, Leprechaun Lattes was a great local program that made a large coffee chain like Starbucks feel like the hometown hero.

Figure 16-2:
Starbucks
Leprechaun
Lattes
began at
one Boston
store in
2002, but
eventually
grew into a
St. Patrick's
Day tradition
across the
Northeast.

Figure 16-2:
Starbucks
Leprechaun
Lattes
began at
one Boston
store in
2002, but
eventually
grew into a
St. Patrick's
Day tradition
across the
Northeast.

Absolut "City" Vodkas

Absolut has had many "city" vodkas that have benefited local causes. The first, New Orleans, raised $2 million for Katrina relief. The Los Angeles Edition raised $250,000 for the environmental mission of Green Way Los Angeles. Absolut Boston raised $50,000 for the Charles River Conservancy, the environmental group that oversees the Charles River watershed that snakes through Boston and its suburbs.

Absolut added an interesting twist to the program in our hometown of Boston. The spirit maker created a freestanding "Wall of Pride" to celebrate the launch of the new vodka (see Figure 16-3). The city's most beloved personalities memorialized their favorite Boston moments on the wall — iconic sports figures, historic monuments, dining, and more. (One of our favorites was of legendary Red Sox great Carlton Fisk.) After being displayed, the tiles were sold on eBay with the proceeds going to CRC.

Figure 16-3:
Absolut's
Wall of
Pride in
Boston
benefitted
the Charles
River
Conser-
vancy.

SXSW Check-In for Charity

South by Southwest (SXSW) is the internationally recognized Music and Media Conference & Festival held annually in Austin, Texas. In 2010, SXSW attendees got to check out the first major location-based cause marketing programs. Whenever a Foursquare user checked-in to a designated location in Austin, PayPal, and Microsoft donated 25 cents to the international children's charity, Save the Children. In just 48 hours, attendees had logged over 135,000 check-ins and had reached the maximum donation of $15,000 (see Figure 16-4).

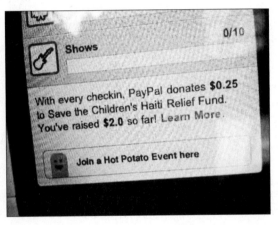

Figure 16-4: SXSW's Check-in for Charity raised $15,000 for Save the Children's Haiti Relief Fund.

Check-in for Charity demonstrated the potential of location-based services for cause marketing and served as a model throughout 2010 of how causes and companies could work together to build awareness and raise money. We cover Foursquare and other location-based services in Chapter 10.

A.C. Moore's Act for Autism

With 136 locations on the East Coast, A.C. Moore's work on Easter Seals' *Act for Autism* campaign may not seem local, but it is. A.C. Moore stores in the Philadelphia and Wilmington, Delaware region collected more than half of the total funds, with the Wilmington store earning the top fundraising spot. The chain also added a craft event at stores that gave the cause marketing program a nice local touch (see Figure 16-5).

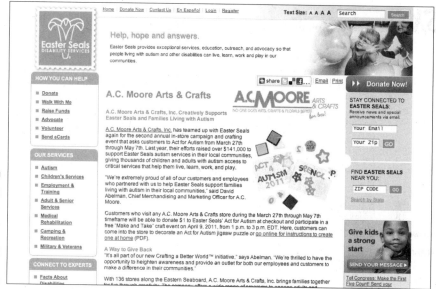

Figure 16-5:
A.C.
Moore's
make-and-
take craft
materials.

During the point-of-sale campaign, which raised $141,000 for Easter Seals, A.C. Moore invited customers to a make-and-take crafting event in stores that involved a jigsaw puzzle (for autism awareness). What a great combination of crafting and cause!

There's another reason we like this program. A.C. Moore stores are not as heavily trafficked as supermarkets or department stores, yet they still raised a lot of money for Easter Seals. This speaks to the commitment and discipline of the craft chain's employees, especially those workers in mid-Atlantic stores.

The number of locations and foot traffic a retailer has will play an important role in your cause marketing success. But you should not underestimate or undervalue enthusiasm as a key factor in your success. It's the human element that makes a good program great.

FedEx Trees for Troops

This cause marketing program brought together FedEx, The Christmas Spirit Foundation, and local tree growers from across the country to donate trees to troops at home and abroad. In 2010, Trees for Troops delivered over 17,000 trees, including to U.S. military bases all over the world.

A highlight of the program is the Trees for Troops Weekend. Growers and retail volunteers agree to host a FedEx trailer, where customers can purchase a tree and donate it to Trees for Troops. About 3,000 do each year (see Figure 16-6).

Figure 16-6:
Soldiers unload trees delivered by FedEx.

Dine Out for No Kid Hungry

Share Our Strength, a Washington D.C.–based anti-hunger organization, has big plans for Dine Out for No Kid Hungry: to end childhood hunger in America by 2015.

To achieve this goal, Share Our Strength enlisted the help of 4,000 restaurants, many independently owned, across the United States in 2010. Together, they raised $1.5 million.

Cause marketing programs varied by business, but point-of-sale and purchase-triggered programs were particularly popular with restaurants of all sizes. For example, during September, Joe's Crab Shack restaurants gave one order of key lime pie to customers who donated $1 and one order of crab nachos to customers who donated $5 (see Figure 16-7). The restaurants added to their donation by giving the proceeds from their signature T-shirts to No Kid Hungry. The cherry on the . . . umm . . . crab cake, however, was that Joe's matched the donation bringing their total gift to $325,000.

Local restaurants, cause marketing, and matching gifts? Dine Out is one dish you have to love.

Figure 16-7: Joe's Crab Shack thanked donors with either key lime pie or crab nachos. Yum!

Whole Foods Supports Local Causes

With nearly 300 stores, Whole Foods could partner with any nonprofit they want. But it flexes its register muscle for local causes that directly support the communities where stores are located.

We know this for a fact because, like many other Whole Foods customers across the company, we've supported these programs at the register of our hometown stores. Unlike many cause marketing programs in supermarkets, Whole Foods cashiers don't typically ask customers to donate. Instead, signage inviting the shopper to give is visible at checkout, usually on or near where shoppers swipe their bank card. The shopper chooses between a $2 or $5 donation, which is scanned by the cashier just like any other item in the store.

The month-long program that benefited the YMCA raised close to $1,500 (see Figure 16-8).

Figure 16-8:
Whole Foods' program for the YMCA wasn't part of a national effort to support Y's. It was a month-long fundraiser for the Y down the street from the super-market.

Dickies Detroit 874

Not all cause marketing is gold. Sometimes it comes in dark navy twill with red stitching, red pocketing, and a Detroit 874 logo.

Work apparel maker Dickies' program for the Salvation Army of Metro Detroit is a great example of product cause marketing. Dickies donated 5,000 pants to the local nonprofit with the promise to donate an additional pair for each 874 sold for a total potential donation of 10,000 pants (see Figure 16-9).

Dickies' goal is simple: To help one of the nation's most economically disadvantaged cities get their residents back on their feet (and dressed!). Dickies also put some money in those pant pockets: They made a $25,000 gift to the Army alongside its product donation.

Massage Envy Social Media Challenge

We love digital cause marketing programs that use Facebook Likes and Twitter hashtags to raise money for good causes. We like these programs even more when we see local businesses and causes executing them with the same commitment and skill as large organizations with national campaigns.

The Massage Envy Social Media Challenge (see Figure 16-10) was the brainchild of Charles Goodwin, a regional developer of the Massage Envy franchise. He and his wife are longtime supporters of Second Harvest Food Bank, which serves the San Mateo and Santa Clara counties in California. Confident in the power and speed of social networks to get the word out about local hunger, he offered $15,000 for the challenge, which would provide 30,000 meals for hungry neighbors.

To receive the full $15,000, supporters of the food bank had to earn it in the following ways:

✔ Like the food bank's Facebook page ($5)

✔ Comment on the page or Like any posting ($2)

✔ Follow the food bank on Twitter ($5)

✔ RT (that's retweet for those of you still stuck in 2008) or mention the Twitter handle @2ndharvest ($2)

✔ Post a photo showing your support of the cause on the food bank's Facebook Page, on Twitter with the handle, or to a Flickr group (bonus $5 each!)

The local chain of Massage Envy and the food bank promoted the challenge heavily throughout December 2010. In January, the food bank celebrated the New Year with a new check for $15,000!

Figure 16-10:
The Massage Envy Social Media Challenge.

Chapter 17

Ten Ways to Nail Your Next Cause Marketing Presentation

*E*ver since we became cause marketers, presentations have become a regular part of our lives. Sometimes we speak to 2 people, sometimes to 20 or to 200.

The writer Ralph Waldo Emerson said, "Every good speaker was once a bad speaker." Good speaking and good presentations come from practice, experience, reflection, training, and still more practice and experience.

In this chapter, we share ten things we've discovered along the way to deliver powerful, persuasive, and ultimately successful presentations.

Know the Who, When, Where, and Why

The first response most people have to preparing a speech is to start thinking about what to say, how many PowerPoint slides they'll need, and maybe even what they'll wear.

All important stuff, for sure, but the first order of business is to take a closer look at your audience, which may be 1 person or 50 or 500. Regardless of the size, audience analysis will be critical to your success.

Ask of your audience who, when, where, and why:

- ✔ **Whom are you speaking to?** Are you addressing the president of a company or a group of middle managers from the marketing department? Who your audience is will impact your speaking decisions. The president may want to hear more about your organization and the larger benefits of cause marketing. The marketing folks may be looking for specific metrics on return-on-investment and how the program works.

- ✔ **When are you speaking?** Are you speaking first thing in the morning, midafternoon, or just before quitting time in the evening? If you're speaking in the late afternoon, you need to be more high energy and brief because your listeners have already endured a long day, and their attention will be divided between you and the comforts of home. If you're speaking at lunchtime, you'll want to make sure that you speak after everyone has eaten — or at least provide lunch. Given the choice between listening to you or listening to their growling stomachs, listeners will always choose the food that's waiting for them back at their desk.

- ✔ **Where are you speaking?** Find out this information well in advance of your presentation. We've shown up at a speaking engagement with a laptop and projector in tow only to discover we were meeting in a room no bigger than a broom closet! One time, the room didn't have an electrical outlet. The goal here is no surprises. Control your environment, or your environment will control you!

- ✔ **Why are you speaking?** This question will help you hone your Famous Last Words (FLW). For each presentation, you want a very clear objective of why you're speaking and what you hope to accomplish. Remember, presentations aren't like poetry or paintings; they're not created just because someone wanted to write or paint that day. Speeches are prepared to do some type of work in the world. What will yours accomplish?

Include Famous Last Words (FLW)

Every speech needs Famous Last Words (an FLW). An FLW is what you want the listener to remember when everything else has been forgotten.

For example:

> *"The keys to a successful speech are audience analysis, organization, and delivery."*

> *"Cause marketing is a great way to raise money and build awareness for your cause."*

Limit your FLW to one sentence and focus each one of your speaking points on reinforcing it. If you want to be subtle and complicated, write a novel. Speaking requires directness, clarity, and laser-like focus.

Limit Your Presentation to 20 Minutes

Mark Twain said, "Few sinners are saved after the first 20 minutes of a sermon." And Twain said this more than 100 years ago when the average attention span was a lot longer than it is now! These days, people prefer 90-minute movies, half-hour sitcoms, tweets that are limited to 140 characters, e-mails without attachments, and books like this one that have lots of bullets, figures, and sidebars.

Why would anyone think that a listener would prefer a speaker who would drone on 30, 40, or 60 minutes! Looking for inspiration for the 20-minute presentation we recommend? Check out the website TED Talks www.ted.com, which highlights a global set of conferences formed to disseminate "ideas worth spreading." TED Talks features some of the best speakers in the world, who have just 18 minutes to present their ideas in the most innovative and engaging ways they can.

Tap the Power of Three

There's something special about grouping things in threes. It's not just us, either:

> *"The Father, the Son, and the Holy Ghost."*
>
> *"Life, liberty, and the pursuit of happiness."*
>
> *"Government of the people, by the people, for the people."*

Humans have a natural ear for things in threes. It has a rhythm that listeners can easily follow and is memorable and persuasive. Limiting your speech to three major themes can help ensure your speech stays within our 20-minute rule (see preceding section).

Finally, Joe believes that the success of your speech really hinges on three important factors: audience analysis, organization, and delivery. He calls them analyze, organize, energize!

President Franklin Delano Roosevelt probably gave the three best tips for public speaking success: "Be sincere. Be brief. And be seated." But FDR forgot one more: Amen! Your audience will thank you if you follow his advice.

Listen to Your High School English Teacher

Like a high school composition paper, every good presentation needs a beginning, middle, and ending:

- ✔ Your beginning should grab your listener's interest and attention and introduce your famous last words (see the section on FLW earlier in this chapter). This is where you state your point of view. "Your company should work with us on a cause marketing partnership because it will build your credibility with customers and potentially drive sales."

- ✔ Your middle is where you prove your point. You support your FLW with arguments that move your listeners to join your program.

- ✔ Your ending is where you drive your point home. You briefly summarize your main points and reinforce your FLW. Finally, knowing that final remarks leave lasting impressions, you finish your speech with a key, memorable message that hopefully closes the deal!

Good speeches are like good books. They vary widely in theme, tone, and length, but they all share one thing in common: a beginning, middle, and ending.

Balance Emotion with Other Appeals

Whenever you talk about a cause, it's always tempting to focus on emotion, appeals that pull at a listener's heartstrings. We do so with good reason: It works. Listeners should connect with causes deeply, emotionally, and viscerally. But emotions can be overdone. If we push them too hard, people will start to pull back as their brains deflect their hearts and force them to consider other critical information.

Balance your emotion with other appeals, such as arguments that include evidence or highlight your credibility. For example, listeners will love the stories you tell about the needy children or animals your cause has helped. But also tell them about your organization's commitment to keeping expenses low and your recent recognition as a top charity.

Next, share with listeners all the things you've learned about cause marketing from this book, how it works, and the evidence that supports your claim. In other fields the risk is that there will be too much evidence, too many stats and figures and nothing for listeners to *feel*. The challenge in cause marketing is just the opposite. It's easy to make our listeners feel joyful, sad, or excited — we have powerful information to share! — but to earn their trust and commitment, we have to make them think.

Be Your Best Visual Aid

PowerPoint is one of the most overused presentation tools ever. PowerPoint is best used to explain and enhance a speech, but instead people use it as a crutch or replacement for engagement or for something to hide behind so people won't look at them.

Don't get us wrong; we love PowerPoint. Used correctly, PowerPoint can help organize, explain, entertain, educate, and even excite your audience. But limit PowerPoint slides to the things that can't be said with words or are best said or explained with slides.

A few basic rules for PowerPoint:

- **PowerPoint is for your audience, not for you.** Don't use PowerPoint as an oversized, electronic notecard for your speaking points. Rely instead on a speaking outline you can easily reference. Save the PowerPoint for informing, educating, and entertaining your listeners.

- **Use PowerPoint to say things that can't be said.** In general, use your slides to powerfully communicate something you can't say. Remember, images clarify, demonstrate, and inspire.

- **If you must use text, use as few words as possible and include no more than three or four lines per slide.** Resist the urge to include *everything*. Give your listeners just enough to comprehend your point but not so much that they don't need you there to explain it.

It's really quite simple. You only have one chance to make a meaningful human connection with your listeners in a presentation. Yet every PowerPoint slide you add decreases the chances of that happening.

Use an Outline to Stay on Track

Everyone has this vision of a speaker taking the stage and speaking passionately and extemporaneously without the aid of notes or cards. What we see on television and at the movies seem to prove that the best speakers are unfettered and unrehearsed. Of course, nothing could be further from the truth.

Comedians, talk show hosts, and speakers go to great lengths to prepare their skits, monologues, and speeches. They also use a speaking outline to stay on track and use placards, note cards, and Teleprompters to keep their outline front and center.

The outline itself can take many forms. Some people prefer to jot down a few words and phrases to jog their memory. Others write down their key ideas on index cards and number them so that they easily recall their key points. Joe is a former public speaking teacher and remembers one student who drew out his speech and used the drawing as an outline!

What shape the outline takes is up to you. But with all the other important things you need to cover during a presentation, your time is better spent on something besides remembering what you had planned to say next.

Let Your Nervousness Energize You

The nervousness you feel before speaking is normal, expected, and important. You heard us right. We believe nervousness is a key ingredient of an effective presentation.

We think that a lot of athletes, actors, and musicians would agree that a few butterflies are a good thing. They energize, motivate, and force you to focus. But tapping nervousness as a power source only works if those butterflies are flying in formation.

You can manage your nervousness in a number of ways. The key is to know what is making you so nervous so that you can address it! Here are a few tips for some common nerve triggers:

- ✔ If you're worried that you're going to lose your train of thought, keep your speech on notecards near you.

- ✔ If you're afraid of being in front of a crowd, spend some time before your speech at the front of the room introducing yourself to audience members so that you can later focus on at a few friendly faces in the room.

- ✔ If you're concerned that you might look incompetent, be competent. Give your presentation extra time and attention beforehand and practice, practice, practice.

Also, comfort yourself knowing that while you may not know as much about cause marketing as you would like, your audience probably knows even less. After all, you are the expert!

Unleash the Nonverbal You

What we say is important, but so, too, is how we say it. Your nonverbal cues — posture, eyes, voice, and gestures — can either impair or empower your verbal message. Here's a quick rundown for managing each cue:

- **Posture:** Stand up straight and move toward your audience. Walking around the stage area is a great way to connect with different listeners and release nervous energy. Just remember that you're not running a footrace.

- **Eyes:** The eyes are the windows to the soul. They should convey sincerity, passion, and conviction. Don't scan your audience; look at different audience members and just talk to them one on one, even if it's just for a moment.

- **Voice:** There's nothing worse than a monotone voice. Add inflection and vocal variety to your speeches to keep listeners engaged. Remember that not every moment of a speech needs to be filled with your voice. Some of the most powerful things you can say are said with silence.

- **Gestures:** Your arms and hands are extensions of your words. When you talk about the reach of your program, outstretch your arms. When you talk about its strength, clench your fists. When you mention the closeness of your partnership, clasp your hands together. You and your words are one.

Index

• J •

• K •

• L •

• **Q** •

• **R** •

Apple & Macs

iPad For Dummies
978-0-470-58027-1

iPhone For Dummies,
4th Edition
978-0-470-87870-5

MacBook For Dummies, 3rd
Edition
978-0-470-76918-8

Mac OS X Snow Leopard For
Dummies
978-0-470-43543-4

Business

Bookkeeping For Dummies
978-0-7645-9848-7

Job Interviews
For Dummies,
3rd Edition
978-0-470-17748-8

Resumes For Dummies,
5th Edition
978-0-470-08037-5

Starting an
Online Business
For Dummies,
6th Edition
978-0-470-60210-2

Stock Investing
For Dummies,
3rd Edition
978-0-470-40114-9

Successful
Time Management
For Dummies
978-0-470-29034-7

Computer Hardware

BlackBerry
For Dummies,
4th Edition
978-0-470-60700-8

Computers For Seniors
For Dummies,
2nd Edition
978-0-470-53483-0

PCs For Dummies,
Windows
7 Edition
978-0-470-46542-4

Laptops For Dummies,
4th Edition
978-0-470-57829-2

Cooking & Entertaining

Cooking Basics
For Dummies,
3rd Edition
978-0-7645-7206-7

Wine For Dummies,
4th Edition
978-0-470-04579-4

Diet & Nutrition

Dieting For Dummies,
2nd Edition
978-0-7645-4149-0

Nutrition For Dummies,
4th Edition
978-0-471-79868-2

Weight Training
For Dummies,
3rd Edition
978-0-471-76845-6

Digital Photography

Digital SLR Cameras &
Photography For Dummies,
3rd Edition
978-0-470-46606-3

Photoshop Elements 8
For Dummies
978-0-470-52967-6

Gardening

Gardening Basics
For Dummies
978-0-470-03749-2

Organic Gardening
For Dummies,
2nd Edition
978-0-470-43067-5

Green/Sustainable

Raising Chickens
For Dummies
978-0-470-46544-8

Green Cleaning
For Dummies
978-0-470-39106-8

Health

Diabetes For Dummies,
3rd Edition
978-0-470-27086-8

Food Allergies
For Dummies
978-0-470-09584-3

Living Gluten-Free
For Dummies,
2nd Edition
978-0-470-58589-4

Hobbies/General

Chess For Dummies,
2nd Edition
978-0-7645-8404-6

Drawing
Cartoons & Comics
For Dummies
978-0-470-42683-8

Knitting For Dummies,
2nd Edition
978-0-470-28747-7

Organizing
For Dummies
978-0-7645-5300-4

Su Doku For Dummies
978-0-470-01892-7

Home Improvement

Home Maintenance
For Dummies,
2nd Edition
978-0-470-43063-7

Home Theater
For Dummies,
3rd Edition
978-0-470-41189-6

Living the
Country Lifestyle
All-in-One
For Dummies
978-0-470-43061-3

Solar Power Your Home
For Dummies,
2nd Edition
978-0-470-59678-4

Internet

Blogging For Dummies,
3rd Edition
978-0-470-61996-4

eBay For Dummies,
6th Edition
978-0-470-49741-8

Facebook For Dummies,
3rd Edition
978-0-470-87804-0

Web Marketing
For Dummies,
2nd Edition
978-0-470-37181-7

WordPress
For Dummies,
3rd Edition
978-0-470-59274-8

Language & Foreign Language

French For Dummies
978-0-7645-5193-2

Italian Phrases
For Dummies
978-0-7645-7203-6

Spanish For Dummies,
2nd Edition
978-0-470-87855-2

Spanish
For Dummies,
Audio Set
978-0-470-09585-0

Math & Science

Algebra I
For Dummies,
2nd Edition
978-0-470-55964-2

Biology For Dummies,
2nd Edition
978-0-470-59875-7

Calculus For Dummies
978-0-7645-2498-1

Chemistry For Dummies
978-0-7645-5430-8

Microsoft Office

Excel 2010 For Dummies
978-0-470-48953-6

Office 2010 All-in-One
For Dummies
978-0-470-49748-7

Office 2010 For Dummies,
Book + DVD Bundle
978-0-470-62698-6

Word 2010 For Dummies
978-0-470-48772-3

Music

Guitar For Dummies,
2nd Edition
978-0-7645-9904-0

iPod & iTunes For
Dummies, 8th Edition
978-0-470-87871-2

Piano Exercises
For Dummies
978-0-470-38765-8

Parenting & Education

Parenting For Dummies,
2nd Edition
978-0-7645-5418-6

Type 1 Diabetes
For Dummies
978-0-470-17811-9

Pets

Cats For Dummies,
2nd Edition
978-0-7645-5275-5

Dog Training For Dummies,
3rd Edition
978-0-470-60029-0

Puppies For Dummies,
2nd Edition
978-0-470-03717-1

Religion & Inspiration

The Bible For Dummies
978-0-7645-5296-0

Catholicism For Dummies
978-0-7645-5391-2

Women in the Bible
For Dummies
978-0-7645-8475-6

Self-Help & Relationship

Anger Management
For Dummies
978-0-470-03715-7

Overcoming Anxiety
For Dummies,
2nd Edition
978-0-470-57441-6

Sports

Baseball
For Dummies,
3rd Edition
978-0-7645-7537-2

Basketball
For Dummies,
2nd Edition
978-0-7645-5248-9

Golf For Dummies,
3rd Edition
978-0-471-76871-5

Web Development

Web Design
All-in-One
For Dummies
978-0-470-41796-6

Web Sites
Do-It-Yourself
For Dummies,
2nd Edition
978-0-470-56520-9

Windows 7

Windows 7
For Dummies
978-0-470-49743-2

Windows 7
For Dummies,
Book + DVD Bundle
978-0-470-52398-8

Windows 7 All-in-One
For Dummies
978-0-470-48763-1

Available wherever books are sold. For more information or to order direct: U.S. customers visit www.dummies.com or call 1-877-762-297
U.K. customers visit www.wileyeurope.com or call (0) 1243 843291. Canadian customers visit www.wiley.ca or call 1-800-567-4797.

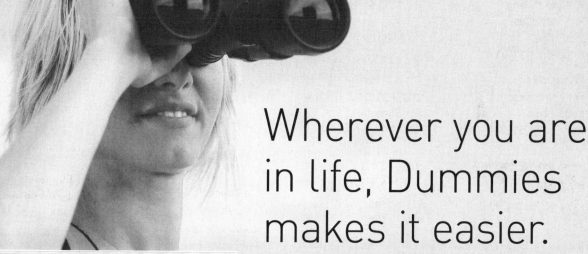